The Theory and Interpretation of Narrative Series

The figure and imagination of American women

Ordinary Pleasures

Couples, Conversation, and Comedy

Kay Young

The Ohio State University Press
Columbus

Library of Congress Cataloging-in-Publication Data

Young, Kay, 1959–
Ordinary pleasures : couples, conversation, and comedy/Kay Young.
p. cm.—(The theory and interpretation of narrative series)
Includes bibliographical references and index.
ISBN 0-8142-0884-3 (alk. paper)—ISBN 0-8142-5082-3 (pbk. : alk. paper)
1. Man-woman relationships in literature. 2. Man-woman relationships in
motion pictures. 3. Man-woman relationships on television. I. Title. II. Series.
PN56.M255 Y68 2001
809'.93355—dc21

2001002256

Cover design by Dan O'Dair.
Text design by Typographics West.
Type set in Adobe Garamond by Typographics West.
Printed by Thomson-Shore Inc.

9 8 7 6 5 4 3 2 1

To Jeff Saver,
my own Nick Charles

Does this make sense does it matter anyway
Is it coincidence or was it meant to be
'Cause there's something about what happens
when we talk

—Lucinda Williams

I don't love him because he is a fine match . . . I should never like scolding anyone else so well; and that is a point to be thought of in a husband.

—George Eliot

I wish as well as every body else to be perfectly happy; but like every body else it must be in my own way. Greatness will not make it so.

—Jane Austen

Contents

Acknowledgments

Fred Astaire and Ginger Rogers, William Powell and Myrna Loy, Clark Gable and Claudette Colbert, Katharine Hepburn and Spencer Tracy, Cary Grant and anyone, Lucy and Ricky, Nick and Nora . . . Without them, it's fair to say, this book could not have been written. I'm grateful for the time I've spent in their company and for how they make me feel.

I owe a great thanks to the editors of Ohio State University Press—most especially Darrin Pratt, Ruth Melville, James Phelan, and Peter Rabinowitz—for their thoughtful, generous, and timely support of this project.

During the years of bringing this book into being I've come to know some remarkable people who have helped me with tangible things like research, reading drafts, making clearer the way inside the world of publishing, and with intangible things like offering me the chance to know them and to better know myself. Many thanks to Porter Abbott, Margaret Allan, Peter Balestrieri, Betsy Carlisle, Julie Carlson, John Cecchini, Elizabeth Heckendorn Cook, Chris Craft, Susan Derwin, Paddy Fumerton, Giles Gunn, Raphael Gunner, Richard Helgerson, Jennifer Jones, Cassie Kircher, Margaret Koch, Ben Leisure, Dr. Joseph Lewis, Alan Liu, Linda Loomis, Leslie Nix, Marina Perez de Mendiola, Linda Raphael, Susan Rodgers, Mark Rose, Kristen Rowe, and Faye Thompson.

Jay Semel, Director of the Center for Advanced Study at the University of Iowa, welcomed me with warmth and good humor into a world that became the writing home of the book's first draft. Treated like a writer, I became a writer in the gracious company of the other members of the center. I am grateful to have had such a year.

And I had such a year because of Antonio and Hanna Damasio, the sponsors of the journey to Iowa. For believing in this project from its inception, for opening doors to different intellectual worlds, for our conversations over dinner and between musicals, and for our friendship—many thanks.

Philip Fisher and Stanley Cavell first challenged and inspired me when I was their student, and later supported and guided me in my academic career. I am very fortunate to have been trained by such rigorous and creative brilliance and to have known such caring mentoring.

I grew up watching old movies with my family. Staying up late and eating grinders from Bell's Pizza was often what it meant to be "us." My father would ask where a quotation was from, my mother would correct the line and then name the movie, and my sister and I would watch and listen and eat and learn much of what we know about narrative and Italian takeout. Thank you for what you've taught me and for your love.

Finally, Jeff and Dashiell and Cleo, with you, over time, I am learning the most about ordinary pleasures.

Ordinary Pleasures

Couples, Conversation, and Comedy

Cary Grant and Deborah Kerr in *An Affair to Remember,* 20th Century-Fox, 1957
Courtesy Academy of Motion Pictures Arts and Sciences

Introduction

DEBORAH KERR: What makes life so difficult?

CARY GRANT: People . . . Are you in love with him?

DEBORAH KERR: I'm not now.

CARY GRANT: Hmm. You know I've never done a day's work in my whole life . . .

DEBORAH KERR: I know. I've been thinking about that . . . hmm? What did you say?

CARY GRANT: I didn't say anything.

DEBORAH KERR: Hmm . . . yes, you did. Ah, you said, I was very fond of expensive things, furs and diamonds, and stuff like that.

CARY GRANT: Did I say that?

DEBORAH KERR: Pink champagne. That's the kind of life we've both been used to. Difficult to . . . Do you like beer? . . . (Theme song begins.) Winter must be cold for those with no warm memories. We've already missed the spring.

CARY GRANT: Probably my last chance. (They look at each other.) It's now or never.

DEBORAH KERR: "Never" is a frightening word.

CARY GRANT: We'd be fools to let happiness pass us by. (Grant turns his back to us to look at her, as she nods.)

DEBORAH KERR: And just because you . . .

CARY GRANT: . . . doesn't mean to say that I couldn't work. Of course not. Suppose I, well, you know, it takes some time, say six months . . .

DEBORAH KERR: What? Now be realistic.

1

CARY GRANT: All right. Say I work long enough and hard enough for, say, six months—where would you be?
DEBORAH KERR: What are you trying to say, Nickie?
CARY GRANT: I just want to be worthy (voice cracks) of asking you to marry me.
DEBORAH KERR: Nickie, that's just about the nicest . . . your voice cracked.
CARY GRANT: Well, that's because—
DEBORAH KERR: Yes, I know, I know . . . I'm going to turn in now. Do some more rolling and tossing. Let me tell you in the morning.
CARY GRANT: It's going to be a long night. (Kisses her hand.)
DEBORAH KERR: For me too. (She walks away and turns back.) Marriage is a very serious step for a girl like me.
CARY GRANT: Yes, I know.
DEBORAH KERR: (She walks away further and turns back again.) Do you like children?
CARY GRANT: Yes. Yes I do. (She leaves; he turns back to face us.)

Kerr, as Terry McKay, and Grant, as Nickie Ferranti, perform that moment of a romantic comedy/melodrama that defines an epiphany of the couple's story—the proposal—in the middle of Leo McCarey's 1957 *An Affair to Remember*. The repetitions of "yes" between them let us know that while it may be a long night for each of tossing and turning, she will accept his offer. Like Western culture's first couple (Adam, expelled from Eden and cursed to know hard labor, and Eve, fated to know the pain of childbirth), Nickie chooses work and Terry the possibility of children over the luxurious ease of being kept by wealthy partners. Both pairs must discover what it means to be together in time and over time in post-Edenic states. And if what is lost for these couples is paradise (or something like it), what is found is a knowledge that justifies that loss. Adam and Eve come to consciousness; Terry and Nickie come to happiness.

The scene can be cut out from the film to stand alone as a great performance piece—to be watched on video by the characters of *Sleepless in Seattle* and held up as their model for a proposal, or to be read here as a historic, unrepeatable moment in the story of the couple, Terry and Nickie. However, what is remarkable about the proposal scene has less, I think, to do with "the work" accomplished by the scene (namely, the couple's promise: to break from being kept by their wealthy partners, work hard, and meet in six months atop the Empire State Building to marry each other) than with what that work enables the couple to perform again and again. And what Grant and Kerr do together here and again and again in their other exchanges is what we most desire from a narrative couple—they show us how they understand each other; and they delight with us in that little miracle. He knows what she means by the highly metaphoric "Winter must be cold for those with no warm memories. We've already missed the spring." Theirs is a "winter's tale," a second go-around, she tells him. He acknowledges this when he renames it "my last chance." We witness them knowing, therefore, how to speak to each other in a symbolic language.

However, their ability to penetrate the other runs far deeper than the swapping of poetic clichés. Kerr's "What did you say?" follows no uttered remark from him that we can hear. But she can. He is thinking of her fondness for expensive things; and his thoughts are loud enough for her to hear, presumably because they are her thoughts as well. Grant and Kerr can, we learn, read each other's minds and discover their sameness, at times, of mind. If the thoughts are not the same, they can be easily finished by each other. He completes her thought about how the past doesn't determine the present—just because he's never worked doesn't mean he couldn't now. And she doesn't even need to speak what it means that his voice cracked: "Yes, I know, I know." What she knows is both why his voice failed him and that hers would too were she to be doing the proposing (that in fact her voice is failing her in that she isn't telling him/us what it is that she knows). But then she does tell us why her voice would crack—"Marriage is a very serious step for a girl like me"—and he responds in harmony, "Yes, I know." Such a shared talent for knowing how to read each other's spoken and unspoken languages means what they sang earlier to each other, "You make it easy to be true." The search is over. Intimacy is under way. The threat of others will not be what is most of interest to this couple: instead, it will entail things like showing up where and when each promised, learning again how to walk and how to trust, waiting to complicate the fantasy of their sharing between them only "one mind" to allow for the hard work of two separate people struggling to come back together. The mystical play of two mind readers needs to experience the "wounds" of separateness for happiness not to pass by this couple in *An Affair to Remember*.

~

Fascinated by and wedded to fundamental doubt regarding the knowability of the other, we as heirs of Descartes continue to be drawn to the drama of escaping our individualism. Couples in stories like *An Affair to Remember* enable us to witness moments of exchange which posit a "betweenness" and suggest forms of contact where the boundaries of the self and the unknowability of the other are at least for those moments of their interaction questioned, and perhaps even forgotten. Approaching the other in conversation, or building a joke together, or meeting in the choral rhapsody of a time step reveal occasions of shared experience. As the audience to a film's or novel's "couple-play," we may feel at the moment of observation the pleasure of a performed union. However, the moment passes, often without our knowing to what to attribute our lingering sense of joy. My desire here is to stay with that lingering joy, to name it, and to account for how a story invites us to feel it. This desire has led me to search in many directions. And because the experience of a third narrative space (not of the "self," not of the "other," but of an "us") is difficult to recognize, I have been prompted to look broadly, beyond the confines of a narrowly defined historical field or genre.

I am exploring in this book a very particular kind of pleasure, couple's pleasure. My notion of pleasure is not that, for instance, of Aristotle, who would make it be the chief end of virtue, or of Plato, who might define it in terms of the realm of the forms. Couple pleasure need not entail a chief virtue or an unknowable noumena, but it does entail, in my telling of it, two people struggling with the everyday challenges of knowing each other and being known, and turning that process of mutual knowing into play. Nor are the pleasures defined here about those of the self alone. Rather, this book explores ways of understanding how we generate pleasure as communities of two, and how stories reveal that pleasure.[1] It is the ordinary pleasures of marriage that concern me, what can come of the experience of mutuality, how play between a couple makes present an intimacy and happiness of the everyday.

Marriage has been compellingly explored by feminist critics for the state of "compliance" it can demand, a word/state D. W. Winnicott defines as adapting oneself to the creativity of someone else, or living so as to "fit in," which is to say not living according to one's own creative impulse (65). However, marriages at times reveal how heterosexual pairs are interesting for reasons other than the display of power relations or reproduction. Marriage stories can reveal moments of mutually derived, creative living. What if aspects of the narrative of a marriage were like that of a comedy team, where the story told—the joke—requires both partners to construct it, where the ability of one to create depends on the creativity of the other?

Winnicott also writes, "It is in playing and only in playing that the individual child or adult is able to be creative and to use the whole personality, and it is only in being creative that the individual discovers the self" (54). My work examines stories that put at their center a couple, a couple exploring the question of marriage as a state to be embraced, or worked through, or returned to, or resisted, but in all cases taken up.

I move mostly between novels of nineteenth-century England and Russia and films and television shows of twentieth-century America. While my focus is the novel and film, at times I inevitably turn to plays because of what they teach us about the dialogues and comedies of couples in narrative. I understand plays, films, television shows, and novels to be narratives, different in the stories they tell, different in their modes of telling, yet fundamentally similar in what they make—the representation of a/the world. Unlike Genette, whom I understand to take narrative to be a construction in words told, not performed, Seymour Chatman also defines plays and films as narratives because of their shared properties with written, non-acted texts and because of his desire to open up the conception of narrative discourse. He writes:

> [T]here is no particular reason why "to narrate" should mean *only* "to tell." Once we decide to define Narrative as a composite of story and discourse (on the basis of its unique double chronology), then *logically*, at least, narratives can be said to be actualizable on the stage or in other iconic media. The burden of disproof falls on theories that would deny the name Narrative to "performed" texts. They would need to explain why—having agreed that "mimesis" is a way of conveying Narrative (even in such nontheatrical texts as dialogue-only novels)—it should not be called an *act* of narration. (*Coming to Terms* 114)

Chatman grounds his claim that films and plays are narratives in the proposition that narratives are a "composite of story and discourse."[2] Simply put, if story is the "what" of the narrative and discourse is the "how," Chatman's proposition leads the way to include the performative media of film and plays as narratives because of their necessary reliance on events, character, and setting (the "what") wedded to techniques/acts of rendering the story (the "how") in their representations of a world. Borrowing from Genette, Chatman takes into account the fundamental difference between the "telling" discourse of the written novel ("diegesis") and the "showing" discourse of the performed play and film ("mimesis").[3] However, he does not allow this difference between telling-a-world-into-being and showing-a-world-into-being to divide performative, embodied representations from unperformed, unembodied language representations.

I am interested in what follows in how novels "tell" the world of a couple as written text, and how plays and films "show" a couple's world acted/performed (if watched) or tell/show the possibility of its embodiment (if read as scripts). I engage in linguistic analyses of what is said between couples on the written page of a text and performed between them on film. While there is the fact of the visual and the aural informing the filmed couple's "play" or the absence of that fact in a couple's exchanges in a novel, what these narratives share is the presence of the partners' dialogues and the "work" these conversations accomplish. My emphasis for discussion in both cases—written narrative and performed narrative—is on the words spoken, though I gesture toward describing the presence of the visual and aural cues that envelop the words on film. However, because my written text cannot reproduce those sights and sounds, my focus remains fixed on what my words can reproduce and analyze—the actual words themselves of the partners' exchanges.

When I cite dialogue from plays, I use the names of the characters from the texts. However, when analyzing the dialogues from film, I identify those words with the actors who speak them. As with a novel, I would suggest that a play's dialogues stand as the utterances of their characters. In the case of a drama, no matter who plays those parts, the words stand ready to be embodied and performed. In the case of the novel, the words are read silently in our heads: we can speak out their words or imagine how they would be performed; however, they need not be spoken out loud; they need not hold a "readiness" to be acted because as their readers, we know those dialogic words are held at large by a "told" narrative. The words of a play are not "owned" by any one actor, even though they may be highly associated with one, as in the case of a musical or a highly acclaimed and often repeated production of a drama. Erwin Panofsky, in the now classic "Style and Medium in the Motion Pictures," writes:

[T]he screenplay, in contrast to the theater play, *has no aesthetic existence independent of its performance, and that its characters have no aesthetic existence outside the actors.* . . .

Othello or Nora are definite, substantial figures created by the playwright. They can be played well or badly, and they can be "interpreted" in one way or another; but they most definitely exist, no matter who plays them or even whether they are played at all. The character in film, however, lives and dies with the actor. It is not the entity "Othello" interpreted by Robeson or the entity "Nora" interpreted by Duse; it is the entity "Greta Garbo" incarnate in a figure called Anna Christie or the entity "Robert Montgomery" incarnate in a murderer who, for all we know or care to know, may forever remain anonymous but will never cease to haunt our memories. (227–28)

Because no one performance stands as *the* performance of a play, the words cannot be wholly identified with just one actor or one production. However, a film is one performance. It is *the* performance by "stars" who are stars because only they "light up the screen" in close-up, embodying only one performance, able to be screened again, but not reperformed in the sense of performed differently.

Our viewing of stars playing couples performing to one another and to us on the screen, our watching of actors performing to one another and to us on stage, our reading of characters "speaking" to one another and to us on the written page present their interactions through remarkably different discourses—embodied, performed, potentially acted, told—and make different stories that represent the worlds of couples. And it is how these narratives represent the worlds of couples—as stories, as discourses—that leads me to desire their juxtaposition and analysis, primarily at the level of their written or performed language.

To ask how intimacy is felt between a couple, how it takes root, how it deepens and continues to re-create itself over the course of a story, means that we must look at the presence and nature of conversation. Embedded within the novel and the chief linguistic mode of storytelling in film,[4] conversation is the primary mode of interaction between narrative partners. In conversation, language is traded: voices are brought side by side, respond to each other, play together. Conversations between lovers insist on the ongoing, mutual adjustments of style and word choice, on working to be understood and trying to understand. The moments in the text of a couple's conversations are about the relinquishing of individual control and the possibility of shaping an interactional account of a couple's selves and their world. Speech creates a possible groundwork for mutual understanding—how "we" talk together determines so much of how "we" know each other. The talk of a couple (what distinguishes their particular talk) is the couple. And so my discussion begins with what it means to speak, in order to move to the making of love talk, and the making of a story's couple.

Chapter 1 opens with a critique of what we might consider the first instance of conversation, the Socratic dialogue, and its example of what it means for two people to talk; I then go on to offer another model of conversation. This chapter addresses a set of questions fundamental to the book: How does a conversation work to create a story, no matter the textual site in which it is found? What other forms of knowledge are to be found embedded in the scene of conversation, in addition to the stated "subject" of discourse? And, most important, what is the relation between holding a conversation and being or becoming a couple?

Looking at how scenes from *Jane Eyre, Pride and Prejudice,* the film *Gone with the Wind,* and *Casablanca* use lovers' conversations to define what it means to be "Jane and Rochester," "Lizzy and Darcy," "Scarlett and Rhett," "Ilsa and Rick," chapter 2 asserts that lovers' talk creates not just couples but the turns of plot of the stories that hold them. By way of contrast, chapter 3 explores other conversations from *Jane Eyre* and *Pride and Prejudice,* along with Dashiell Hammett's novel *The Thin Man,* Shakespeare's *Antony and Cleopatra,* and Hollywood's remarriage comedies, to distinguish how moments of conversational intimacy enable their stories to be "on holiday" from the driving/linear work of plot in the sustained, relational plane of the talk that is "just talk."

The talk of couples can work as the precursor to other modes of partnered play in a story—paired encounters with music, dance, and slapstick. Couples need to be able to talk together (which does not mean understand each other but does mean understand how to play with language together) in order to do other kinds of talk with their feet, their voices, and everything in-between. Shared "conversation," be it in words or in movement, in sound or in silence, defines moments of performance. Talk creates intimacy and the pleasures that accompany the mutual knowledge of that intimacy. The whole range of performed play between couples accounts for some of a narrative's bursts of happiness. To understand happiness as something performed between two people requires that we understand first the performing of intimacy in words. Granting the presence of intimacy's pleasures in narrative makes possible the granting of happiness.

Or does it? Happiness presents itself perhaps even more than intimacy as an impossible site of narrative, reserved for a mythic realm of "happily ever after." In stories, we're told, the happy state toward which the action of the plot has been directed is lived elsewhere, outside the boundary of the narratable present. Stories depend on problem states in order for there to be a "plot," that which must get "solved." However, narrative also depends on the creation of a nonproblem. What I mean is this: it is possible for a story to tell itself through non-plot advancement. When, for example, Astaire and Rogers break into dance, what they do together is not about making plot through problem production or resolution. What they create together is about the dance itself, that moment of play, and the pleasure it gives them—the pleasure of making romantic comedy together. That narratives need not perpetuate their stories only in the linear drive from problem to solution reveals itself in the comic outburst by partners which "stops" the show, or in the subversions/variations tried by partners to upset the expected comic rhythm of stasis, crisis, stasis. Comic play by lovers—the movement of feedline to punchline, song lyric to dance step, wisecrack to pratfall, gesture to joke—makes moments of "ordinary" happiness.

The second half of the book, therefore, posits a relation between the making of comedy between lovers and knowing states of "ordinary happiness." Beginning with a model of New or romantic comedy, chapter 4 makes a case for what still makes romantic comedy new and vital, namely, New Comedy's invention of the male/female comedy team. In the next three chapters I look at different genres of romantic comedy—the novel of domestic comedy, the situation comedy, and screwball comedy—to see how they figure the male/female comedy team.

Chapter 5 examines how the domestic novel creates "everyday" comedy by naming what is present, which includes washstands and bees, and the terrors and pleasures of being in a partnership. A reading of the Kitty/Levin portion of *Anna Karenina* unearths from that "extraordinary" novel of adultery an embedded, less visible (because ordinary) marriage story that depicts an ongoing, worked-on happiness. Looking at the repeated situations of *I Love Lucy* and the particular, non-repeatable improvisations of Nichols and May, in chapter 6 I explore the physical and verbal comedy of seemingly "opposite" teams who find ways to reinvent and perpetuate their unions in their very embracing of or resistance to repetition. Hollywood's screwball comedies of the 1930s and '40s define the high-water mark of team comedy. Chapter 7 explores how these partners know how to talk to, dance with, sing about, and trip one another with a kind of unrivaled inventiveness and joy. The stories of screwball couples willingly turn their plots over to these performances by forestalling problem creation and resolution in favor of making in-the-moment play. Their smart, sustained play is something like the best moments of vaudeville and Broadway musical team comedy.

While I do not devote chapters to the stage performances of the male/female comedy teams of vaudeville and radio, or to the lovers in musical comedy and opera, my hope is that the analysis of comic structures explored in these three chapters will be applicable as well to the aesthetic of those and other forms of comedy. The choice of looking at the interaction of a few words spoken in conversation in the opening half of the book versus giving readings of whole scenes and examining how the form of a genre depends on the presence of the comedy team in the second half has to do, at some literal level, with the *size* of what I'm seeking to uncover. And what I want to bring forward is, first, the relatively small space in which a narrative displays a speech act (the conversation of lovers) and then how it makes the larger space of a whole mode of narrative (New or romantic comedy). While the narrative couple I most often write about is a woman and a man engaged in the pursuit, living, or leaving of marriage, this is not always the case. Some of the couples I discuss engage in "as if" marriages, and some are same-sex partners who help to define what it means to do love talk (as in the case of Socrates and Alcibiades), or to perform a comic "marriage" (as do Laurel and Hardy). While my interest lies, in particular, with uncovering/recovering the pleasures of discovered and performed mutuality between a male/female partnership, my hope is that the work is applicable to the same-sex narrative couple.

To "see" often requires seeing differently; it may require striving to see what has never been visible, or what has grown invisible. I pay serious attention to some of the narratives that have been so strongly assimilated into the American culture and mind as to constitute the stories we are raised on (stories that define how we understand what is a novel or what is a film). All too frequently, these core narratives are the objects of warm, nostalgic feelings and little thought. I've deliberately chosen "classic" American films and television shows and "classic" European novels that we, as their audience/readers, have been schooled to consider "treasures." We tend to resist subjecting to analysis that which is so comfortably a part of who we are, and of whose value we are so sure. That I want to return to them as objects of study comes from my desire to encourage an active, engaged re-seeing not just of these stories but of stories in general and how they make the intimacy and happiness I'm defining be "close to home." Intimacy and happiness can be discovered in our own narrative backyards.

I bring together works that seem to have no business standing in relation to each other so as to startle the reader into encountering these narratives with a fresh eye. I juxtapose the "high" and "low," "difficult" and "easy," known by the few and known by the many, in part as a means of forcing attention. But more important, these works are useful to one another. Most of the philosophical texts I use make claims about how ordinary language works, claims that require testing. The stories I've chosen offer themselves as representations of the world, of how we communicate; they stand, therefore, as ripe linguistic fields for proving or falsifying assertions of language-centered philosophy. And while paying philosophically rigorous attention to the language of a novel or film scene risks the discovery of shallowness if the story cannot support the analysis, it can reveal an unsuspected depth, or unearth a variety of meanings, or make clear why we hold a narrative to be dear. In part, the act of taking *I Love Lucy* or *Gone with the Wind* or even *Jane Eyre* seriously does mean mingling these works with the self-evidently serious writings of Grice or Habermas or Gadamer. However, it also means putting Wittgenstein's words, for instance, in "mixed company" (what does it mean for texts to relate to each other as unexpected/inappropriate guests?), which frees serious works to play in not so serious ways, or at least to know themselves as not just serious, and playful works to know themselves as not just playful. Both sets of texts—story and theory/philosophy—transmute when engaged in each other's company, and I want the liveliness that accompanies the presence of both moods, the serious and the light, to inform my analysis of what constitutes narrative intimacy and happiness. The surprise encounter between different kinds of writing allows works more room to be known differently, makes them surprising in what they share (that a conversation from *Pride and Prejudice* and phrases from *The Philosophical Investigations* resonate is not what we expect) and clarifying in what they do not.

Finally, texts as strange bedfellows or odd partners mimic in the friction of their encounters what the couples of these narratives navigate in their confrontations with the boundaries of their difference/separation. What the narrative couples tirelessly explore is how to acknowledge what makes the other always other and partner in the creation of a third being called "the couple." That acknowledgment happens, I claim, in their moments of play, in all its variety (for instance, as banter, dancing, fighting, singing, screaming), that is, as the outbreaks of self-toward-other expression that being together demands. Reading a couple's interaction as speech, or summarized in language by a narrator, we imagine its sounds, looks. We must lend our own embodiment to the written text, and so mingle what we know of perception with conception, in order to "experience" how the couples of a written narrative are engaged in performance inside the linguistic world of the novel and inside our imaginations. As audience to an embodied couple in a film or on stage, we perceive bodies speaking and moving, most often without the mediating presence of a narrator. Our eyes and ears are fed by the sensory presence of an "actual" couple. The immediacy of the experience of being their audience quiets the need to perceive what is absent from a written text because the couple is physically present, even if merely as the moving images and taped sounds of film; we don't need to fill in sensory experience to know their performances. However, while we gain immediate, perceptual knowledge of the embodied couples, we lose the closeness of mingling our imaginations with the unembodied couple, as we "lend ourselves" (what we know in our bodies of sound, sight, movement) to perform their words. As different as the process of "reading couples" is from that of "being audience to couples," both narrative experiences—written and embodied—prompt us to witness/enact through ourselves how couples negotiate the thorny ground of their boundaries in their moments of performance. We experience something like it again in the partnering of story to theory/philosophy.

I look most often at narrative's "usual,"[5] not at moments of the extraordinary—scenes of birth, seduction, weddings, divorce, death, psychic undoing or restoration or epiphany—where the novel or film displays those life markers which seem to advance or turn the plot. Instead, my focus is most often on middles, on relationships under way, on repetitions, and on what fills in the space between a work's changes of direction. Narrative's extraordinary is nonrepeating; narrative's ordinary insists on its return. Edward Said's *Beginnings* and Frank Kermode's *The Sense of an Ending* have explored the importance of the sites of the text which mark the "beginning" and "ending," or which pitch their content to discussions of those imagined moments, or which take up the philosophic implications of the very ideas "beginning," "ending."[6] Edges, like "origins" and "closings," fascinate for the drama of their boundedness, for the potentiality of what they inspire or for their finality, for the fantasy they prompt that there be nothing prior to or following their being. Middles, on the other hand, do not inspire the romance of edges because they remove the pressure of the boundary. We often approach consideration of the middle with fear—will I reach an end? will there be a beginning? when will I again know the new? when will I again know closure? To lose the new or the experience of finishing seems to imply the loss of clarity, order, freshness, and the wisdom born from making meaning at an event's end. However, the constructedness and artifice of these apparent positions of beginning and ending belie their continuity with before and after. By acknowledging and resisting the drama of how stories construct life markers that declare "beginning," "ending," or the to-be-experienced-only-once, I've sought here to reveal how narratives depend as well on repetitions of rhetorical strategies, how they create a continuum of the ordinary and of meaning in their engagement with the process of making the known unknown and re-known in new ways.

In the way that a narrative has a "usual," or way of working, which it repeats as what it knows and then plays with through a process of re-creation, a story's couple has its "usual" way of being. In response to its own ordinariness, the pair comes to navigate or not its self-(re)invention over time. The partnership that finds pleasure in inventing new material out of the old embraces comedy as the performance mode most responsive to the fact of living with repetition. Knowing "the routine" (which also means knowing how to make it "unroutine") means knowing how to love in romantic comedy—a knowledge that makes present a happiness merely promised in the ending of "happily ever after."

INTIMACY

~

CHAPTER I

Conversation
Makes the Couple

When are we said to *tell* anything?—What is the language game of telling?
I should like to say: you regard it much too much as a matter of course
that one can tell anything to anyone. That is to say: we are so much
accustomed to communication through language, in conversation, that it
looks as if the whole point of communication lay in this: someone else
grasps the sense of my words—which is something mutual: he as it were
takes it into his mind.

—Ludwig Wittgenstein, *Philosophical Investigations*

Socrates and Agathon

"Speak low if you speak of love" (*Much Ado about Nothing,* II, i, 102–3). A
masked Don Pedro stages what it means to woo when he utters these words
to Hero. His hidden identity and speaking "low" theatricalize the conversation of love by associating it with costumes and a self-consciousness
about its sounds. What matters most about the performance of the love
scene, Don Pedro tells Hero, is its pitch or tone: its speaker does not need
to be known, but its sounds do. But what is this "low"? A deeper tone, a
quieter voice? And is it the sound of the words or the way they are spoken
which prompts us to know "this," as opposed to "that," is a conversation
of love, or the one addressed is the object of love talk? His words invite us
to wonder: What are the sounds of love? Is there a right way to speak it?
And why does knowing love's sounds take precedence perhaps over knowing its speaker?

Henry Tilney in *Northanger Abbey* suggests that even to arrive at the
conversation of love requires first other forms of shared talk, which have,
apparently, nothing to do with love. Upon first encountering Catherine
Morland and the blush that reveals her "unsatisfactory" first impressions
of him, he declares: "Thank you; for now we shall be soon acquainted, as

I am authorized to tease you and the subject [the blush and its meaning] whenever we meet, and nothing in the world advances intimacy so much" (27). The shared connection that enables acquaintance—an embarrass-ment—will lead to teasing and the referencing of a shared past. Embar-rassment, and especially ensuing conversations regarding it, signify the beginning, as Tilney describes it, of a relationship. Such an account of how intimacy advances in the Austen universe suggests questions like: How does a plot come finally to a conversation of love? Once there, what does one speak to tell of love, to pass on what that means to the self? And how is love's telling to be registered as "known" and responded to? In Wittgenstein's musings above, we are asked to wonder even more broadly how "to tell anything," and whether we can hold the sense of each other's words in our heads in something like mutual understanding, be that in the telling of love or a review of one's day.

I take all three of these moments to be invitations, invitations for us as readers/listeners to consider what it means to pursue and understand the nature of talk, in particular between lovers. What follows is a response to these invitations which explores the sounds and kinds of conversations between lovers in narrative, a response that interrogates what the presence of love conversations does to the narratives that hold them, and a response that examines the possibility or impossibility of mutuality between couples in the language games of telling, listening, and telling back, in the sound, look, and content of love exchanges. Bakhtin, in "The Problem of Speech Genres," asserts that utterances exist in discernible spheres as "relatively stable types . . . [which] we may call speech genres" (60). Utterances of love function as a speech genre that contributes to the identity of narra-tives. To understand how that contribution works, we need to consider the constituent features of the speech genre, and how it interacts with narra-tives' other forms of utterance.

Dialogue, as a rhetorical device, stands apart from the other forms of a novel's linguistic practice, or from how a film presents itself in its essen-tial telling through photography (sound comes second in film and hence could come second in its evolution). In addition to constructing the nar-rative's present tense as scene, dialogue reveals couples sometimes at play, even acts as the primary narrative space for doing so. And yet the functions of dialogue in general do not make self-evident the distinctive features and functions of the different conversations' speech genres and subtypes, how they work in relation to their speakers and the overall narrative, and specifically how the conversations of a novel or film pursue talk of love, and what the significance of love talk is to the narrative.

To consider these questions, it is useful to begin with a Socratic dialogue, if only because of its cultural standing as something like the "first" or model conversation of Western thought. It casts a long shadow that, I would assert, both reveals and obscures the nature of conversation.[1] The Socratic corpus suggests that Socrates devoted his philosophic life to the almost monomaniacal pursuit and demonstration of conversation, conversation which set out to encompass all topics of knowledge, including love. In the dialogues, Socrates employs conversation as the means by which the "truth" can be discerned through the rhetorical and philosophical rigors of question and answer. Intriguingly, however, one topic Socrates rarely considers is how conversation itself works, and how fundamental aspects of a topic, like love, are revealed in the form, rather than the content, of lovers' conversations. It is the Socrates of the *Symposium* who, when prompted by the others in his party, proposes to make "a plain statement of the truth about love with only such diction and phrases as may happen to occur to me on the spur of the moment" (74). For Socrates to assert that love can be known in a "plain statement of truth" and in a "spur of the moment" speech suggests that "love" lends itself to a belief in the possibility of an easy, spontaneous access to its "truth." Before delivering his address, however, Socrates chooses to ask the previous speaker, Agathon, a "few small questions so that I may obtain his agreement before I begin my speech" (74):

> "Let us sum up the points on which we have reached agreement. Are they not first that Love exists only in relation to some object, and second that that object must be something of which he is at present in want?"
> "Yes."
> "Now recall also what it was you declared in your speech to be the object of Love. I'll do it for you, if you like. You said, I think, that the troubles among the gods were composed by love of beauty, for there could be no such thing as love of ugliness. Wasn't that it?"
> "Yes."
> "Quite right, my dear friend, and if that is so, Love will be love of beauty, will he not, and not love of ugliness?"
> Agathon agreed.
> "Now we have agreed that Love is in love with what he lacks and does not possess."
> "Yes."
> "So after all Love lacks and does not possess beauty?"

"Inevitably."

"Well then, would you call what lacks and in no way possesses beauty beautiful?"

"Certainly not."

"Do you still think then that Love is beautiful, if this is so?"

"It looks, Socrates, as if I didn't know what I was talking about when I said that."

"Still, it was a beautiful speech." (77–78)

Set in the home of Agathon, where good friends meet for food, drink, and conversation, this scene, which demarcates an environment of the private, invites the topic of discourse, the nature of love. We are drawn into an easy acceptance of the accord of talk to scene and can focus attention on the "what" of the words spoken. As a work of philosophy, the *Symposium* prompts us to forget the narrative structures of setting and speakers in order that we attend to the logic of the arguments presented and to the arguments' ends, namely, "the truth." But while the Socratic dialogue foregrounds the process of question and answer as the model of conversation that brings us to knowledge, it is the nondialogic components, the features of storytelling surrounding the discourse as narrative background, which seem to call for the structuring form of this text to be conversation. Talking philosophically, as opposed to writing philosophy, requires a narrative concern with scene because it happens between voices who must be somewhere, and who must stand in some form of relation to each other.

Hans-Georg Gadamer, in *Truth and Method*, is drawn to take up the idea of the Socratic dialogue as a model for how we come to the "truth." Gadamer is interested in conversation, not for how it functions as a narrative scene, but for what he takes to be its object: arrival at the "truth." The "essence" of the question, he writes, is to have "sense," which includes a sense of "direction" (362).[2] A question, as a sentence, Gadamer asserts, must have a definite sense and a definite direction in order that it be taken as a real question. He continues, "Hence the sense of the question is the only direction from which the answer can be given if it is to make sense. A question places what is questioned in a particular perspective. When a question arises, it breaks open the being of the object, as it were" (362).

In keeping with Gadamer's depiction, Socrates directs Agathon through six questions as a means of breaking open Agathon's notion of love as "love of beauty." The first question prompts reassurance that Socrates has summarized appropriately their agreement on the ideas discussed ("Let us sum up the points on which we have reached agreement. Are they not . . . ?"). Another asks if Socrates has acceptably restated Agathon's earlier argument ("Now recall also what it was that you declared in your speech to be the object of Love. I'll do it for you, if you like. . . . Wasn't that it?"). The next question serves as the "then" response to an "if" assertion prompted by the agreement reached prior to it ("If that is so, Love will be love of beauty, will he not, and not love of ugliness?"). The subsequent question works to tie an idea earlier agreed upon to the current discussion ("So after all Love lacks and does not possess beauty?"), and the next question tests its logic ("Well then, would you call what lacks and in no way possesses beauty beautiful?"). Once all pieces of the argument are questioned and answered, the final question calls for a conclusion ("Do you still think then that Love is beautiful, if this is so?").

Socrates, then, illustrates Gadamer's notion of a dialogue by raising the questions that prompt the direction the conversation takes. This particular movement or choice of a concrete "this" or "that," this question followed by that answer versus that question versus this answer, cause the subject of what is being questioned to be understood from one vantage point. Agathon's subject, love as love of what is beautiful, inspires Socrates' questions, which prompt the answers of the conversation: if love loves an object of which it is in want, and if love loves the beautiful and not the ugly, then love lacks the beautiful and hence itself cannot be beautiful. The sense of direction created by the questions is itself limited by the nature of the subject; this limitation creates the "horizon" of the questions. For Socrates to ask questions about the relationship between good food and love would be beyond the boundaries of the subject as Agathon determined it.

Further, there is a "trying on" of each partner's words so that Socrates works within the framework of Agathon's vocabulary in summarizing his argument, asking questions about the meaning of his words and turning the words around so that new words juxtapose and prompt a new perspective. Likewise, Agathon can enter Socrates' recasting of his language in order to see the logic of this revision of his definition of love. Agathon's "reiterated yesses," as Gadamer casts it, reveal the first condition of conversation, "that the other person is with us" (367). "The inner logic" of the subject proceeds unhampered by interruption and digression so that the subject matter seems to conduct the partners, rather than the partners conducting the subject matter. Opposed to a notion of conversation as an act of *argument*, Gadamer embraces the Platonic dialogue because it creates a sense of "falling into" conversation where questions act not to present differing takes on the subject but instead lead to an increasingly refined, clear notion of the truth of the subject.[3] This reflects his belief that "when a question arises, it breaks open the being of the object, as it were" (362). For Gadamer, then, the speaking subjects do not lead the conversation; instead, it is their subject which leads and which leads them to knowledge.

Construing the Platonic dialogue to be the embodiment of what occurs during the process of conversation leads Gadamer to conclude:

> Our first point is that the language in which something comes to speak is not a possession at the disposal of one or the other of the interlocutors. Every conversation presupposes a common language, or better, creates a common language. Something is placed in the center, as the Greeks say, which the partners in dialogue both share, and concerning which they can exchange ideas with one another. Hence reaching an understanding on the subject matter of a conversation necessarily means that a common language must first be worked out in the conversation. This is not an external matter of simply adjusting our tools; nor is it even right to say that the partners adapt themselves to one another but, rather, in a successful conversation *they both come under the influence of the truth of the object* and are thus *bound to one another in a new community.* To reach an understanding in a dialogue is not merely a matter of putting oneself forward and successfully asserting one's own point of view, but being *transformed into a communion in which we do not remain who we were.* (378–79, emphasis mine)

If love is the "something" placed at the center of Socrates and Agathon's conversation, then a common language about the relation of love to beauty is what arises between them. For Gadamer it is the subject that insists on this language. Once engaged in the discovery of the language and aware of the dawning of the truth of the subject, the partners experience a transcendent bonding—conversation makes a community of two out of two strangers. Religious in overtone, Gadamer's description transforms separate conversants into partners joined in "communion" with the almost "divine" truth of a subject. The act of engaging in conversation means experiencing a transfiguration of the self: "we do not remain who we were." Who the partners were before, or who they have become as transfigured selves, or what it means to be in a community of two is not, though, Gadamer's concern. The pressure of the subject has prompted change; however, what the change means is left to silence. Still, Gadamer comes to the conclusion that the pursuit of the truth through conversation does transform separate selves into partners and into different selves. However, are Socrates and Agathon transformed? Do we no longer recognize Socrates? Does Agathon's voice of "reiterated yesses" differentiate him finally from any of the other speakers with whom Socrates engages in dialogue?

If we return to the dialogue and to Socrates' prefatory remarks before he begins his series of questions, we discover his motive in addressing Agathon: to "obtain his agreement before I begin my speech." It is not, therefore, the truth of the subject which causes Socrates and Agathon to fall into this conversation on love, but rather Socrates' need to prompt Agathon to understand the faults of his depiction of love. We do not see the voice of Socrates transformed, nor do we discover a fully realized, re-created Agathon. Instead, we hear the relentless questions and affirmative responses that cause us to recall other Platonic dialogues from past reading. The echo is not of a moment when two conversants' language was transformed into a communal, iterative approach of the truth of the subject, but rather of the repetition of a particular scene. We hear again a figure of some note in Greek culture (call him Agathon, Phaedrus, Aristophanes) offer a description of an idea. And we experience again the dismantling of that idea and its speaker's identity in the Socratic questions that overwhelm and dismiss with the pressure of their logic. Short, certain replies of "yes" or "no" are all that seem possible in response to the prompting of Socrates' questions. The Socratic dialectic leaves little room for the possibility of another's ideas or the particularity of another. Out of the retraction of Agathon's theory will come the Socratic answer—an idea derived from the process of question and answer, built on the ruins of Agathon's argument.

While we do not, therefore, see a new language of the subject emerge from the joint interaction of Socrates and Agathon, nor a mutual falling away of the individuality of the speakers to where they both no longer know themselves (though this seems to be true of Agathon), we do see a conversation that highlights the primacy of the question. Every address Socrates makes to Agathon is in the form of a question, except one, "Now we have agreed that Love is in Love with what he lacks and does not possess," to which Agathon says, "Yes." Here too Socrates' statement could have ended with a question mark as it calls for the same response from Agathon as did his "questions," namely, confirmation. His only other noninterrogative is the final remark, "Still, it was a beautiful speech," a closing move toward irony. After having caused Agathon to retract his equation of love and beauty, Socrates tells him that his words are beautiful and, therefore, empty because love is not beauty.

Gadamer asserts that, in order for a question to be a "real" question, its answer must not already be known by the questioner. The conversation evolves out of a mutual sense of a genuine search for knowledge wherein the process of questioning and answering is reciprocal between the partners. Both experience the surprise of the language and its subject that emerges as a result. When Socrates creates questions as a summary of what was previously said and merely asks for affirmation that he "got it right," or when he asks a question to which there can only be one answer, which Agathon and Socrates alike know, or when he leads Agathon through a series of questions to a conclusion that can only refute Agathon's original claim, we must consider, are these "real" questions? Gadamer could claim that the truth of the subject leads Socrates to ask these particular questions, which will lead to their particular answers. But the subject does not lead Socrates; rather, Socrates leads the subject and Agathon. Socrates acts as the master builder of knowledge who sets out to gain Agathon's agreement. The order of his questions reveals a plan of analysis based on two premises: that love exists in relation to some object, and that the object must be something of which love is in want. The conclusion that love is the beautiful fails then because if it seeks the beautiful (the object it lacks) it must be ugly, or if it is beautiful it must seek the ugly (the object it lacks). In either instance, Love cannot be understood wholly as the beautiful. Socrates asks questions whose answers he knows; he does not, therefore, ask "real" questions.

One way to make sense of the Socratic dialogue is to let go of the notion that it is about the mutual adjustments of partners engaged in the joint discovery of a subject or of the understanding of each other's position. Instead, if we understand Socrates to be a "midwife" of knowledge, we can understand how he performs the method of *maieusis* to enable the birth of an idea in another person. "Midwiving" knowledge is best accomplished by questions and hints. David Fordyce comments that the mind of the Socratic model was "richly impregnated with the Principles of all Knowledge, but that these lay hid like rude Embryo's in the dark Womb of Thought—and that it required an artful Midwife to deliver them" (qtd. in Berland 101–2). The expression of surprise or a difference of opinion in conversation would mean that "knowledge" had not been born in one or both partners: how can there be surprise or opinion in the face of know-ing "the truth"? And it is clear Socrates knows the conclusion he desires to reach because he knows the truth about love; his challenge lies in how as midwife to show Agathon the faults of his logic.

If the Socratic method functions successfully as a particular scene of teaching/birthing, it fails as a scene of conversation. As Socrates' questions grow increasingly suspect in our eyes and we see his methodic control over where the conversation must advance, our suspicions of Agathon's answers mount. Are the questions so loaded that they already contain the only answer that Agathon can provide? Or do they allow room for a different direction of thought from that which the horizon of the question seems to demand? Agathon could object to the opening premises, or he could allow for the possibility of the love of the ugly; to make either of these moves would be to upset the direction of Socrates' questions. However, the power of Socrates' hold on the scene is so inviolable that we sense, regardless of Agathon's reply, that the Socratic voice would construct other questions that would still lead Agathon to the negation of his theory. Because Agathon's answers only reiterate the answer already contained in Socrates' questions and because we doubt any answer could sway the Socratic direction of the conversation, we can conclude that Agathon's are not "real" answers.

A Model of Conversation

Finding Gadamer's choice of the Socratic dialogue to be wanting as a par-adigm for his description of the nature of conversation, we need to look again at the description. Is it the case that conversation is a process of com-ing to an understanding, that "it belongs to every true conversation that each person opens himself to the other, truly accepts his point of view as valid and transposes himself into the other to such an extent that *he under-stands not the particular individual but what he says*" (385)? Is a true con-versation about reaching a mutual understanding of a subject? Is a process of transposition attainable, in which each partner "enters" the other in the act of coming to understand the other's position? Is it possible to separate knowledge of the individual from knowledge of what he or she says? Is the goal of conversation to reach the "truth" of the idea addressed, or to reach the partner co-addressing the idea? Are these distinguishable? I need to ask again, What is a conversation? And what is its significance, in the sense of, what does it accomplish?

The verb "to converse" is from the Latin *conversare,* to turn round frequently, or to direct. (The Socratic dialogue works as the great instance of conversing as directing.) Both of these root definitions—to turn round frequently and to direct—create a picture of an active, changing verb. Turning round frequently suggests a going between, a back and forth, or a circling. The phrase also implies something that bears ongoing analysis, as in turning an idea over again and again. *Conversatio,* the Latin root of the noun conversation, means frequent sojourn to or abode in a place, or regular dealings with a person. Whereas the verb insists on movement, the noun carries with it a sense of continuity, as in the ongoing relation of one person to another or to a place. If the roots of *conversation* insist on the same "players" over time, the roots of *converse* insist that those players change, move, realign. Of the definitions the *O.E.D.* cites for the meanings of conversation, all eleven insist on some form of "engagement with" or "being in the company of." The definitions include living in a place with others; consorting or having dealings with others; sexual intercourse; acquaintance or intimacy with a matter, company, or society; the manner of how one conducts oneself in society; the interchange of thoughts and words, familiar discourse or talk; a public debate; having an "at home" (gathering); a painting representing a group of figures; a card with the sentence for a game. Whether it is conversation as sexual intercourse, or the interchange of words and ideas, or living in the society of others, conversation carries with it some form of company and some stated or implied interaction. While it is conversation as "interchange of thoughts and words, familiar discourse or talk" that concerns me generally, more specifically I will pursue *how* conversation as talk mediates a relationship between the same couple over time (the root of conversation), and *how* conversing creates a context for the dynamics of making meaning together and for what it means to be together as something that necessarily shifts and changes (the root of converse).

The nineteenth-century linguist Wilhelm von Humboldt's sense of the function and form of speech as that "which is a necessary condition for reflection, even in solitude" characterizes one philosophical take on language which requires only one speaker and an object of his speech set in isolation (in Bakhtin, "Speech Genres" 67). Such a position makes secondary the presence of another and the desire for and activity of communication. However, what Bakhtin will come to call "real-life dialogue" (75) *requires* the presence of an other who must respond to hearing speech and discerning meaning from it, because listening and understanding for Bakhtin are inherently responsive. One "either agrees or disagrees with it (completely or partially), augments it, applies it, prepares for its execution, and so on" (68). A conversation between two partners, whether textually portrayed in a medium such as a novel or film or occurring in actual life, does not happen in isolation; rather, it is located within a scene or context.[4] Embedded within a setting of visual and auditory components (depending on the medium), the words exchanged in "real-life dialogue" demand the primary attention of the rhetors. Between them they create the "narrative present" of a rhetorical situation where the story of the scene is about the act of two people talking.[5] Whereas Gadamer allows the Socratic method of question and answer to best represent the work of conversation, we have seen that the figure of Agathon could not feel as if he were engaged in the act of exchanging thoughts or opinions. Real speech for Bakhtin presupposes not only the presence of a listening other but also the speaker's "expect[ation of] a response from [the listener], an active responsive understanding. The entire utterance is constructed, as it were, in anticipation of encountering this response" (94). The passive head nodder in Socrates' dialogues cannot be taken for such a partner in communication.[6] What does it mean to be a real partner in conversation? And how do real partners make a real conversation?

A conversation depends first on the gathering together of two or more people who speak collectively—but not all at once. There must be a rhythm of mutual exchange where turns are taken. Without this process of "turn-taking," the scene becomes something else, a lecture to students, a soliloquy from a tragedy, a comedic monologue, a psychoanalytic session, a giving of a medical history, a reporting of the news, a telling of a story. Words are exchanged between the conversants in their turn-taking; each must be responsible for holding up his or her end of the conversation. The demands of mutual exchange make clear the benefits and risks of participation: speaking and misspeaking what is meant, being understood and misunderstood, connecting to and missing each other, being informed and informing or bored and boring, creating a revelation or passing the time, revealing or hiding oneself, discovering or obscuring the other.

The rhythm of turn-taking indicates a conversation underway, but a conversation must first begin. That initiation happens because one person gestures to another to engage in a talking partnership. Words of conviviality, such as greetings or questions to convey interest in the other, may act as the initiating step of a conversation. Or there may be a topic of pressing concern to one or more of the participants; then the topic itself may initiate and direct where the discourse moves. Likewise, talk inevitably must end—and this act must be signaled by one rhetor to the other. Conversations have the sense then of being structured with a beginning and ending, or are framed by the words of who initiates and who closes the exchange.

Sociolinguists such as Deborah Tannen recognize that conversations are shaped not only by a large-scale narrative structure of the "opening," "working through," and "closing" but also by micro-scale formal contributions from a conversant's structuring behavior.[7] Evaluating when to speak (the concept of knowing when it's one's turn), showing how ideas relate to each other (the act of summarizing or making connections), revealing one's relation to the conversation (listening, being interested, appreciative, friendly, hostile, critical, angry, apologetic, seeking help, offering it), and indicating how one feels at the time of the conversation (facial expressions of excitation, sadness, boredom, body posture of fatigue, energy, attraction, hostility, eye movement of interest or lack of concentration, tone of voice, gestures) work together to create the *scene* of a conversation. What Tannen defines, in essence, is the performance elements of conversation. Paul Grice calls this act of knowing when and how to interact with another the "Cooperative Effort" or the "Cooperative Principle." He defines it as making "your conversational contribution such as is required, at the stage at which it occurs, by the accepted purpose or direction of the talk exchange in which you are engaged" (26). However, Grice applies his notion of cooperation only to the semantic content of rhetors' language, the message or linguistic part of an interaction, to how the "what" chosen to say shows we understand each other. Tannen and other sociolinguists recognize in addition metamessage or paralinguistic elements of conversation, by which information is conveyed not in words but in the "how" of what is said. Sociolinguists' emphasis on the metamessage goes beyond the implicature of actual words spoken and requires an understanding of the totality of a speaker's actions in relation to the context or scene in which the words are spoken.

The vocal signals of pacing, pausing, loudness, pitch, intonation, and using particular forms of address are the conversational devices through which we control and choose how and when to speak. For example, using the exclamatory or imperative statement with an intensity of loudness or pitch reveals the conversational device of "expressive reaction." Likewise, the interrogative statement combined with a rising intonation creates the conversational device of the question. Other assertions made through the declarative combined with varying signals can produce the conversational devices of complaining, apologizing, claiming, and relaying information.[8] The conversational devices of expressive reaction, questioning, apologizing, complaining, claiming, or relaying information act as the means of revealing the speaker's intent. However, the idea of intentionality raises complications for which the concept of conversational device cannot fully account. Is the intent of the speaker fully or adequately revealed in one of the six structures of address cited above? How does the receiver of the message perceive what is offered?

What is at stake here is the relationship between what is stated, implied, meant, and what is received, or how we mean and come to understand another's meaning. Early in his description of "language and the actions into which it is woven" as the "language-game," Wittgenstein explores an account of the word as that which names or labels a thing (5e(7)). The word points like a linguistic gesture to the thing. Wittgenstein discusses what it means to understand a word: "What really comes before our mind when we understand a word?—Isn't it something like a picture? Can't it *be* a picture?" (54e(139)). "To understand a sentence means to understand a language. To understand a language means to be master of a technique" (81e(199)). To allow Wittgenstein's claim means to accept the notion that conversants do understand each other because they can picture the words, understand the sentence, be masters of the technique that informs the language they exchange. Within this framework, we may explore the relationship between the stated, implied, meant, and received and other cognitive elements of transmitted and received thought. The "implied" surfaces for Wittgenstein in the idea of a sentence contained within a sentence, against a background of language containing a vast array of sentences:

If you shout "slab!" you really mean: "Bring me a slab!"—But how do you do this: how do you mean that while you say "slab!" Do you say the unshortened sentence to yourself? And why should I translate the call "slab!" into a different expression in order to say what someone means by it? And if they mean the same thing—why should I not say: "When he says 'slab!' he means 'slab!'"? [8e(19)] . . . We say that we use the command in contrast with other sentences because our language contains the possibility of other sentences. . . . But doesn't the fact that sentences have the same sense consist in their having the same use? (9e(20))

If "Slab!" contains the implied sense "Bring me a slab!" it contains that sentence. Because both sentences have the same sense, they have the same use. And a language, Wittgenstein writes, has the possibility of sentences containing the same meaning of other sentences—of different sentences having the same use—which I choose to distinguish here as the stated and the implied. Understanding the "sentence within a sentence" as a condition of language means for Wittgenstein that we take on both the stated and the implied when we process the stated, in other words, that that is part of the work of being engaged in conversation.

Grice also differentiates between stated wording and intended meaning, but he develops a more formalized idea of implicature. He first casts conversation as an act characterizable through Kant's categories of distinctions of quantity, quality, relation, and manner. To adhere to these rules is to state one's meaning directly. Whereas following the rule of quantity would be to "make contributions as informative as required for the purposes of the exchange and not more so," following the distinction of quality would be to "make contributions that are true." Likewise, following the rule of manner is to "be perspicuous," whereas following the distinction of relevancy is to "make conversation something reasonable to follow" (27–29). Implicature "flouts" these four rules through the use of silence or through an unstated or less than fully realized connection, as in a figure of speech made between remarks (violations of quantity); use of irony, metaphor, hyperbole, meiosis (violations of quality); use of a disconnected rejoinder to a statement so as to change the subject (violation of relevance); and use of ambiguity so as to overtly obscure meaning so that, for example, a child present cannot understand (violation of perspicuity) (35). In each instance of implicature, the speaker intends a meaning that is perceivable if the person present understands which "rule" of conversation is being bent. Grice determines, then, that a conversant can state directly what is meant by adhering to the four distinctions and can imply what is meant by playing with these distinctions.

In contrast, Tannen considers how conversations are framed by silent extralinguistic indicators of intent.[9] Whereas words stated directly or implied may reveal the frame to be "I intend seriousness or humor or anger or confusion," conversants also determine frames nonlinguistically. Pitch, tone, use of pauses, physical expression, silence may all work to reveal how partners are to read the frame of the conversation, or the structure that indicates how conversants are relating. A frame shift occurs when one of the partners recognizes that he or she has read the frame incorrectly. This is the moment of dawning when a rhetor sees this misreading of intent and wanders between frames, or finds the appropriate frame in which to perceive the intent. "Getting" a joke works this way in that moment before one realizes it is a joke, or at once understands what it is about the joke that is funny. Whereas Gadamer and Grice think about conversation for how it reveals the "truth" or "knowledge" or "information" of a topic, and Wittgenstein plays with how the language games of conversation give us the sense of knowing, Tannen concerns herself with understanding the social dynamic between the conversants. She puts at the center of her discussion the fact of performers engaged in a performance, performers who must read both the linguistic and nonlinguistic elements of their scene of shared speech to discern meaning.

Further, taking up the idea of indirect meaning leads Gadamer, Grice, and Wittgenstein to consider how the implied is embedded within language itself. Tannen instead allows for conversants to negotiate implication through a process of reading what is silently going on between them. Unlike Grice, when Tannen considers verbal cues that create implication through the idea of speaking indirectly, she emphasizes what this does between the conversants relationally (*That's Not* 55–59). She points to the "rapport" that is created through indirection: not having to "spell it out" produces an unstated moment of relational congratulations (we understand each other so well that we don't have to speak).[10] Tannen brings together how the language between speakers works and what it means that there are two people physically present to one another—what they do to "act out" their conversation, and what starts to happen between them as a result of these actions. To understand the nature of conversation as a speech act necessitates an engaged analysis of how its words mean and how its speakers perform that meaning: both the words and the speakers speak and act.

Socrates and Alcibiades

While a model of conversation can be understood as the unstated, even unconscious, structure that is in effect as talking occurs, we need to consider how the model changes as the nature of conversation changes. The conversation between Socrates and Agathon sounds strange, hollow. Different languages and different means of using them in conversation are appropriate for different occasions: this is the premise of Bakhtin's notion of "speech genres." Conversations use a particular kind of language for a friendly chat, another for gossip, another for confrontation, another for establishing or speaking about intimacy (Duck and Pond 19). Words about love do not have the right ring to them when they are spoken to a group as a reasoned, well-turned speech. The Socrates of the *Symposium,* Martha Nussbaum tells us in *The Fragility of Goodness,*

> is put before us as an example of a man in the process of making himself self-sufficient—put before us, in our own still unregenerate state, as a troublesome question mark and a challenge. Is this the life we want for ourselves? Is that the way we want, or need, to see and hear? We are not allowed to have the cozy thought that the transformed person will be just like us, only happier. Socrates is weird. He is, in fact, "not similar to any human being." We feel, as we look at him, both awestruck and queasy, timidly homesick for ourselves. We feel that we must look back at what we currently are, our loves, our ways of seeing, the problems these cause for practical reason. We need to see ourselves more clearly before we can say whether we would like to become this sort of being, excellent and deaf. (184)

Revealingly, Nussbaum chooses "deaf" to describe Socrates, an attribute that questions the very possibility that he can converse. One must be able to hear another in order to interact. Being "deaf to argument" is how Habermas describes the figure whose words are presented as beyond criticism, unable to be improved (18). Socrates, as the founding father of dialectic argumentation, can strangely be recast as an outsider to it.

It is only when Alcibiades literally falls into the conversation drunk and declares his love for one particular man, Socrates, that something of the language of love, performed to Socrates as if in conversation with only him, can be heard. The arrival of Alcibiades signals a shift in Socrates' speech, in his sentence construction. The Socrates whose speech depends on the lack of particularity of his interlocutor (call him Agathon, Phaedrus, Aristophanes) disappears. A Socrates whose speech has everything to do with the individuality of the listener takes his place. The characteristic sounds of Socrates throughout his dialogues, what K. J. H. Berland calls "his questioning method, his assumed ignorance, his irony, his dry wit" (96), disappear in the face of, or when confronted with, the sounds of Alcibiades. Socrates, it turns out, is not deaf; he had just stopped listening (out of boredom, arrogance?). The presence and responsiveness of Alcibiades transform Socrates' speech from "signifying units of a language—words and sentences—that are impersonal, belonging to nobody and addressed

to nobody" to what Bakhtin calls "utterances" that are "directed to someone," and hence embody a chief marker of the utterance, "addressivity"
("Speech Genres" 95). Alcibiades insists that Socrates direct his words
to him; likewise, Socrates' presence demands the same from Alcibiades.
Nussbaum writes, "*The Symposium* is a work about passionate, erotic
love. . . . Its only speech [Alcibiades'] that claims to tell the 'truth' is a story
of complex passion, both sexual and intellectual, for a particular person"
(167). Before the arrival of Alcibiades, Socrates delivers a monologue on
the nature of love. Significantly, the *Symposium* does not end with this
speech, words based on a remembrance of hearing Diotima of Mantinea's
discussion of the topic. What is revealing about Socrates' borrowed words
is their formality, their repeatability, their lack of connection to one particular author who speaks them because he feels them and who addresses
them to the particular object of his love. Could such a speech approach
the nature of love? While Alcibiades too delivers a speech about love, it is
his "own," his panegyric about *the* man *he* loves, *Socrates.*

Before Alcibiades' speech, a very different conversation from others
heard in the *Symposium* occurs between him and Socrates:

> "If I praise any person but him in his presence, be it god or man,
> he won't be able to keep his hands off of me."
> "Be quiet," said Socrates.
> "It's no good your protesting," Alcibiades said. "I won't make a
> speech in praise of any other person in your presence."
> "Very well," said Eryximachus, "adopt that course, if you like, and
> make a speech in praise of Socrates."
> "What?" said Alcibiades. "Do you think I ought, Eryximachus?
> Shall I set about the fellow and pay him out in the presence of you
> all?"
> "Here, I say!" said Socrates; "what have you in mind? Are you
> going to make fun of me by a mocking panegyric? Or what?"
> "I shall tell the truth. Do you allow that? . . . don't be surprised if
> I get into a muddle in my reminiscences; it isn't easy for a man in my
> condition to sum up your extraordinary character in a smooth and
> orderly sequence." (99–100)

The sound of this interaction is remarkably different from that between
Agathon and Socrates. Whereas Socrates leads Agathon through an analysis of his errors in logic about the nature of love, Alcibiades speaks of the

man Socrates, about whom making a speech in a "smooth and orderly sequence" seems impossible. This movement in language from one distinct voice to another, from one speech type to another, reveals Bakhtin's notion of "heteroglossia." We feel the pressure of Alcibiades' presence in the scene because of the individuality of his voice in the dialogue and because of the shift of speech type he introduces. Alcibiades utters a new language of love. While he displays Grice's rules in that he claims he will speak only of what is necessary, truthful, relevant, and clear to reveal this man who is his love, he violates the rules of "good social behavior" because his very presence and what he might reveal are impositions. In not giving Socrates the option of stopping these words (though he will allow Socrates to correct him if he lies) and in agitating Socrates to the point of anger because of the embarrassment of the situation, Alcibiades does not create with Socrates a conversation of friendly, distanced camaraderie. Where Alcibiades will go with the words that he addresses to Socrates (as if this is his part in an ongoing conversation between them, which we have the privilege to overhear, not as its audience but as its eavesdroppers) is to say finally that "the really wonderful thing about him is that he is like no other human being, living or dead" (110).

The confusion of the moment—Alcibiades drunk, Socrates embarrassed, Eryximachus goading Alcibiades on—marks a break from the previous text of the *Symposium*. The dialogue of teacher correcting student for faults in logic gives way to a scene of talk between lovers. We hear a difference in the sounds of the words used which stems from the mens' knowledge of and particular feelings for each other. We feel drawn into the moment because of how words are put together between these men— the energy of that engagement—and by the sense that something is going to happen here by virtue of their responsiveness. We stop knowing this text as a work of philosophy whose ideas we are to try on in abstraction, even with the presence of a setting and speakers, and come again to remember, or perhaps experience for the first time, the *Symposium* as narrative. This is a scene. This is a plot happening. This is a moment of mimesis because these two men are present to each other as "performers" of a love conversation. A conversation between lovers makes a text of philosophy for a few pages seem no longer to know itself, or to force from it a brief molting into another mode of being.

What's curious is how and why this transformation occurs. This is not a question for Gadamer, Grice, Wittgenstein, or Habermas. Philosophers of language do not as a rule make it their business to discuss shifts in speech kind or the transformations in genre that may result. While Socrates may discuss in a philosophical dialogue (*dialogus* is Latin for philosophical conversation) the nature of love, he is not concerned with how love talk actually sounds, or with the relationship it creates between its performers, or with how it alters the structure of the dialogue. What concerns philosophers is not the impact of different modes of conversation but rather how and why an idealized "dialogue" leads to meaning. They explore propositions in the dialogic context, not to understand the context, but to better understand the propositions.

What is it about the specifics of a conversation between lovers in the *Symposium* that makes narrative happen so spontaneously, so surprisingly, even in the midst of another textual form? Bakhtin's interest in heteroglossia—in how languages differentiate themselves, mingle, coexist to create the buzzing linguistic activity of the text "as life"—leads him to acknowledge levels of intimate talk. That his focus is primarily the novel and not philosophy also prompts his recognition of ranges of public and private speech. Bakhtin might explain such an outbreak of a novel-like scene in a philosophical dialogue by the nearness of speaker to addressee and the attitudes between them, the ways these facts interact to create a genre's "style" and a genre's resistance to or willingness for intimacy:

> Intimate genres and styles are based on a maximum internal proximity of the speaker and addressee, in his sympathy, in the sensitivity and goodwill of his responsive understanding. In this atmosphere of profound trust, the speaker reveals his internal depths. This determines the special expressiveness and internal candor of these styles (as distinct from the loud street-language candor of familiar speech). Familiar and intimate genres and styles (as yet very little studied) reveal extremely clearly the dependence of style on a certain sense and understanding of the addressee (the addressee of the utterance) on the part of the speaker, and on the addressee's actively responsive understanding that is anticipated by the speaker. These styles reveal especially clearly the narrowness and incorrectness of traditional stylistics, which tries to understand and define style solely from the standpoint of the semantic and thematic content of speech and the speaker's expressive attitude toward this content. Unless one accounts for the speaker's attitude toward the *other* and his utterance (existing or anticipated), one can understand neither the genre nor style of speech. ("Speech Genres" 97–98)

Like Don Pedro, Bakhtin knows that to inhabit the genre of intimacy means to affect its style, as in "speaking low" to make for its "special expressiveness" or "internal candor." Likewise, Bakhtin understands that a speech genre can switch with transformations in context: a text of philosophy can become a narrative with the displayed nearness of a Socrates to an Alcibiades, and the presence of their threatened, adoring, "overwhelmed by" attitudes toward each other and their utterances. Not the content of their speech but their *attitudes* toward each other, Bakhtin tells us, are what make for the possibility of an intimate style and genre. Intimacy, it seems, can break out in some styles of speech but not in others. That the Socrates/Alcibiades conversation has a "feeling" to it stems from the mens' feelings for each other, not from the "truth" or logic of what they have to say about the nature of love. Swept up all at once into their scene, the assembled become those who are "around them," those who function now as their suddenly uninvited audience. Alcibiades and Socrates create a configuration of two who perform to each other, stand apart from the others, and exist as "together": in essence, they become a couple.

Narratives tell us conversations are not just about their apparent subjects, or the making of knowledge, or the arrival at the truth. Conversations set in the context of a story are performances between people who have attitudes and feelings about each other in addition to concerns about the ostensible subject of their conversation. While their talk may do nothing to advance the pursuit of truth (though it may), it may do everything to create a context for shared speech, time, and ways of knowing each other—for being in the world together. Narrative speech may at times function as philosophic dialogue. On these occasions (they are few), we may use philosophers' analyses of how conversation creates subjects to explore some general structures of conversation and how narratives mean or define a world. However, a narrative's insistence on love talk requires much more—that we consider how states of feeling and modes of performance enter into and emerge from conversation. In essence, the presence of partnered speech in a novel or film opens new possibilities for experiencing an intimacy that is not our own, for understanding how we come to know the intimacies of a couple, for imagining how those intimacies make their "coupleness," and for exploring what the relation is between the couple and the narrative world that holds them. Narrative conversations promise an experience that skepticism claims we cannot have—witnessing something like shared feelings or knowledge.

CHAPTER 2

Word-Work:
Couples and Their Plots

Few hours spent in the *hard labour of incessant talking* will dispatch
more subjects than can really be in common between any two rational
creatures, yet with lovers it is different. Between *them* no subject is finished,
no communication is even made, till it has been made at least twenty
times over.

> —Jane Austen, *Sense and Sensibility*

In the way that we remember an action narrative by virtue of its starred,
event-defining deeds, we remember a marriage narrative through its starred,
event-defining conversations. Crux conversations function as destinations
toward which a narrative directs its energy; they stand out from the rest
of the narrative as "keys," or as necessary points of arrival in order for the
plot to come into full being. They are the moments from which we mark
off how a narrative charts its passing of time, or path of development, or
places of knowledge gaining. In particular, they embody a partnership's
turns, as in how that partnership discovers itself, understands itself, ends
itself. In marriage narratives, the strategies for how the narrative plots have
everything to do with how its couples turn. Therefore, couples' conversations display both how the narrative works through its whole structural
design and the thing it works hardest at representing, the couple. Crux
conversations uncover the pleasures that accompany the experience of intimate knowledge, knowledge that unfolds in defining, often shattering, in
the sense of groundbreaking, instances of speech.

Beginnings

Within the array of moments in a couple's history when plot turns upon
the fact of a conversation, the "first meeting" requires that words be exchanged, that each future partner hear the other speak, observe his or her

manner, and in turn be observed. Because the "first-time" conversation functions to define the narrative, how the two interact becomes a model for subsequent meetings and for how the plot proceeds by acting as a reference point for all that follows. It prompts from the events/exchanges to follow questions like, Does that exchange justly define us? or, Are we still like that? Therefore, it is a rare narrative that presents what we would consider a generic or repeatable conversation of introduction. We do not witness just the sharing of names, work, interests which exhibits Grice's rules of telling the necessary in a truthful, relevant, clear manner, or Lakoff's formula of negotiating distance and involvement. Instead, we find an odd exchange or strange form of meeting which shakes itself subtly or deliberately from out of the comfortable procession of plot to demand a different attention, in terms of our expectation both of conversation and of plot development.[1] The novel or film proceeds by stopping at this meeting. Therefore, narratives cue us by marking off as distinct the first conversation between "the couple." Aware that we are hearing something unusual, we know to attend to this dialogue, and come to know in time that it is from these opening words that the important work of the couple commences.

So that in *Pride and Prejudice,* for instance, a forestalled conversation functions to mark the first meeting of Elizabeth and Darcy. Each stands in a position to overhear the other. Elaborate plotting strategies for both bringing together and keeping apart these future lovers surround the very possibility of their first coming to speak to each other. What their first conversation plots is suspense: the ironic suspense of a meeting actually happening in that it doesn't happen, and the suspense that builds around our anticipation of what will be said when it does. First we read:

> Elizabeth Bennet had been obliged, by the scarcity of gentlemen to sit down for two dances; and during that time Mr. Darcy had been standing near enough for her to overhear a conversation between him and Mr. Bingley. . . .
>
> "Come, Darcy," said he, "I must have you. I hate to see you standing about by yourself in this stupid manner. You had much better dance."
>
> "I certainly shall not. You know how I detest it, unless I am particularly acquainted with my partner. At such an assembly as this, it would be insupportable. Your sisters are engaged, and there is not another woman in the room, with whom it would not be a punishment to me to stand up with." (59)

Eleven pages later at another social gathering, with still no words exchanged directly between them, Darcy stages himself to overhear Elizabeth:

> He began to wish to know more of her, and as a step towards conversing with her himself, attended to her conversation with others. His doing so drew her notice.
> "What does Mr. Darcy mean," she said to Charlotte, "by listening to my conversation with Colonel Forster?"
> "That is a question which Mr. Darcy only can answer."
> "But if he does it any more I shall certainly let him know that I see what he is about. He has a very satirical eye, and if I do not begin by being impertinent myself, I shall soon grow afraid of him." . . .
> "Did not you think, Mr. Darcy, that I expressed myself uncommonly well just now, when I was teasing Colonel Forster to give us a ball at Maryton?"
> "With great energy;—but it is a subject which always makes a lady energetic." (70–71)

The scene of Elizabeth and Darcy's meeting is set, not around their conversation, but rather around their acting as *eavesdroppers* to each others' conversations. Significantly, both overhear words about themselves. This picture of each character speaking of the other to his or her closest friend while the other listens in figures the means by which knowledge of the other is attained throughout the text. Triangles, in which words are exchanged between two while a third listens or in which words are exchanged behind the scenes and the third surmises what has been said without having been a witness to them, generate the misinformation and misperception that drive the novel. The act of acquiring knowledge of and judging character is the novel's preoccupation; therefore, how that knowledge is acquired and judged is of vital importance to the workings of the plot.

For Elizabeth, her position of "unknown surveillant" will color her perception of Darcy's character in accordance with how it is portrayed to her. If conversations occur directly between them, these words will not be taken at "face value" because Darcy can have no face value. Her first encounter with him is staged in a scene of the hidden and masked, that which she had access to because of her own position of being hidden to him. If, therefore, conversations are overheard or are reported from other sources, Elizabeth takes them to be trustworthy forms of knowledge. The rules then for how Darcy's character is to be understood are modeled in Elizabeth's relationship to her first "conversation" with him.

Whereas Elizabeth happens accidentally to stand near enough to Darcy to overhear his rejection of the women of Longbourn and in particular his rejection of her, Darcy overhears Lizzy deliberately. Her action functions as a response to him; she confronts him for his seeming impropriety: "Did you not think, Mr. Darcy, that I expressed myself uncommonly well just now?" The progression of the plot will proceed with Darcy's deliberately generative actions: he observes Elizabeth openly, proposes, writes a letter, and proposes again. In his first meeting and "conversation" with Lizzy he places himself in the position of "observable surveillant," whereby he acts in openness and in silence. Darcy's first known position to Elizabeth will function as a model for how his knowledge of her and his generative actions of plot will recur—through a public information gathering about her (as if she were a kind of observable datum), through the actions he takes to marry her, and through the silence in which he shrouds himself. While his is a project of collecting knowledge in a publicly observable form, hers is collection acquired through secrets and the privately passed on. His are perceptions of her digested through observation and in silence; hers are perceptions of him collected through varied conversations where each account acts as a piece of evidence to further her privately derived understanding. Whereas his process of information gathering leads to events of plot to which Lizzy must respond, Lizzy's process of amassing the hidden leads her to the avoidance of generating plot between herself and Darcy. Thus public, silent participation in conversation leads to the generating of plot; and private, verbal participation in conversation leads to reacting to plot.

The openness of his act of eavesdropping combined with her private knowledge of his hasty evaluation of the women of Longbourn inform Elizabeth's prejudice against him. Whatever he says after these two scenes of first meeting will be rendered false or impertinent to Lizzy's ears until his written speech, his letter to her, forces her to see his words and therefore himself anew. Overhearing and seeing him overhear make Darcy's presence and "living words" suspect. The unseen presence of himself in the letter allows the words to "speak for themselves." Likewise, not knowing of Lizzy's private means of formulating her knowledge of his character enables Darcy's sense of pride. Of course she will accept his first proposal, what could she know (or have heard) of him that would make him less than wholly desirable as a suitor? Their sense of mutual surprise when

Darcy first proposes and Elizabeth first refuses is the moment of conversation when their two frames for acquiring information or their rules of knowledge collection collide. They find, in fact, that they cannot converse, that they cannot, therefore, be a couple. They do not yet share a language because they do not yet share a means of participating in conversation, and so cannot share each other. That is, they do not yet understand Bakhtin's notion of "addressivity": neither knows how to address the other. Darcy's public pursuit of, versus Lizzy's private involvement in, conversation keeps them worlds apart; the possibility of intimacy between them seems impossible. And yet they do share an excited focus from their misunderstanding, in that Darcy can come to love Lizzy in his open preoccupation with her, and Lizzy can enjoy her dislike of Darcy in her cutting responses to him. The early pleasures they feel in response to their first conversation are the early gains that come of misreading.

Acknowledgments

The scene of mutual acknowledgment of love is a pivotal moment toward which the marriage narrative moves. It may constitute something like the middle or the close of the plot's line, and in some cases both. This is the place a narrative has often worked hardest to reach and so stands as a "hot" point in response to the narrative's own longing. And yet, strangely, the most often desired or worked toward conversation is the one we imagine we've heard too many times already. We think we know the sound of this conversation (from hackneyed overuse? fantasy?). The sounds of this scene come almost too easily to mind: the atmosphere of tension; the halting starts and stops of the partner who first braves the revealing of this secret that can no longer remain secret; the encouragement by the other to say more because the same is felt; the increased pace and escalating level of excitation; the other partner's assent and additions; the pause to mark physically the sharing of words; the retracing of "our history," or how we perceived all that we said and did before this moment of acknowledgment (what we thought each piece meant versus what we see now it actually meant); the spirit of giddiness because this moment has finally come to be. How can a plot devote itself to solving or arriving at an end whose "being" is already so well known? However, in the way that conversations of the first meeting may veer in narrative away from our lived experience of that moment and shape the plot in response to the obliquity of that first encounter, scenes in narrative of mutually acknowledged love can surprise for how they rewrite our anticipation of their gestalt. They can, therefore, "deserve" the work that led to them in the inventiveness or power of how they meet their plot's longing for them.

In *Pride and Prejudice* we are not invited as readers even to overhear Darcy and Elizabeth's conversation of acknowledgment. Here too it seems Lizzy's tendency toward the private precludes a "public hearing" where Darcy cannot be silent and Lizzy cannot allow us to hear. We read through reported speech of the acknowledgment of their feelings and her acceptance of his proposal. What reported speech of the events for which we've been preparing the length of the novel does is signal an "endpoint," or place of rest. Nothing more about the "problem" of love needs to be worked through because the work is already done. Hence a crux conversation need not take place.

Crux conversations take on a problem or topic that is ongoing and "process" it in the back-and-forth of speech, as is the case with the first acknowledgment scene in *Jane Eyre.* Or, crux conversations enact some last piece of work that must be accomplished between the speakers for this part of the plot to come to rest, which is the case with *Jane Eyre's* second acknowledgment scene. We need not hear the acknowledgment in *Pride and Prejudice* because we've known Darcy's position for half the novel and have come to learn of its transformation within Lizzy as she learns of it. Plotted around the concept of repetition and revision, *Jane Eyre's* first narrative of Jane and Rochester's union leads to a "midway" acknowledgment in the plot and in the actual content of the acknowledgment, given the absence of full disclosure (that Rochester is married, that his wife is the mad woman upstairs who periodically haunts the house). The second acknowledgment plots the narrative's end and arises out of the passage of time and a full digesting of what has been disclosed. Displays of the "acknowledgment of us," in the sense of displaying an "us" as married, are repeated as a model for Jane to process until she designs, controls, masters that model for herself. That is, until she acts as the initiator of conversation and so too of the plot of her life, Jane is often the victim of conversations about her, or brought to her, where she acts as the responder to someone else's vision of her or to the desires they have of her. If the topic of *Pride and Prejudice* is the *business* of getting married,[2] *Jane Eyre* explores what it means to *get* married. The narrative presents endless restagings of the event of marriage: the actual scene of the marriage interrupted by Mason; its theatrical staging in Rochester's home with Blanche and Rochester acting out their marriage; the metaphoric telling of the wedding night in Rochester's recounting to Jane of the affair with Céline Varens, which may have led to Adèle's conception; Jane's position as governess to Adèle as a form of wife to Rochester and mother to Adèle; Rochester's marriage to Bertha; the proposal to Jane from St. John of what their marriage could be; and Jane and Rochester's actual marriage.[3] The movement from "others" controlling the discourse on marriage to Jane's mastery of its speech plots the evolution both of the novel and of Jane into her Janeness. Therefore, the acknowledgment conversations, which demand not just that Jane and Rochester declare their feelings but that they translate those feelings into being a couple who marry, present themselves over the course of the novel as crucial moments of plotting.

The first acknowledgment conversation of "us" occurs in Rochester's Garden of Eden with Rochester as serpent to Jane's unknowing Eve. Jane declares:

"I grieve to leave Thornfield: I love Thornfield:—I love it because I have lived in it a full and delightful life,—momentarily at least. I have not been trampled on. . . . I have talked, face to face, with what I reverence; with what I delight in,—with an original, a vigorous, an expanded mind. I have known you, Mr. Rochester; and it strikes me with terror and anguish to feel I absolutely must be torn from you for ever. I see the necessity of departure; and it is like looking on the necessity of death."

"Where do you see the necessity?" he asked, suddenly.

"Where? You, sir, have placed it before me."

"In what shape?"

"In the shape of Miss Ingram; a noble and beautiful woman,—your bride."

"My bride! What bride? I have no bride!"

"But you will have."

"Yes:—I will!—I will!" He set his teeth.

"Then I must go:—you have said it yourself."

"No: you must stay! I swear it—and the oath shall be kept." . . .

"Do you think I can stay to become nothing to you? Do you think I am an automaton?—a machine without feelings? . . . —it is my spirit that addresses your spirit; just as if both had passed through the grave, and we stood at God's feet, equal—as we are!"

"As we are!" repeated Mr. Rochester—"so," he added, enclosing me in his arms, gathering me to his breast, pressing his lips on my lips: "so, Jane!" . . .

"My bride is here," he said, again drawing me to him, "because my equal is here, and my likeness. Jane, will you marry me?" (252–56)

The conversation centers on a conflict of intention and meaning. Rochester creates a reason why Jane believes she must leave Thornfield: his apparent desire to marry Blanche Ingram. Masterminding this frame of an intended marriage to another forces Jane to speak to that frame, to acknowledge that she must leave Thornfield because she loves Rochester. As the architect of the frame, Rochester removes himself from involvement with the urgency of Jane's words. He may continue to speak of the charade of the "other" marriage so as to press Jane to declare her love more vehemently, or call a halt to the game and propose. Jane displays what Grice defines as the rules of conversation in that she says what she takes to be necessary according to Rochester's plan of marrying another; she admits to her true feelings, her statement is relevant to the topic raised, and she speaks out clearly.

Rochester, however, as the creator/recipient of the scene, demonstrates Lakoff's description of conversation: not imposing, he keeps his distance and allows Jane the freedom to make her declarations. He asks questions that suggest to Jane varying options her responses might take; he maintains a friendly stance even in the face of her increasingly heated statements. When one speaker addresses the linguistic side of a conversation (Grice's depiction of what one does when one speaks) and the other addresses the paralinguistic (Lakoff's sense of how conversants maneuver to allow the other to speak), a clash of frames occurs. Rochester, as the one who constructs the collision, knows how to see the two pictures of intent, whereas Jane can only see what she takes Rochester to be asking her, not his intent.

The difference in duration of speech indicates a reverse form of control or knowledge of what the scene is really about. Although it first appears that Jane's outpouring dominates the scene, in fact these words are pulled from her by Rochester's creation of a false conflict. His punchy, short questions are not just questions but rather devices for demanding Jane's acknowledgment. Provoking her into an admission of feeling, Rochester acts the teacher or psychotherapist, justifying the fabrication of a false marriage-to-be (while hiding a false marriage-that-is) by Jane's need to hear herself say and so admit to herself these feelings, as much as his own need to hear her say them. The escalating use of "!" and "?" as Rochester responds to Jane's statements reveals the conversational devices he uses of expressive reaction and questioning. The writing on the page—the sparseness of words combined with the presence of device-defining punctuation ("!" and "?")—creates visually or serves as the stage directions for what the auditory in a non-book-based narrative would provide as conversational signals. Seeing the visual cues, we hear the pace increase, the loudness escalate, the intonation seem more impassioned and urgent. The relentlessness of Rochester's interrogative and imperative statements migrates into Jane's own speech; this migration exemplifies Bakhtin's sense of the "assimilation" that occurs between speakers and their utterances. As Jane progresses from hinting to saying to meaning, her words and punctuation grow bolder, more reactive, more exclamatory. While the subject of Rochester's "impending marriage" serves as the apparent prompt of the conversation, in fact it is Rochester's desire to force Jane's acknowledgment of passion which controls its movement. What we witness then in the baiting diction of Rochester and the reacting diction of Jane is the negotiation of speech types prompted by the different intents or levels of "control" of the speakers. We experience in the kiss something like the momentary "meeting" of speech types at the momentary meeting of their lips. In finally proposing to Jane, Rochester allows the masquerading frame to dissolve and Jane to see his true intent; they meet in one frame when she accepts his proposal as a true one, though ironically it is not. In their first speech of acknowledgment, therefore, what Jane and Rochester acknowledge is that they both are and are not yet a couple.

The frame within a frame as a structure of conversation, as a model for the plot of scenes of marriages embedded within each other, repeats itself in the second acknowledgment conversation in *Jane Eyre*. However, the locus of who creates and thus who controls the negotiation of inner to outer frame, and the confinement of the other to only one of the frames until the frame shift is allowed, changes as the roles of proposer and proposee reverses. Jane uses Rochester's creation of a false threat of marriage to another as a means herself of forcing acknowledgment and maintaining control. She remembers her partner's prior performance and assimilates that performance by repeating it. And in response, Rochester acts the part of the former emotionally pushed Jane. This is a couple whose conversations show that they know how to swap roles. She first tells of her relationship to St. John:

"He intended me to go with him to India."

"Ah! here I reach the root of the matter. He wanted you to marry him."

"He asked me to marry him."

"That is a fiction—an impudent invention to vex me."

"I beg your pardon, it is the literal truth: he asked more than once, and was as stiff about urging his point as ever you could be."

"Miss Eyre, I repeat it, you can leave me. How often am I to say the same thing? Why do you remain pertinaciously perched on my knee, when I have given you notice to quit?"

"Because I am comfortable there."

"No, Jane, you are not comfortable there, because your heart is not with me: it is with this cousin—this St. John. Oh, till this moment, I thought my little Jane was all mine! I had a belief she loved me even when she left me: that was an atom of sweet in much bitter. Long as we have been parted, hot tears have I wept over our separation, I never thought that while I was mourning her, she was loving another! But it is useless grieving. Jane, leave me: go and marry Rivers."

"Shake me off, then, sir,—push me away, for I'll not leave you of my own accord."

"Jane, I ever like your tone of voice: it still renews hope, it sounds so truthful. When I hear it carries me back a year. I forget that you have formed a new tie. But I am not a fool—go—"

"Where must I go, sir?"

"Your own way—with the husband you have chosen."

"Who is that?"

"You know—this St. John Rivers."

"He is not my husband, nor ever will be. He does not love me: I do not love him." . . .

"What, Jane! Is this true? Is such really the state of matters between you and Rivers?"

"Absolutely, sir. Oh, you need not be jealous! I wanted to tease you a little to make you less sad: I thought anger would be better than grief. But if you wish me to love you, could you but see how much I *do* love you, you would be proud and content. All my heart is yours, sir: it belongs to you; and with you it would remain, were fate to exile the rest of me from your presence for ever." . . .

"Choose then, sir—*her who loves you best.*"

"I will at least choose—*her I love best.* Jane, will you marry me?"
"Yes, sir." (446–48)

Where Rochester uses a supposed proposal to Blanche, an invented conversation, Jane uses a real proposal from St. John, a noninvented conversation, as the means to open the discussion of marriage. Each acts as the initiator of the frame; but because Rochester invents the play into which Jane enters as unrequited lover, he cannot see Jane's proposal from St. John as anything but an "invention." He had needed to use fictions, to use the signifier, Blanche, in order to veil the signified, Bertha—the dark beauty of one transformed into the dark madness of the other, the idea of the appearance of the bride-to-be covering the interior essence of the wife-once-wed—as a means of achieving his desired end, Jane, the new sign. His reliance on fictions causes him to see this strategy in Jane's account of a proposal from St. John. Her denial causes him to rethink his belief in the "fiction" because he knows that Jane does not lie. ("Liar" is the name first used to embody Jane at Lowood when she wears the sign "LIAR." Brocklehurst's pointing to her as an example for the others as being the thing named works as a reverse literalization of Wittgenstein's description of the relationship between name and thing. She lives in the narrative refusing endlessly to be the thing named.)[4]

Whereas Rochester's use of a fiction to begin his proposal to Jane prefaces a dialogue that hides his story with Bertha, Jane's use of the truth to introduce her own proposal to Rochester initiates a conversation that hides nothing. Rochester in his proposal emits obscure references, such as "No: you must stay! I swear it—and the oath shall be kept," and later, "It will atone—it will atone" (257–58). What is the "oath" and what is the "it" that will atone? Why must it? Rochester's almost biblical diction keeps something not only from Jane but from us. Her language, however, while teasing, is also almost immediately self-explanatory. While Rochester creates a system of embedded frames from which all but he are excluded as a device of plot (the plot unfolds in accordance with the process of Jane's discoveries of the knowledge kept from her), Jane as the guiding voice of the text leaves "no frame unturned." We know the truth of Jane's proposal from St. John because we heard that conversation. Further, we know that Jane keeps nothing else from Rochester because she has told us her whole story as the plot progressed in the frame of her linear, autobiographical narrative.

In the first acknowledgment conversation, Jane must endure being the one who does not control the elaborate dialogic dance of mingling voices and speech types. She makes two impassioned speeches about her love for Rochester before he makes the frame shift. Rochester, in the second conversation, speaks one extended passage in which he uses a voice of melodramatic jealousy and tells her to go to St. John in much the same way that Jane states she must leave Thornfield for Ireland. Jane encourages Rochester by using what Grice calls implicature: "Shake me off, then sir,—push me away, for I'll not leave of my own accord" (446). Here, Jane's making a less than fully realized connection (violation of quantity) causes Rochester to "read into" Jane's refusal to leave his lap. The questioner in each scene of proposal maintains the controlling intent that steers the answerer. While Rochester's prolonging of Jane's agony extends through pages of conversation, Jane relieves Rochester's misery almost immediately, "He is not my husband, nor ever will be. He does not love me: I do not love him" (447). In the second acknowledgment conversation, Jane and Rochester share speaking time because there is nothing to hide. Rochester's need to maintain a secret accounts for his resistance to speak in the first acknowledgment, other than to question and assert finality, "It will be done." The openness of the concluding acknowledgment reflects the achievement of intimacy between the speakers: the second acknowledgment conversation has completed their transformation into a couple because there are "no secrets" left to be discovered.

Curiously, in the first conversation, the assertion that the two stand before each other as "equals" needs to be voiced. Their sense of equality has evolved from Jane's varying instances of "raising" a fallen or vulnerable Rochester (meeting after his fall from his horse, inciting him to rise from his bed after Bertha set it on fire, leading a blind, partially paralyzed Rochester) and from their verbal sparring. The first acknowledgment speech is as much about establishing their equality of souls as it is about establishing their love. Their spirits must be well matched or the social mismatching of landed gentry to penniless governess would make the union not only improbable but inappropriate. The ability of the two to be married is in part grounded in the possibility of them moving away from the names "governess" and "landed gentry" to meeting in a liminal space where spiritual compatibility is as defining of state as one's economic or lineal background. (This is the Cinderella plot of narrative where poor girl not only deserves wealthy man but effects his spiritual transformation. Think of *Pamela,* or the plot made American in the Hollywood films of the secretary or housekeeper who "saves" her employer: Loretta Young as maid to Joseph Cotton's aspiring senator in the 1947 *The Farmer's Daughter,* and Greer Garson as housekeeper to Gregory Peck's mill owner in the 1945 *Valley of Decision,* women who first transform and then marry their employers.)

Inspired by the twofold need in the first conversation of acknowledgment to attest to their equality and to her love, Jane drops the words "Mr." and "sir," the terms of social distinction which divide them, and uses the personal pronouns "you" and "we"—words that voice her sense that they are approaching partnership. Subsequently, the narrative reverses their worldly inequality by revealing Rochester to be the "liar," or at least an aspiring polygamist, and Jane not to be penniless. By contrast, with Rochester sightless, without the use of his right arm, and repentant, his "equality" of spirit at the moment of the second acknowledgment conversation approaches Jane's even as her equality of economic worth approaches Rochester's. However, now Jane uses a term, "sir," to distinguish his status from hers:

> "Ah! Jane. But I want a wife."
> "Do you, sir?" . . .
> "Is it unwelcome news?"
> "That depends on circumstances, sir—on your choice."
> "Which you shall make for me, Jane. I will abide by your decision."
> "Choose then, sir—*her who loves you best.*"
> "I will at least choose—*her I love best.* Jane, will you marry me?"
> "Yes, sir." (448, emphasis mine)

What began as a moment of teasing for Jane and despair for Rochester has evolved into a conversation of delight, of comedy. Both know the question and both are asking it—"Will you marry me?" Both also know the answer—"Yes." The game evolves out of the maneuvering over what it means to ask and answer in a conversation where neither position is stable, where the question is not a question and the answer not an answer, where the act of "choosing" is not an act because the implications have already told each rhetor that each has already chosen and been chosen by the other. For one partner to tell the other to make his choice for him is not to make the choice; for that same partner not to choose the answer given is to destabilize deliberately the positions of who controls and who is controlled, who asks and who answers. They are now a couple because their speech no longer needs to "work" for them, or the narrative, in the sense of reveal information or accomplish a point of plot. Instead, they are free to play or invent the routines of their partnered speech.

The comedy of the conversation makes itself felt in Jane's use of "sir." Though they have been made "equals" by the course of the narrative, Jane's constant insistence on "sir" calls back teasingly to the earlier phase of their intimacy when the passion of the moment so drove Jane that she refused to utter "sir" and therein made a dramatic break from the codes of social language that declared a nonnegotiable difference. The movement from "sir" to "you" worked as a dramatic gesture of social defiance and of self-disclosure. The first acknowledgment conversation then moved from the socially informed speech type, where class difference as revealed in choice of language prohibited a language of love, to a dropping of the language of social division in order that the revelations of a self and of a consciousness of "us" speak. A sign of deepened intimacy reveals itself in an ironic return to the term which first signified separation and prohibitions to speak, and therefore to love. The repetition of "sir," like a choral rejoinder to every phrase, laughs at itself. The sense of mastery and social division it connotes falls away in the now revised positions that the partners occupy in relation to themselves and each other. "Yes, sir," Jane's reply to Rochester's proposal, which was her proposal that he choose the one who loves him best, plays a textual joke of mocking the earlier stage of their intimacy where that would be an appropriate response. Transformed by experience, the language used in the second conversation reveals the distance Jane and Rochester have traveled. No longer a name for or marker of division, "sir" becomes an idiom or term of endearment, like "dear." That trans-conversation joke reveals something of the pleasure these partners now know about who they are together: about their history together, about their successful arrival together at a "now" out of a "then," about what words mean to them together over time. There's a giddiness displayed here that has to do with shared survival, rediscovery, and the capacity to transform the fraught-with-danger into a joke.

This later intimacy, born from the discovery of secrets, endurance of individual suffering, and separation from each other, is necessarily a deeper intimacy by virtue of what has been discovered, experienced, and felt because of and apart from each other. For each to have brought him- or herself back to this moment of acknowledging their love again reveals more deeply the equality of their selves and their worth. The acknowledgment of love appears not only in the second half of the text but at its end. Whereas first Jane and Rochester can only strain to assert the appropriateness of their desire to marry, at the finale they can laugh at the fact of having this conversation at all.

When information exchange in a conversation is no longer necessary because the speakers know too well where the conversation will move, when they know the questions and answers and outcome already, when the point of the conversation, therefore, is no longer the "subject" in Gadamer's sense, and when the structure is all implicature in Grice's sense, then the conversation acts not as a linguistic exchange but as a paralinguistic moment. Speech acts become a symbol or celebration of "us": we now are and now know what it means to be an "us." Jane and Rochester's second acknowledgment conversation exhibits what Gadamer means by the making of a common language. From positions of separation, the truth of "us" bonds them in a new community of understanding where each no longer knows who s/he is in separation and instead knows without having to say who s/he is in union. If the underlying concern of *Jane Eyre* is, what does it mean to get married? then the repetition and working through of this conversation of acknowledgment is the narrative's response.

Endings

In marriage narratives, the ending of divorce or departure allows for the possibility of an ending that is not death. Twentieth-century film and modern dramas beginning with Ibsen's *A Doll's House* build plots most successfully around this possibility. These explorations have been shaped by the peculiar features of film and plays as narrative mediums: Dramatic and cinematic narratives require the audience physically to enter and depart from a theater, and to participate in the ephemeral act of viewing.[5] They require something like our own "divorce" from the narrative—we must walk out on it. If an audience has limited access to the text and if that text requires unstopped movement through it, then the creation of the memorable becomes a primary feature of the text.

Film conversations between couples that acknowledge the end of an "us" or "our final meeting" perform double work. They emphasize the fleeting quality of the couple's relationship on screen and the fleeting quality of the audience's relationship to the screen. It means something about films made before the age of video that those movies could not be "owned," put before one's eyes whenever desired, and revisited with the same freedom that one could a novel. How could they be memorable? The novel can always be returned to and demands its readers' temporal control. Reading a novel requires starting and stopping, choosing when and where to read it, even deciding what part to read first or reread. The temporal

process of reading and the ability to control when one reads, where, and
how often inscribe within the medium a relation to "the end" as something we can determine, even interminably delay. And yet, inevitably, the
novel ends. According to Benjamin, this is its ineluctable fact, not what we
resist but that from which we derive our sense of its meaning. It is the
ending over which we have no control—death—that gives us the greatest
pleasure because the greatest sense of meaning. He writes in "The Storyteller" that the novelist "invites the reader to a divinatory realization of
the meaning of life by writing 'finis'" (100). I take its meaning to be "divinatory," on that scale, because the novel invites us to control its passage
of time. In our loss of that control—confronting "the end," and in particular the end that is death—we encounter our limits and ourselves. We
cannot in "the end" control time, avoid death, be as gods. Benjamin writes
further,

> The nature of the character in a novel cannot be presented any
> better than is done in this statement, which says that "the meaning"
> of his life is revealed only in his death. But the reader of a novel actu-
> ally does look for human beings from whom he derives the "meaning
> of life." Therefore he must, no matter what, know in advance that he
> will share their experience of death—the death of the novel—but
> preferably their actual one. . . . What draws the reader to the novel is
> the hope of warming his shivering life with a death he reads about.
> (100–101)

Film originated as an ephemeral medium. Its viewing experience insisted
on passing encounters that brought its audience out to public theaters,
with showings scheduled at fixed times, controlled by a projection that
couldn't be stopped or made to skip, a process of motion that the viewers
experienced by moving themselves to it. The medium of film is the unin-
terruptible flow of motion—moving pictures, ongoing sounds, ephemera.
To stop the film is to no longer know it as itself but as a frozen still without sound. And yet it is its very ephemeral nature, the motion that can't
be stopped, held onto, or controlled, that leads to its powerful revision of
the novel's most powerful (because memorable) end in death. The promise of motion, more motion, is what the film raises in its audience—the
end that isn't "the end." What I'm suggesting is that on film the loss of a
partner to the door is more memorable than the loss in death. The ache
of death that we witness on film prompts us not to hope for return: we

must accept the lover is gone forever (unless the couple inhabits a magical narrative universe). However, the lover who walks out may someday walk back in. And it is the hope that accompanies the possibility of return that wrenches and tugs and resists forgetting. Recall *Shane, Brief Encounter, Roman Holiday, The Way We Were* (or almost any Barbra Streisand noncomedy).

Perhaps the most remembered acknowledgment in the Hollywood narrative of the spoken end of a couple is the conclusion to *Gone with the Wind*. While the novel portrays the same end, it is its telling through the larger-than-life Selznick production and its stars, the celestial figures of Vivien Leigh and Clark Gable (still known as "the King"), that makes the conversation unendurable. When we think of Rhett's departure, we're not thinking of Margaret Mitchell's words printed on the page, "'My dear, I don't give a damn.'" What we hear and see are Clark Gable's embodiment and transformation of them. Neither Scarlett nor the "Windies," the fan club of the 1939 production, can bear it:

CLARK GABLE: I'm leaving you, my dear. All you need now is a divorce and your dreams of Ashley can come true.

VIVIEN LEIGH: No, you're wrong. Terribly, terribly wrong. I don't want a divorce. Oh, Rhett, when I knew I loved you I ran home to tell you, oh darling.

CLARK GABLE: Please don't go on with this. Leave us some dignity to remember out of our marriage.

VIVIEN LEIGH: Oh, Rhett, I must have loved you for years only I didn't know it. Please believe me. You must care. Mellie said you did.

CLARK GABLE: I believe you. What about Ashley Wilkes?

VIVIEN LEIGH: I never really loved Ashley.

CLARK GABLE: You certainly gave a good imitation of it up till this morning. No, Scarlett, I tried everything. If you only met me halfway, even when I came back from London.

VIVIEN LEIGH: Oh, Rhett, I was so glad to see you. I was, Rhett. But you were so nasty.

CLARK GABLE: Or when you were sick, and it was all my fault. I hoped against hope that you'd call for me, but you didn't.

VIVIEN LEIGH: I wanted you, I wanted you desperately, but I didn't think that you wanted me.

CLARK GABLE: It seems we've been at cross purposes, doesn't it? But

Vivien Leigh and Clark Gable in *Gone with the Wind,* MGM, 1939
Courtesy Academy of Motion Pictures Arts and Sciences

it's no use now. As long as there was Bonnie there was a chance that we'd be happy. I liked to think that Bonnie was you, my little girl again, before the war and poverty had done things to you. She was so like you, and I could pet her and spoil her as I wanted to spoil you. When she went, she took everything.

VIVIEN LEIGH: Rhett, please don't say that. I'm so sorry for everything.

CLARK GABLE: My darling, you're such a child. You think that by saying "I'm sorry" that all the past could be corrected. Here, take my handkerchief. Never at any crisis of your life have I known you to have a handkerchief.

VIVIEN LEIGH: Rhett. Rhett, where are you going?

CLARK GABLE: I'm going to Charleston, back where I belong.

VIVIEN LEIGH: Please take me with you.

CLARK GABLE: No. I'm through with everything here. I want peace. I want to see if somewhere there isn't something left in life full of charm and grace. Do you know what I'm talking about?

VIVIEN LEIGH: No. I only know that I love you.

CLARK GABLE: That's your misfortune.

VIVIEN LEIGH: Rhett. Rhett. Rhett! If you go, where shall I go, what shall I do?

CLARK GABLE: Frankly, my dear, I don't give a damn. (Door opens and closes.)

VIVIEN LEIGH: I can't let him go, I can't. There must be some way to bring him back. I can't think about this now, I'll go crazy if I do. I'll think about it tomorrow. But I must think about it. What is there to do, what is there that matters? . . . Tara! Home! I'll go home, and I'll think of some way to get him back. After all, tomorrow is another day!

The script's words on the page render little of the reality of their sound in film, the sweeping Max Steiner score, Vivien Leigh's cries and gasps, Gable's stiffness and certainty, nor of the visual splendor of the massive stairway, chandeliers, Tiffany glass, the height and erectness of Gable set against the petite shape and beauty of Leigh. Waiting for Scarlett's recognition of her love for Rhett is the preoccupation of the movie; with its dawning comes the least expected end, his departure. How can he leave her? What makes the scene memorable is the metamorphosis of the expected, long-awaited end into its surprising reality. The audience experiences in one moment the satisfaction of their desire and its frustration with the departure of Rhett from us and from Scarlett. Perhaps Rhett has reached "his end" with Scarlett—he can no longer endure her resistance to him; he can no longer tolerate her love of Ashley. Worn out by Scarlett, perhaps Rhett feels nothing. It's over.[6]

However, the ending is not about the closure of resolution but rather the perpetuation of desire, relocated. Rhett's acknowledgment of his having reached the end with her, "Frankly, my dear, I don't give a damn," prompts an assertion of new beginning, "I'll think of some way to get him back. After all, tomorrow is another day!" With the belief in certain givens comes the possibility of the occurrence of other events, of the fulfillment of desire. We, with Rhett, have waited through the narrative for Scarlett's acknowledgment that she and Rhett *are* the partnership (Rhett's words to Scarlett over brandy go directly to this: "We're not gentlemen"). We, with Rhett, have known since the beginning what Scarlett apparently has not known until the ending (from Rhett's unyielding smile of delight/leer of desire when he first sees Scarlett from the bottom of the stairs at Twelve Oaks, to his exit down their shared flight of stairs and out their door). But in fact, the maintenance of Rhett and Scarlett as a couple has had everything to do with Scarlett's resisting acknowledgment. Their "us" is about one who pursues and one who is pursued, one who loves and one who is loved. Her admission speech is prompted by his assertion that "they" have ended. As soon as he gives up the pursuit of her, she takes up the pursuit of him. This reversal of roles sustains their version of partnership, a state defined by the tension of desire meeting resistance in a perpetual scene of chase. Therefore, this seeming conversation of "the end" does not actually perform the end. Instead, it sustains what it means to be "Rhett and Scarlett" by making possible the ongoing performance of their partnered bouts of desiring and (apparently) resisting in return. The end simply adds a new twist to their by now old routine. The pleasure registered on Vivien Leigh's tear-stained face when she rises up from being in a heap has to do with the challenge of the role reversal. But more than that, it has to do with the dawning recognition that Rhett's departure has made possible that they go on together, the knowledge that this is who they are, and that she loves it. Without the fight between them of wanting differently, there could be no mutual ground between them, instead just the "likeness" of being a Mellie and an Ashley, doomed to die young because of their cousinly sameness.

The film's narrative closes with an acknowledged end that, not mutually agreed to, creates a beginning. Something needs fixing. Floating desire must be located, but because its apparent satisfaction can occur only after the text, the text continues or plays outside itself. The conversation of "our" end, therefore, does end conversation or the couple if it brings to life or light ongoing desire left unattached.⁷ And desire must always be left unattached if this couple, as they understand their "coupleness," are to remain themselves.

~

If certain films create powerful endings in conversation which are not endings—and *Gone with the Wind* closes with perhaps the most famous discourse about acknowledging a relationship's end coupled with the possibility of its new beginning—the best remembered conversation in Hollywood filmmaking of the "final meeting" where the end truly is "the end" is the denouement of *Casablanca*.⁸ A couple narrative that ends in separation makes the "final conversation" an ultimate destination of the plot, a marker of where the action has moved to and from which it disbands. The memorability of *Casablanca*'s end, however, comes, as with *Gone with the*

Claude Reins, Humphrey Bogart, Paul Henreid, and Ingrid Bergman in
Casablanca, Warner Brothers, 1942
Courtesy Academy of Motion Pictures Arts and Sciences

Humphrey Bogart and Ingrid Bergman in *Casablanca,* Warner Brothers, 1942
Courtesy Academy of Motion Pictures Arts and Sciences

Wind, from a concatenation of surprising reversals, overwhelming loss, and recognition of a nobility that underlies that loss. But it also comes from the embodied performance of the conversation: the camera's study of the beauty of Bergman's face, it's complex unmasking of Bogart's toughness, and the poignant return of "As Time Goes By" holding together in music the close-ups of their profiles and studies of their faces alone.

We watch and listen and know too well the final parting from each other these stars/this couple must perform. Ingrid Bergman's "Ilsa" asks Humphrey Bogart's "Rick" to do the thinking for both of them once she realizes she cannot tear herself away from him again. Arriving at the airport, Paul Henreid's "Victor Laszlo" leaves them briefly enough for their private conversation to occur within a frame of the public discourse that includes Laszlo and Claude Rains's "Inspector Renault":

HUMPHREY BOGART: If you don't mind, you fill in the names. That will make it even more official.

CLAUDE RAINS: You think of everything, don't you.

HUMPHREY BOGART: And the names are Mr. and Mrs. Victor Laszlo.

INGRID BERGMAN: But why my name, Richard?
(Camera zooms into close-up, profile shots of Bergman and Bogart. His trench coat. Her suit. The gorgeous hats framing their profiles. "As Time Goes By" begins its accompaniment of the moment.)

HUMPHREY BOGART: Because you're getting on that plane.

INGRID BERGMAN: I don't understand. What about you?

HUMPHREY BOGART: I'm staying here with him until the plane gets safely away.

INGRID BERGMAN: No, Richard. No. What has happened to you? Last night . . .

HUMPHREY BOGART: Last night we said a great many things. You said I was to do the thinking for both of us. Well, I've done a lot of it since then and it all adds up to one thing—you're getting on that plane with Victor, where you belong.

INGRID BERGMAN: But Richard, no, I . . .

HUMPHREY BOGART: Now you've got to listen to me. Do you have any idea what you'd have to look forward to if you stayed here? Nine chances out of ten we'd both wind up in a concentration camp. Isn't that true, Louis?
(Camera shot of Claude Rains alone.)

CLAUDE RAINS: I'm afraid Major Strasser would insist.
(Zoom back in for close-up shot of the lovers, and then a deeper
close-up of Bergman's face with just the back of Bogart's head.)
INGRID BERGMAN: You're saying this only to make me go.
HUMPHREY BOGART: I'm saying this because it's true. Inside of us we
both know that you belong with Victor; you're part of his work,
the thing that keeps him going. If that plane leaves the ground and
you're not with him, you'll regret it.
INGRID BERGMAN: (whispered) No.
(Close-up of just Bogart's face.)
HUMPHREY BOGART: Maybe not today, maybe not tomorrow, but
soon, and for the rest of your life.
(Close-up of Bergman's face.)
INGRID BERGMAN: But what about us?
(Close-up of Bogart's face.)
HUMPHREY BOGART: We'll always have Paris. We didn't have, we'd lost
it until you came to Casablanca. (Close-up of Bergman's face.) We
got it back last night.
INGRID BERGMAN: When I said I would never leave you . . .
HUMPHREY BOGART: And you never will. (Close-up of Bogart's face.)
But I've got a job to do too. Where I'm going you can't follow.
What I've got to do you can't be any part of. (Closest close-up of
Bergman; no Bogart visible; her tear-stained face.) Ilsa, I'm no
good at being noble, but it doesn't take much to see that the
problems of three little people don't amount to a hill of beans in
this crazy world. Some day you'll understand that. (She drops her
head. His left hand reaches up and touches her chin. Her eyes
look up and meet his.) Now, now. (Back to Bogart's face.) Here's
looking at you, kid. (Closing bars of "As Time Goes By." No
words. Final close-up of her face. The fall of her tears. The movement of her lips. Final close-up of his face. She looks away. His
eyes, which had been looking reassuring and "noble," now when
only looking on her without her returned gaze, show the beginnings of tears. Their final gazes upon each other are ours in this
final sequence of shots.)

Inscribed within the public context, the privacy of this conversation is
created from its placement within a larger spatial sphere of a third figure
(Renault) situated on the edge between the conversation and the plane

which suggests worlds beyond. Rick's pronouncing the names Mr. and Mrs. Victor Laszlo prompts the literal inscription of the names onto the letters of transport and the disruption of Ilsa's connection to Rick. He gives her away by transforming this scene to be about the making of a marriage license, but not of their marriage to each other. He renames her "Mrs. Victor Laszlo." Renault, therefore, writes officially both the possibility of their departure and their identification as the Victor Laszlos. While Renault writes Ilsa into Victor's space, that of the plane and other worlds, she and Rick have their last conversation about their parting.

Curiously, Renault stays an invited eavesdropper throughout the conversation (in much the same way that Sam does as "their" piano player/minstrel throughout the film), although we only see Claude Rains at the beginning of the conversation, during one shot in the middle, and after the conversation's close. His proximity and solicited participation make him the bridge between what is outside and what is inside with regard to this conversation.[9] Rick speaks as the one "thinking for both of us"; he tells Ilsa what must be done and explains "why," while she prompts him with short questions or assertions. Offering the worth of Victor's cause and Ilsa's role as "the thing that keeps him going," Rick defines her place as being in union with another man and his work. However, of his own work she can be no part; where he goes, she cannot. At issue for Ilsa, therefore, is the definition of her role—not that of whose lover she will be, but whose companion in work. The idea of an "us" is crystallized and ended with this moment, an "us" that now includes with this conversation their prior relation in Paris, her return to Casablanca, their declaration of their love "last night," and with it, their "getting back" of Paris. Her return to him does not work to mean their second loss of each other, but their rediscovery, their recovery of each other in memory. Rick cannot speak of an "us" of Ilsa and Victor. He can only address the appropriateness of their recasted work positions. There Ilsa and Victor must be joined; there he must be alone. The romance of an "us" must be reserved for him and Ilsa: this is in their private sharing of their getting back Paris, of her never leaving him. What follows their exchange is Rick's repetition for Victor, recast so that Victor hears a "public" version, not theirs, not "their" truth. Renault remains audience to both conversations and reveals to Rick that he knows "their" truth, which he asserts to be the truth.

The good-bye works as a means of negating itself. The reversal of Ilsa's and Rick's positions of who wants who to stay, and with whom, leads to their recognition of what has been gained in their moment of reunion and future of separation. "Getting it back," "never leaving" are positions of the mind which enable these conversations about their acknowledgment and their leave-taking to live beyond both the life of the conversations themselves and the possibility of further lived discourse. This conversation instructs them that what it will mean for them to be a couple is to be so in memory. And for us they have only been a couple in memory, as seen in the "flashback," which tells the story of Ilsa and Rick's romance (it is not lived in the narrative, only recalled), and from their modes of being throughout the film. Both Bogart and Bergman act haunted, as if their present lives (which are something like a living death—living in Casablanca, living with Victor, living in exile from each other and so too from their selves) reflect only what was lost to them somewhere in the past. Their "presentness" of being alive is what is gotten back with Ilsa's return and their conversation of "the end": each can live again in "now" because the "then" has been restored, mutually remembered, mutually understood, and mutually felt. The series of close-ups of Bergman and Bogart in profile frame for us their partnership, their getting it back, its permanence for our minds' eyes. The studies of each face alone put us in the position of the other not pictured, the partner who gazes upon the beloved. We see him for the last time; we see her for the last time; we inhabit each partner's position of the couple and, therefore, "perform" it by looking at him, looking at her. And in the way that she will now never leave him, we have been instructed from having occupied each position in the partnership to stay with this narrative, to remember this parting, and so not to part from it. Sam sings it to us as he sings it to them, "You must remember this"; and Rick tells it to us as he tells it to Ilsa, "We'll always have Paris."

Not the greatest film ever made, only the most perfect, *Casablanca* leaves us with this sense of its perfection in the imprinting of the ending in our memories. Like Ilsa, who leaves Rick after this conversation but comes to understand in the conversation that she will never leave him, viewers leave *Casablanca* and never leave it: we will "always have Paris" in the act of remembering. In the pressure, which is the pleasure of the last conversation, this plot declares that this couple will share the same memory of what it means to be "us" (which includes being a "we" who remembers). This pressure/pleasure then migrates throughout the narrative and insists that we remember this plot that is about remembering, and this couple that knows itself again in remembering. *Casablanca* and its final conversation know the pleasures of remembering are not just about the recovery of the past but about the integration of the past with the present and, most of all, the integration of the past with the future by retrieving a shared history that will continue to connect one lover to the other over time.

~

Love stories use conversations to embody the starred moments a plot traces through the life of the relationship—the first meeting, the acknowledgment of love, the acknowledgment of the end of love, and/or the final meeting. These dialogues serve and shape linear marriage narratives by marking plot places called "the beginning," "the middle," and "the end." Only shared conversations can represent these discrete, knowable points of a love plotline, which cannot be constructed by events of a solitary "I." Dialogues are interactive, mutually made moments of a partnered story that function to mark off "our story," around which a "we" works to build the quotidian that constitutes that we. The moments of collective making that mark the turns around which a partnership moves will come to constitute that couple's history, the remembered bits that will stand for what this couple "means" or "has been," and the pleasures that can accompany coming to that knowledge. These pleasures include experiencing an uncertainty that needs to be solved (what is happening here/between us?), and the clarity of the known (this is who we are/what is), and the memory of what was made, lost, recovered (this is who we were/what was/what can be again). The narrative of an "us," whose plot is the history of a couple, relies then on rhetorical structures that tell the life events of the marriage/narrative free from one controlling vision. Crux conversations "speak" the marriage narrative as a storytelling of collective consciousness.

CHAPTER 3

Word-Play:
Couples and Stories on Holiday

I suggest that we must expect to find playing just as evident in the analyses
of adults as it is in the case of our work with children. It manifests itself, for
instance, in the choice of words, in the inflections of the voice, and indeed
in the sense of humour.

—D. W. Winnicott, *Playing and Reality*

Over the course of a novel or film, the recurrent form of a couple's "usual"
speech gives a distinct, privileged voice to the pair, makes them singers in
a duet set in relation to a chorus of others. Whereas ends-seeking plot
speech decides and does away with issues, no declarations accompany
the repeated talk that constitutes the accumulated world of a pair. Plot-
forming, crux conversations function as word-acts; these are the moments
when a novel, in particular, gets things done. Between these declarations,
however, are the conversations in which a couple "live" their coupleness
through how they putter, tinker, and mess around together with their
words. How much space a narrative turns over to a couple's playtime has
everything to do with how "active" it takes itself to be. The "lazier" the
narrative, in its avoidance of linear progression, the more complicated its
structure in that it must continuously invent some other geometry for its
being, in addition to the line with its desire for action. And the difficulty
of creating lazy, inactive narratives has everything to do with the paucity
of narratives that devote themselves to the play of an established couple
over time. What follows here are instances of repeated or "in-between" conversations of couples. These conversations make up the bulk of exchanges
between their couples and demonstrate the "lives" of their partnerships,
rather than marking the evolution of their partnerships' lives. The usual
talk of couples is not a conversation that measures or marks or defines or
draws lines. Instead, it is speech that functions as the "norm" in that it
shows how the narrative/couple generally interacts. What makes these

lines of talk less memorable has to do with their function: these conversations do not do the work of the plot; they do not get things done. Or, what they do is different. Even if the plot is not advanced, the couple's understanding of "who we are" is. Not event-connected or defining, the speech which is just about "how we talk" embeds itself inside the narrative world as part of what composes its *texture*.

Who Are You?

Knowing the other in narrative's lengthiness is a continuous process, as is knowing the self. The world-making and world-exhibiting conversations of couples play interactively with the subtleties and ongoingness of the process of knowing. I return to *Jane Eyre* and *Pride and Prejudice* because these novels reveal how fiction depends on the movement between conversations that plot and those that repeat a pair's history. In both texts, discussions of the nature of the other with whom one keeps talking occur early and extend to the novels' ends. These exchanges demonstrate how the pair interact repeatedly over time.

Early in *Jane Eyre*, Rochester discusses his state of degeneracy without yet describing what events occurred to bring about the decline of his moral self. Jane responds, and Rochester begins his evaluation of her:

> "To speak truth, sir, I don't understand you at all: I cannot keep up the conversation, because it has got out of my depth. Only one thing I know: you said you were not as good as you should like to be, and that you regretted your imperfection; one thing I can comprehend: you have intimated that to have a sullied memory was a perpetual bane. It seems to me, that if you tried hard, you would in time find it possible to become what you yourself would approve; and if from this day you began with resolution to correct your thoughts and actions, you would in a few years have laid up a new and stainless store of recollections, to which you might revert with pleasure."
> "Justly thought; rightly said, Miss Eyre; and, at this moment, I am paving hell with energy."
> "Sir?"
> "I am laying down good intentions, which I believe durable as flint. Certainly my associates and pursuits shall be other than they have been."
> "And better?"

"And better—so much better as pure ore is than foul dross. You seem to doubt me; I don't doubt myself: I know what my aim is, and what my motives are; and at the moment I pass a law, unalterable as that of the Medes and Persians, that both are right."

"They cannot be, sir, if they require a new statute to legalize them."

"They are, Miss Eyre, though they absolutely require a new statute: unheard-of combinations of circumstances demand unheard-of rules."

"That sounds a dangerous maxim, sir; because one can see at once that it is liable to abuse."

"Sententious sage! so it is: but I swear by my household gods not to abuse it."

"You are human and fallible."

"I am: so are you—what then?"

"The human and fallible should not arrogate a power with which the divine and perfect alone can be safely entrusted." ...

"You are afraid of me, because I talk like a sphynx."

"Your language is enigmatical, sir: but though I am bewildered, I am certainly not afraid."

"You *are* afraid—your self-love dreads a blunder."

"In that sense I do feel apprehensive—I have no wish to talk nonsense."

"If you did, it would be in a grave, quiet manner, I should mistake it for sense. Do you never laugh, Miss Eyre? Don't trouble yourself to answer—I see, you laugh rarely; but you can laugh very merrily: believe me, you are not naturally austere, any more than I am naturally vicious. The Lowood constraint still clings to you somewhat; controlling your features, muffling your voice, and restricting your limbs; and you fear in the presence of a man and a brother—or father, or master, or what you will—to smile too gaily, speak too freely, or move too quickly: but, in time, I think you will learn to be natural with me, as I find it impossible to be conventional with you; and then your looks and movements will have more vivacity and variety than they dare offer now." (140–42)

The dialogue opens and closes with the partners' discussing at length their understanding of each other. Jane seems to exemplify Grice's rules of conversation: she speaks only to what she knows, asserts that her knowledge of the "truth" of Rochester is limited, focuses on the moral makeup of Rochester to which he himself has alluded, and articulates her mind with such perspicacity that her sentences have a mechanical sound—they are almost too correct, too controlled, too precise. Little affect is expressed; instead, Jane's words are declarative. Her part in this two-part construction of voices is to make transparent the work of conversations: taking her turn, Jane waits until Rochester has made his statement about himself, which she then challenges. Working only from the previous text about himself that Rochester provides, Jane's responses work to interconnect his thoughts with her own. Throughout the discourse, Jane's manner remains attentive, measured, and "proper." The reiterations of "sir" acknowledge her constant awareness of their different positions. However, while her logical, almost robotic utterances joined with the social frame she maintains with the use of "sir" work to make it seem as if Jane's speech never loses its self-control, in fact the power of her directness crosses that line. She prefaces her remarks with an appeal to simplicity and lack of expertise: "'I don't understand you at all: I cannot keep up the conversation, because it has got out of my depth." But she continues: "Only one thing I know . . . one thing I can comprehend. . . . It seems to me, that if you . . . and that if from this day you . . . you would in a few years . . .'" (140). By the conclusion of her speech, Jane has moved from a disclaimer to a fully developed remedy to Rochester's proposed vicious condition—not the act of a servant who remains within the confines of restricted linguistic interaction with the "master." Further, she challenges every statement Rochester makes; her turn in speaking never strays either to herself or to words of support or acceptance of Rochester's position. According to Lakoff's and Gadamer's descriptions of dialogue, Jane upsets the friendly conversation's need for "reiterated yesses" and other noises of agreement, or at least cordiality. Jane's position as respondent to Rochester's query about his moral predicament gives her the moral "upper hand." And she takes it in an effort both to provide a commonsense solution and to remind him of his humanity and fallibility. Neither the position in which she is placed as conversant nor how she chooses to interact from that position makes hers the expressions of a servant.

Likewise, Rochester engages in the cooperative effort. He does not use his position of power to silence Jane; rather, he encourages her critique by using his turns to respond to her responses. He expresses his sense of respect for her, as well as a sense of distance, in his continuous use of "Miss Eyre." Coded shifts in states of intimacy are often first indicated in changed forms of personal reference. Rochester moves from the address of "Miss Eyre" to "Jane" during the course of the bedroom scene when Jane rouses him from his burning bed. From owing his life to Jane and finding Jane and himself suddenly to be in a room and clothes signifying the greatest intimacy, Rochester tells Jane that he sees her now as "Jane." Only during scenes of intense emotionality does Jane use "you" or even think of him as "Edward Fairfax Rochester," never as just Edward. And only twice in the final chapter does she refer to him as "my Edward," but never in conversation with him. The shift in codes from calling another by family name, the title of a generalizable group, to the "Christian" name, the title of an individualized person, tells of the distance a namer has moved from a form of public to intimate address. As the last name represents the collectivity of its members, the quality of being one of the generalizable "them," the first name represents the individuality of the person for whom it signifies. Therefore, the distance traveled from last to first name is one of backward movement from the outward accessibility of the group to the inward individuality of the person named. To be "Eyre" no longer is not to be an identifiable member of the Eyre group; to be "Miss" no longer is not to be of unmarried, disconnected status. To be "Jane" to someone else is for another to assert knowledge of her and, therefore, to be in relation to her. By calling her "Jane," Rochester claims to know her "Janeness," her private self; he creates a bridge in the name between their selves as one knows and the other is known. To name her "Jane," as opposed to Miss Eyre, is for Rochester to picture her, think of her, know her as "Jane." And because they occupy the positions they do, it is for him to voice this name to her, to signal this assertion of their change in intimacy. Her allowance of Rochester's liberty signifies her unspoken agreement to be named by him and to what he means by that name, an act she will not allow others. (As already noted, Brocklehurst's calling her "liar," or John Reed's calling her "dependent," are the names-made-labels from which she spends portions of the novel detaching herself.) Further, her acceptance of Rochester's speech act reveals her tacit acknowledgment of and growing fascination for the changed form of their relating, from the socially prescribed to their private, ongoing construction of an "us," authored by us and our evolving rules.

Jane's reluctance, even inability, to dispose of "sir" for "Edward" couples with her resistance to speak of herself freely (to share with Rochester moments of her own moral struggles) to create a scene of one who maintains distance of address and self-disclosure versus one who presses on that distance to shorten it. Rochester's position of "mastery" provides him the latitude to test the boundaries of what makes for appropriate speech between landowner and governess. It is his choice to make. He chooses to offer a description of weakness and to make himself available to criticism. The device of revealing something of what one takes to be one's internal self is in part an invitation to another to gain knowledge of one's self; it functions as an act of gift giving where the gift is offered with the tacit understanding that it be treated with care and not be made available for public consideration. This opening forms the basis of an "us," created from the knowledge of the self shared with another, privately. Therefore, self-disclosure also acts as an invitation to the other to offer a piece of his or her own private storehouse of the self. Jane's refusal to respond to this indirect appeal and her insistence on replying as an observer to Rochester's musings about himself prompt him to step back from the topic of the conversation. Her refusal takes the form of moving to leave the room; his response is first to ask where she's going and then to refuse to accept her reply. He then forces the topic of the conversation to turn to Jane's interior self, not as a solitary identity, but as an identity in relation to him: "You are afraid of me because I talk like a sphynx." In Rochester's movement from "I" to "you in relation to I," he raises the question of what she keeps within, or of who she is when she is not "Miss Eyre." He offers a summary of what has just taken place: "[I]n time, I think you will learn to be natural with me, as I find it impossible to be conventional with you."

What this conversation represents, then, is how Rochester will repeatedly reshape the boundaries of what is a "natural" conversation between himself and his governess. However, it also reveals how Jane modifies the configuration of "their" conversation and relationship throughout the novel. Her "truth," her refusal merely to agree or assume the position of static listener—to be in essence Bakhtin's "presupposed other" who must respond to a speaker and be responded to in kind—is what prompts Rochester's desire to reveal more of his internal nature, to entrust this partner in discourse with his self. As in the first instance of Rochester's assuming a position of vulnerability with Jane, requiring her assistance to mount the horse from which he's fallen, and Jane's readiness to respond in a manner true to her "Janeness," the intimacy of interaction deepens as each encounter leads to increased knowledge about the other. These conversations are made possible by their exchanging of positions: Rochester assumes the role of one who needs to be led, or "mastered," and Jane that of the one who guides, or "governs." I would assert that such a conversation

makes evident how they make and live their coupleness. By sharing a language and positions of vulnerability and control, Rochester and Jane forge
a ground of compatibility based on the possibility of a spiritual equality
and intimacy.

~

Whereas it is Rochester's sense of play which invites Jane's earnest response
that ignites one of their many conversations on what it means to explore
the identity of each, it is Elizabeth Bennet's sense of a joke and her critical
eye which prompt her to consider, yet again, who this Darcy is, while he
explores her "Elizabethness," as she promenades with Miss Bingley about
the room:

> "Mr. Darcy is not to be laughed at!" cried Elizabeth. "That is an
> uncommon advantage, and uncommon I hope it will continue, for it
> would be a great loss to *me* to have any such acquaintance. I dearly
> love a laugh."
>
> "Miss Bingley," said he, "has given me credit for more than can be.
> The wisest and best of men, nay the wisest and best of their actions,
> may be rendered ridiculous by a person whose first object in life is
> a joke."
>
> "Certainly," replied Elizabeth—"there are such people, but I hope
> I am not one of *them*. I hope I never ridicule what is wise or good.
> Follies and nonsense, whims and inconsistencies do divert me, I own,
> and I laugh at them whenever I can.—But these, I suppose, are pre-
> cisely what you are without."
>
> "Perhaps that is not possible for any one. But it has been the study
> of my life to avoid those weaknesses which often expose a strong
> understanding to ridicule."
>
> "Such as vanity and pride."
>
> "Yes, vanity is weakness indeed. But pride—where there is real
> superiority of mind, pride will always be under good regulation."
> Elizabeth turned away to hide a smile.
>
> "Your examination of Mr. Darcy is over, I presume," said Miss
> Bingley;—"and pray what is the result?"
>
> "I am perfectly convinced by it that Mr. Darcy has no defect. He
> owns it himself without disguise."
>
> "No"—said Darcy, "I have made no such pretension. I have faults
> enough, but they are not, I hope, of understanding. My temper I
> dare not vouch for.—It is I believe too little yielding—certainly too

little yielding for the convenience of the world. I cannot forget the follies and vices of others so soon as I ought, nor their offenses against myself. My feelings are not puffed about with every attempt to move them. My temper would perhaps be called resentful.—My good opinion once lost is lost forever."

"*That* is a failing indeed!"—cried Elizabeth. "Implacable resentment *is* a shade in a character. But you have chosen your fault well.— I really cannot laugh at it. You are safe from me there."

"There is, I believe, in every disposition a tendency to some particular evil, a natural defect, which not even the best education can overcome."

"And *your* defect is a propensity to hate every body."

"And yours," he replied with a smile, "is willfully to misunderstand them." (101–3)

Initially, it appears that Elizabeth controls the frame of the discussion in that she seems to coerce from Darcy an admission about himself that reveals his vanity or pride, the very qualities he claims make someone worth ridiculing and which he does not possess. With the insertion of a stage direction, Elizabeth's turning away to smile, the joke is taken note of: to assert that he is not subject to the defects of vanity and pride provides further evidence that these are in fact Darcy's faults. She laughs at her partner in the conversation in such a way that neither he nor their audience, Miss Bingley, is made aware of the game. This is Elizabeth's private joke, told to herself at Darcy's expense. She proceeds to ridicule him openly by declaring that he is without defect because he has said so himself. His response, like that to her statement about his not being an object open to laughter, reveals a note of honesty and seriousness. Admitting he has faults, namely, his temper and resentment, he claims he also possesses understanding. Elizabeth cannot hear the extent of Darcy's disclosure of himself to her. Inclined to ridicule and so to finding fault, she seizes on the "failing" of his resentment and extrapolates beyond that to conclude that his "defect is a propensity to hate every body."

However, something has altered the tone and positions of control of the conversation—an alteration that repeats throughout the novel. When at midpoint Elizabeth turns from her partner and audience to laugh to herself—a pleasure-filled, self-congratulatory gesture about her superior wit and understanding—Darcy is the one left openly smiling. Elizabeth has so convinced herself of the shortcomings of Darcy's character that she arrives at a hyperbolic assertion of his defect. Darcy turns Elizabeth's critique of him into a gentle, thoughtful retort about *her* defect: "And yours . . . is willfully to misunderstand them." It is Darcy who ends their discourse with the pleasures of a smile. If we can "hear" Darcy at this moment in a way that Lizzy cannot, then the movement of this speech from her smile to his enables something to happen which we as its readers desired. These non-plotting conversations that display how a couple repeatedly talks can fulfill the reader's desire for plot, even unbeknownst to the couple.

Darcy's first and last comments to Elizabeth move from his definition of the dangers of the "person whose first object in life is a joke" to a working out of the specific danger to which Elizabeth falls prey. Elizabeth's discourse with Darcy is part of her ongoing acquisition of evidence intended to prove him to be a man of defects. While at first it appears that Elizabeth's use of indirection enables her to joke at Darcy's faults while he reveals them unawares, Darcy acts as a partner in indirection in his evaluation of how Elizabeth responds to him. Their camaraderie reveals their mutual ability to use implicature as a means of evaluating each other. While theirs is not a conversation of a shared common language, as Gadamer describes it, it is one of "complementary schismogenesis," which Gregory Bateson describes as the simultaneous act of each member of a conversation staying within the paradigm or frame of how each views what the conversation is meaning. Neither can move into the other's gestalt because each holds vigilantly to the one he or she uses. As a result, conflicts deepen and conversation seems almost impossible because how language is used and how meaning is determined function as points of contention.[1]

Each stays within a self-determined, mutually exclusive frame of reference for understanding the other, which results in misunderstanding. However, misunderstanding works as the means through which they perpetually relate; from the plot conversation of their first meeting to this instance of Darcy-and-Elizabeth-talk-as-usual, to misunderstand is what it means for Darcy and Elizabeth to converse. It is the lifeblood of their partnership, the conversation that gets repeated. Not being "present" to each other and not being able to make the other "present," not understanding the other and not being understood, they need one another's physical presence, time spent together, occasions in which the other is a preoccupation. To misunderstand prompts first the wrong construction of a picture of the other (but still all of the psychic energy that is required by the act of creating that misconstruction). To acknowledge that one has misunderstood is to create a new picture assembled from a negation of knowledge, an understanding based in knowing suddenly all that the other is *not*. The intimacy of knowing is then founded on the intimacy of having not known: this is the process which defines how Lizzy and Darcy use speech to build the sense of intimacy that redefines them as partners. They grow together from an ongoing experience of jointly shattering their misconstrued "truths."

This movement from one way of knowing to another, the recognition that movement is possible because another understanding is possible, shares in Wittgenstein's description of the "dawning of an aspect" in his discussion of the Jastrow drawing of the duck/rabbit: "I contemplate a face, and then suddenly notice its likeness to another. I *see* that it has not changed; and yet I see it differently. But we can also *see* the illustration now as one thing now as another.—So we interpret it, and *see* it as we *interpret* it" (193(xi)). Darcy has another face for Elizabeth when she construes him differently. He has not changed and yet he has changed profoundly in response to the revision of her interpretation. The novel must soon end once the conversation of Darcy and Elizabeth changes to understanding: that change takes place silently, somewhere outside the confines of the narrative's final pages.

I Know You, and I'm Still Here

Conversations *before* the conversation of love's declaration stage the negotiation of selves in relation to each other, the "who are you?" interacting with "who am I in relation to you?" interacting with "who are we?"— multilayered play of discourse. Conversations *after* its declaration are about the sounds made after love has been announced, after the sharing of an "our history." How have the sounds changed? How is surprise to be found in the already discovered?

Nick and Nora Charles are a "we" acknowledged before we meet them. Their plot conversations in Dashiell Hammett's novel *The Thin Man* do not address the approach toward or away from knowledge about themselves, each other, and their relationship but rather consider the solution to Julia Wolf's murder. The problem of the novel is not in their getting married or in their being married; it is elsewhere—in the murdering, stealing, and lying of others who surround them. In their conversations, plot discussions on solving the case and nonplot exchanges displaying their "usness" interact. Because the drama of the plot does not revolve around negotiating the boundaries of individual self and collective selves, their discourse creates a static "us," which comments on the case and its players and itself. As the central character or narrator of the text, the marriage, therefore, is a collective voice that evaluates the meaning of the clues revealed while it "self-displays." Although the actual narrator is Nick—the novel is in his voice—the readers' narrator is Nick and Nora. What I mean by this is that readers make their way through the novel by understanding that Nick actually tells the story and that Nick and Nora together encounter the story, hear the story, think about the story, work to "solve" the story. So if Nick "makes" the plot in his words of narration, Nick and Nora meditate on it. The focalization shifts the reader between the framing perspective of Nick and the interpretive perspective of Nick and Nora. The opening of *The Thin Man* is not about a first meeting of the members of a marriage, but rather the meeting of the marriage with the woman who brings the problem that needs solving:

> Asta jumped up and punched me in the belly with her front feet. Nora, at the other end of the leash, said: "She's had a swell afternoon—knocked over a table of toys at Lord & Taylor's, scared a fat woman silly by licking her leg in Saks, and been patted by three policemen."
>
> I made introductions. "My wife, Dorothy Wynant. Her father was once a client of mine, when she was only so high. A good guy, but screwy."
>
> "I was fascinated by him," Dorothy said, meaning me, "a real live detective, and used to follow him around making him tell me about his experiences. He told me awful lies, but I believed every word."
>
> I said: "You look tired, Nora."
>
> "I am. Let's sit down."
>
> Dorothy Wynant said she had to go back to her table . . . Dorothy patted the dog's head and left us.
>
> We found a table. Nora said: "She's pretty."
>
> "If you like them like that."
>
> She grinned at me. "You got types?"
>
> "Only you, darling—lanky brunettes with wicked jaws."
>
> "And how about the red-head you wandered off with at the Quinn's last night?"
>
> "That's silly," I said. "She just wanted to show me some French etchings." (3–5)

The novel opens with a possible trap. Whereas "Nora" is mentioned in the first line of the novel, she is not present at the start of the first conversation. Instead, a man alone at a speakeasy is alighted upon by an attractive, younger woman. The early moments of the opening prompt us to wonder, is this the relationship of the text to read for? Nora's entrance announces that it is not. Whereas Dorothy must introduce herself to Nick, Asta and Nora are known; without introduction, Nick describes their approach and Nora launches into her depiction of the day. Her words, directed to Nick, sound familiar, as if he would know Asta's actions to be Asta-like, and as if the conversation is an ongoing one. Nora waits for no introduction; being in the presence of Nick requires no gesture of ritualized speech by way of greetings. The introduction Nick provides is one to Nora of Dorothy; its emphasis is not Nick's attempt to bring Dorothy to a closer ground of intimacy by revealing anything to her of Nora. Instead, Nora is told what Nick knows of Dorothy; suddenly, the scene is no longer of single man meeting single woman, but rather of single woman meeting a couple. Dorothy attempts to bring the tone of the conversation back to one of a shared world between her and Nick by describing her fascination with him. In response, by looking at Nora and without asking but seeing that she is tired, Nick brings the discourse back to his knowledge of and concern for Nora. Dorothy's presence feels superfluous; the noise of Nora's entrance and Nick's leap into a realm not of question and answer between estranged acquaintances but of partner in discourses previous to the narrative draw the energy of the text to that partnership. It wants to hear their gestures, asides, jokes, ways of knowing each other which are already well formulated.

When the couple is alone, the routine or "our song" phenomenon reveals itself (Tannen, *That's Not* 60). Nora begins a pattern which Nick identifies and jumps into without skipping a beat. Staging a mock jealousy, "She's pretty," Nick turns the affected jealousy on Nora and then lets go of it: "If you like them like that." She is ready to play back; grinning, she asks Nick to tell her who he desires, namely, herself. He responds; she asks again; he retorts. The ease with which Nora knows how to question and Nick to respond lends to their conversation the quality of daily talk, or at least a way of interacting in which both are versed. Further, the immediacy of the entry by both into the pattern makes the conversation an example of their routine of tease, her slangy "You got types," and his idiomatic "darling," renamed by him as a lanky brunette with a wicked jaw. This is their song, their way of allowing in the sexual tension of possible strayings of desire—"She's pretty," and "And how about the red-head"—

and response of implicature, turning the answer back to Nora, not address-ing it head-on and thereby allowing the tension to exist within the pattern of indirection that says, "you know that I desire you by the act of my not answering directly, by my joking about French etchings."

Because she still asks and because he still answers indirectly or with a joke, they create a "shtick" which is their shtick, which pre- and postdates the narrative itself. Their sense of teamness, which never grows more or less intimate, is never threatened by the possibility of dissolution. Not burdened with the requirement that the development of plot proceed from a development in their relationship, the conversations of their collective entity reveal the rhetorical displays of an ongoing intimacy, static in its history (there is no revealed beginning or development or move toward an end, just middleness), rich in its sounds of an idiomatic dailiness. Their marriage is the collective voice which tells of its private world of discourse, its own form of "twinspeech," and of the public world of clues and mys-teries, which it uses as its subject for further verbal play. They perform conversation as improvisation, their means of making their narrative in and around the detective plot. With a knowing delight that they have had the good fortune to find one another, Nick and Nora perform like a rou-tine the "Nick and Nora marriage."

~

In the way that Nick and Nora's discussion of their mutual desire is cre-ated by the presence of a third figure appearing as the idea of threat or intrusion into their private sphere of desire, the conversations where Shakespeare's Antony and Cleopatra reaffirm without limit their fidelity to each other are predicated on the triangulation of desire. Using René Girard's depiction of the display of X's desire toward Y, who is the desired object of Z, as X's unexpressed desire to be like Z, Nora uses Dorothy's desire for Nick as a means of reaffirming her own desire for Nick in the guise of teasing him about fidelity. Antony and Cleopatra, like Nick and Nora, use the destabilizing formation of the triangle as a means to con-tinue the conversation of their desire for each other.[2] Antony, in the place of Nora, uses the apparently threatening (though clearly not) presence of Thyreus to express in some new way his old love. Shakespeare named only two of his plays for couples—*Antony and Cleopatra* and *Romeo and Juliet,* one a drama of mature love and the other a play of young love. The dia-logues of Antony and Cleopatra offer with a kind of infinite variety the sounds of love perpetuating itself by lovers who do so to perpetuate their already well-established love.

The declaration of their passion occurred earlier: Enobarbus tells of Antony's helplessness before Cleopatra's entrance on the purpled barge. The narrative of conversations, discourse of the play's present, is of a continuous "now" after the acknowledgment. Her hand kissed by the lips of Caesar's servant Thyreus, Cleopatra is named directly a "boggler" by Antony. Nora implies the same with Nick in "She's pretty." However, the ends to which Nora and Antony directly or indirectly address their "critique" are the same:

Cleo. Good my lord—
Ant. You have been a boggler ever.
    But when we in our viciousness grow hard—
    Oh, misery on't!—the wise gods seel our eyes,
    In our own filth drop our clear judgments, make us
    Adore our errors, laugh at's while we strut
    To our confusion.
Cleo. Oh, is't come to this? . . .
Ant. To let a fellow that will take rewards
    And say, "God quit you!" be familiar with
    My playfellow, your hand, this kingly seal
    And plighter of high hearts! . . .
[Thyreus is ordered whipped]
Cleo. Have you done yet?
Ant. Alack, our terrene moon
    Is now eclipsed, and it portends alone
    The fall of Antony.
Cleo. I must stay his time.
Ant. To flatter Caesar, would you mingle eyes
    With one that ties his points?
Cleo. Not know me yet?
Ant. Coldhearted toward me?
Cleo. Ah, dear if it be so,
    From my heart let Heaven engender hail
    And poison it in the source, and the first stone
    Drop in my neck. As it determines, so
    Dissolve my life! . . .
Ant. I am satisfied . . .
    If from the field I shall return once more
    To kiss these lips, I will appear in blood.

I and my sword will earn our chronicle.
There's hope in't yet.
Cleo. That's my brave lord.
Ant. . . . Come,
Let's have one other gaudy night. Call to me
All my sad captains, fill our bowls once more.
Let's mock the midnight bell.
Cleo. It's my birthday.
I had thought to have held it poor, but since my lord
Is Antony again, I will be Cleopatra.

(3.13.109-87)

That Thyreus functions as the catalyst to cause the outburst, to cause
the reunion, redefines him from person as threat to dismembered lips that
kiss her hand, or to reification of the idea of Caesar. As the re-membered
mouth of Caesar (mouthpiece of and lips that kiss), Thyreus embodies
an object of desire worthy of Antony's jealousy and whipping. Cleopatra
becomes a fetishized hand, Antony's "playfellow": to have her hand kissed
by another is to have Antony's object of desire be shared or satisfied by
another. While the conversation between Cleopatra and Antony is that of
a staged melodrama of a lover intercepting his love in a posture of intimacy
with another (imagining himself betrayed by the woman who must plead
her innocence and win him back), it is played as a play both know only
too well. Calling Cleopatra a "boggler," or shifty thing, Antony incites her
to tell him again how she loves him. After the conversation of acknowledgment of "us," the scene that can be construed as a setting to cause jealousy works as a means to restage the acknowledgment conversation with
an equal, though different, sense of urgency. It functions as the means to
make dramatic again the context of discourse, to provide the ground to
have this conversation again, to make the relationship be again at stake
and so need a form of declaration.

Cleopatra is no stranger to what is being asked of her. Throughout the
course of their interactions, Antony and Cleopatra exchange positions of
who demands an address of reaffirmed passion and who offers its evidence.
Their conversation reveals the sound of familiarity or recognition of the
ritual which Nick and Nora display in their game of indirect reacknowl-
edgment of devotion. "Oh, is't come to this," "Have you done yet?" "I
must stay his time," "Not know me yet?" have the feel of, "Oh, not this
again. Are you finished?" "I just have to wait this one out." "Do you know

who you're talking to?" This conversation keeps being had. It works as the response to understanding disrupted, even ruptured, and then as its renewal. Moving between believing in what is seen (the kissing of the hand) and what is known (the endlessness of their hungry passion for each other) makes the scene be at once an urgent attempt to reorder the meaning of what is witnessed and the acting out of a melodramatic performance. Both work to reestablish the understanding of "usness" out of the simultaneous understanding of how to respond to the seriousness/jokiness of what is being called for. "Our speech" becomes in this instance the working through yet again of "our plot," which is "us." What prompts Antony's outburst and their subsequent conversation tells about the nature of their intimacy, that it is worthy of threat, fragile enough to succumb to threat, and requires threat as a means of reestablishing itself.

Antony acts as "intimate critic" of Cleopatra, a position Tannen describes as knowing another so well that the other's weaknesses are readily perceived and the qualities that aggravate are readily taken to be weaknesses (*That's Not* 145–58). To call her a "boggler" is to know what everyone knows about Cleopatra, that she is shifty and fickle. However, for Antony to call her this is for him to cast doubts on her relations to him, on the mutually created entity that defines them both as joined together in separation from others. It is an expression too of the knowledge of that to which she is most sensitive (because it is perhaps the most true), and that which most wounds him in his relation to her. However, while uttering "boggler" performs a critique of Cleopatra, it also works as an idiom of endearment and familiarity. The site of both critique and endearment, "boggler" holds what most repels and attracts Antony. As a word, it reveals the intimacy of Antony's knowledge of Cleopatra because to know what most attracts and repels is to know another intimately. Likewise, Antony's use of "playfellow" as the description for her hand and of "gaudy night" for sexual intercourse create an intimate atmosphere where the references need not be defined in direction but are cast through indirection into an implied state where rapport is insisted upon by the unstated.

As respondent to Antony's charge of betrayal and implicit incitement to act out her fidelity, Cleopatra allows Antony the verbal space to rant until her cue from him, "Coldhearted toward me?" She delivers one speech of defense as an offering to Antony, who tells her this part of the interaction has run its course: "I am satisfied." The route from accusation to defense to acceptance leads to the fruit of the interaction—making up. Antony's call for one more gaudy night solicits Cleopatra's response, "It is my birthday. / I had thought to have held it poor, but since my lord / Is Antony again, I will be Cleopatra." A night of mutual gift givings of the body in celebration of the rebirth of again knowing themselves to be who they are raises the questions, What does it mean to be Antony again? to be Cleopatra? When did they end or begin again to be their identities?

An outburst in conversation where the cause is the accusation of a form of infidelity at once remakes the participants to be new to one another and continues a ritualized pattern of interaction. To stop being the known entity of Antony to Cleopatra and Cleopatra to Antony is to give life to the outburst, to allow its legitimacy. That it is still possible to no longer know the other means to no longer know the relationship, to put it at risk. Movement through the unrecognizable to an end where the partners know where they are, with whom they are, and who they are makes the discourse of intimate conversation be about the negotiation between confirmation (or prediction) and discovery (or rediscovery). This renewal conversation suggests an experienced ritual—this is the structure of a conversation that keeps happening—which is itself about suggesting the possibility of undoing the knownness of the partners who engage in its design. Seeking to test the ground of familiarity by undoing it, the conversation runs the risk of the familiar becoming unrecognizable and recognizable. If a problem of narrative is how to sustain itself after love has been acknowledged, then the undoing and redoing of the conversation of that acknowledgment poses a possible solution.

After Endings: Me, You, Us, Again

What of a narrative that attempts to proceed after the conversation that declares an end of "us," or takes as its topic what ensues after a statement of separation? A genre of film devotes itself to just such a question, to pursuing the narrative exploration of that problem. It's to that genre as an entity that I now turn, as opposed to the analysis of one of its conversations, because I'm interested in how these films function together to address the problem of narrating "after endings" (in that the *whole* of each film explores what can follow "after endings," not just a conversation), and how these films collectively create conversations that reinvent the old marriage. As named and defined by Stanley Cavell in *Pursuits of Happiness,* "comedies of remarriage" are a set of films within the general category of Hollywood screwball comedies that function as a genre in their association with the structure of *The Winter's Tale.* These are narratives where the "drive of [their] plot[s] [is] not to get the central pair together, but to get them *back* together, together *again*. Hence the fact of marriage in it is subjected to the fact or threat of divorce" (2).[3] *The Lady Eve, It Happened One Night, Bringing Up Baby, The Philadelphia Story, His Girl Friday, Adam's Rib,* and *The Awful Truth* are the seven films Cavell explores as responses to Nora's shutting the door on Torvald, as solutions to her call in *A Doll's House* for "the miracle" so that "life between us could become a marriage." Understanding these films to be conversations that lead to "acknowledgment; to the reconciliation of a genuine forgiveness; a reconciliation so profound as to require the metamorphosis of death and revival, the achievement of a new perspective on existence; a perspective that presents itself as a place, one removed from the city of confusion and divorce" (*Pursuits* 19) means recognizing the "miracle" Nora speaks of as *conversation.* However, the conversation cannot take place on the old ground of the marriage, the marriage before its real or threatened end. These films, from the great era of the "talkie," make continuous talk out of what it means to know another and be known almost too well. They make those conversations be a source of urgency and present Antonys and Cleopatras who act as intimate critics, needing to be selves apart from the selves of the marriage or from the other, and yet still needing the marriage. While conversation acts as the medium that brought the marriage to its end, it works too as that which transforms the couple so that a "new perspective" is possible, founded on new ground, creating a remarriage.[4]

How does conversation between the same partners lead to marriage, and then to the desire to end marriage, and then to the need for remarriage? Time passes. People change. Marriages change. And yet, in the remarriage comedies it is the *how* of the conversation (how it is delivered and understood) that leads to an end, not the pressures of time and evolution. Tannen, in *That's Not What I Meant!* asserts that individual speech style and understanding of what it means to converse account generally for the underlying tensions or bonds that sever or unite. These are the paralinguistic perceptions that surround how an individual presents him- or herself, or understands another. Spencer Tracy's slap of Katharine Hepburn during her rubdown in *Adam's Rib* works as a signifier for or way of conversing about their emerging differences over what makes for a marriage— his attempt to keep their interaction within the known boundaries of the intimate, and her recognition that he really *meant* that slap. They must separate after that slap. Katharine Hepburn's (in *The Philadelphia Story*) and Claudette Colbert's (in *It Happened One Night*) sounds of entitlement and perfection as the daughters of old money families or rich fathers lead to Cary Grant's depiction of Hepburn as fancying herself to be a "virgin goddess" and Clark Gable's naming of Colbert as "brat." In their choice of epithets, these men make these women be people with whom they cannot converse because of their distances in social or generational stature. Being named "virgin goddess" and "brat," how can Hepburn and Colbert actually speak to transform those names and make a bridge toward the men who named them? And finally, why would they want to do so? With the breakdown of Lakoff's rules of interaction staged in the film or prior to it comes the figuring of the couple's conversation as that which is no longer tolerable, that which must end. The "what" of the conversation feels inconsequential; regardless of the subject, just having a conversation with the other comes to feel insupportable. And yet not.

The couples of remarriage comedies keep talking to each other, seem never to be free of their exchanges, because even in the need they feel to rage against each other, they finally don't want to be free of their partnered speech, even if it must be shouted. Therefore, the ongoingness of their conversations means the continuation of their relationships, despite its stated or legal end. Conversation *is* the relationship in these films because it is what constitutes the marriages' ends and their perpetuations to follow. To be a "talkie" is to be a film that talks. This particular genre of talkie makes talking be about the cycles of marriage. With the breakdown of Grice's cooperative effort comes the couple's break. However, in *His Girl*

Clark Gable and
Claudette Colbert in
It Happened One Night,
Columbia, 1934

Courtesy Academy of
Motion Pictures Arts
and Sciences

Friday the fact of still having the conversation prompts Hildy's reacceptance of marriage to Walter because nobody wears her down so well. And in *The Philadelphia Story*, Tracy Lord's punishment for being the unforgiving "prig and perennial spinster no matter how many marriages," followed by her melting into the human "lit from within, full of hearthfires and holocausts," occurs because she and Cary Grant keep talking. She melts from the position of "virgin goddess" because of the discovery of her own passion and vulnerability. That she is passionate and vulnerable enables C. K. Dexter Haven to have the woman in remarriage he first wanted in marriage; it also enables her to see C. K. Dexter Haven as desirable. Where once those shared traits in him were "so unattractive," now they make him the right partner.

Understanding disrupted here brings not the end of the film but its beginning, not the end of the conversation but its renewal, not the end of a marriage but its re-creation. There is an assertion of knowing the other so well and of being so well known that the conversation brings an end

Katharine Hepburn
and Cary Grant in
The Philadelphia Story,
MGM, 1940

Courtesy UCLA Arts–
Special Collections

in order that it begin again, so that the marriage can perennially recur. The sequel brings with it the idea of the vehicle of the story having a life of its own after its last words, as in the repeatability of *Star Wars* or *The Thin Man,* where the problem solvers are given new problems to solve. In contrast, the comedy of remarriage is about the marriage having a life of its own in the ongoingness of the conversation that appears at the outset to be at its end and at the end to be at its middle—but a middle that feels oddly like a beginning.

~

Language that enables partners just to talk in narratives, as opposed just to make the narrative's plot, creates conversations that function as their own performances. While plot conversations may reveal how a couple repeats aspects of their linguistic engagement, these crux conversations stand out in their drive to bring the plot to new places, to do new things, to end in their full knowledge of all there is to be known. They function as extraordinary structures of rhetoric in their memorability, a memorability tied to how they define certain desired moments of plot development. The conversations of repetition, or what I refer to here as the words that play, fill the text in their recurrence and work to tell the general story—to show again and again, for instance, *Pride and Prejudice* to be about words misunderstood or *Jane Eyre* to be about exchanges of power in the forging of notions of equality. What these repeated conversations do, therefore, is to tell the text's "usual," or function as the narrative's structural refrain. They tell of the pleasure the narrative/the couple take in these conversations, in that they are the ones repeated, and hence desired.

However, when a narrative seems to have nowhere to go in that its plotting has declared its end, as in the "end of us," the conversations of play enable the continuance of that narrative. In an instance of narrative where plot runs out or dead-ends by virtue of its fulfillment of its self-declared end, these conversations of rhetorical play make possible a genre of narrative, the comedy of remarriage, or a means for the narrative to continue despite its inability to move forward. So it charts something like a circle, or a traveling back and forth between known points, or a flipping over to move along the backside of an already experienced front. The forward-moving line of plot, made possible by the lines of plot-making first conversations, becomes abandoned for the words that form some recurrent or other geometry, or perhaps no geometry at all. Just a sense of being there, or being there again, though differently: these are the partnered words of the moment that creates a "now" or a lifetime together. While these conversations do not obviously advance a narrative, they do represent in their replay what a partnership is about, and therefore what the narrative is about, until it shifts in direction. The comedy of remarriage works as a whole genre of the narrative moments that play because these films are formed from the rhetorical sparring of partners who play, as opposed to plot, because their plots have so little distance to go. The language and the narrative of remarriage couples are about the surprise of our still being present to something, the end of which we seem to know and not know at the same time.

Conclusions

If the "life" of a narrative depends on its conversations for help in its sustaining, this dependence has everything to do with the "aliveness" of exchanged language itself. Wittgenstein writes of the processural quality of language revealed through "countless different kinds of use of what we call 'symbols,' 'words,' 'sentences.' And this multiplicity is not something fixed, given once and for all; but new types of language, new language games, as we may say, come into existence, and others become obsolete and get forgotten. . . . Here the term 'language-game' is meant to bring into prominence the fact that the speaking of language is part of an activity, or a form of life" (11e(23)). In his discussion of this passage in "The Availability of Wittgenstein's Later Philosophy," Cavell states:

> We learn and teach words in certain contexts, and then we are expected, and expect others, to be able to project them into further contexts. Nothing insures that this projection will take place (in particular, not the grasping of books of rules), just as nothing insures that we will make, and understand the same projections. That on the whole we do is a matter of our sharing routes of interest and feeling, modes of response, senses of humor and of significance and of fulfillment, of what is outrageous, of what is similar to what else, what a rebuke, what forgiveness, of when an utterance is an assertion, when an appeal, when an explanation—all the whirl of organism Wittgenstein calls 'forms of life.' (*Must We Mean* 52)

Where Wittgenstein focuses on the multiplicity, changeability, expandability of a language itself, Cavell applies this idea to what people who

87

speak together actually do. How we understand one another and how we learn to extend our knowledge of language into new settings reveal the flexibility both of the language and of the mind which uses language. That language is not fixed, that its games are ongoing, evolving activities, enables one to discover new ways of thinking and being a self, and of understanding the self and other in relation.

The talk between two people affords a means of presenting one self to another, not a fixed self always appearing with the same words, but fluid selves connected at this instant with these words. The inability to freeze the motion of conversation reflects what Bergson would consider the non-atomizable flow of consciousness. A dialogue cannot be stopped or captured in a word or a moment; it is about the movement of language and consciousness between speakers. Habermas emphasizes the *activity* of being engaged in argumentation in his theory of communicative action. If meaning does not come from the subject of the discourse itself, it comes from the involvement of the "actors" who continuously seek consensus by measuring it against the "truth," "rightness," "sincerity" of the "fit" or "misfit" that occurs between the speech act and the tripartite structure of the "lifeworld" we inhabit—the objective of the external state of affairs, the social of the intersubjective interaction, and the subjective of the individual to which no one else has access (100). Further, Cavell writes of the activity of speaking:

> [T]he primary fact of natural language is that it is something spoken, spoken together. Talking together is acting together, not making motions and noises at one another, nor transferring unspeakable messages or essences from the inside of one closed chamber to the inside of another. The difficulties of talking together are, rather, *real* ones: the activities we engage in by talking are intricate and intricately related to one another. (*Must We Mean* 33–34)

Cavell allows for both the possibility and the difficulty that attend the exchange of ordinary language in the activity of "talking together." Speech acts are acts in that their speakers and listeners do things with the words they utter: do what is asked or not, learn what something means or not, laugh or cry or grunt or tune out, but feel prompted to make some form of response. The speaking of words in a scene of conversation demands response (even if it's silence or a deliberate "not hearing"). This demand is compounded from the power of words mixed with the power of what it means to be "with" another. To refuse to acknowledge another's language is to deny the presence of the other's self.

But how is one to acknowledge the other? How is one to do the activity of talking? Kierkegaard's Johannes the Seducer of *Either/Or I*, in his description of a conversation with the object of his seduction, Cordelia, discusses in particular what some of the real difficulties of talking together are, why, in fact, he believes conversation cannot be conveyed:

> It would be interesting, if it were possible, to record exactly the conversations between Cordelia and myself. However, it is easy to see that this is an impossibility; for if I were fortunate enough to remember every single word exchanged between us, still it would always be impossible to express the contemporaneity which really forms the nerve center of the conversation, the surprised outbreak, the passionateness which is the life-principle of conversation. In general, I have not prepared myself, since this would militate against the essential nature of conversation, especially erotic conversation. (394)

Contemporaneity is the central feature, the "nerve center," the erotic heart of conversation. Out of this energy of give and take comes the "surprised outbreak," "the passionateness" which Johannes calls conversation's "life-principle." That conversation has a life-principle, and so has life, comes from this texture of unrehearsed exchange. The spontaneity of conversation works for Johannes as a mirror of the act of seduction, even as a necessary precursor to or part of its execution. Expressions of passionate compliance or disagreement burst into the midst of exchange. In essence, he points to how conversation defies a description that would make it progressive, sequential, plottable on a line. While its result may be seen as a progression or movement away from where it began, looked at during the moments in which it has life or is occurring, it is about ongoingness; its life cannot be divided into determinable stages. To recast discourse as an erotic scene of contemporaneous passion, surprise, outbreak necessarily means to make conversation be a shared, ongoing activity. Film echoes the life of the conversation in its medium: connected frames of image and sound blend into a smooth unity imitating a "natural" conversation. Were the frames to stop, a snapshot and indistinguishable noise would convey the freezing of contemporaneity and, therefore, its distortion. While the novel cannot represent contemporaneity owing to the necessary limitation of reading from one word to the next (we cannot read contemporaneously), directions conveyed in punctuation and the narrator's description inter-jected in the midst of the scene make it possible for the reader to see and hear the conversation as it might look and sound in its contemporaneity.

The presentation of a self of the moment occurs with the exchange of words from one consciousness to another. In contrast, the act of remem-bering one's words creates a snapshot or a frozen representation of the self outside the conversation. A thought like, "These were my words, this is who I am," results from transporting the words from conversation into memory. While talking allows for the shaping of consciousness as an ongo-ing activity, reflection on discourse causes a break in the activity of speak-ing and a determination of intactness. Darcy's letter to Elizabeth stops the flow of conversations that have created an ongoing sense in Elizabeth of his faults. By fixing her attention to unchangeable words on the page, she must accept or reject the static portrait of himself he offers. From this picture, she moves to reinterpret their exchanges to come. The life of the couple is ongoing, daily, changeable, original, and habitual, like the process of talking. That it has a life of its own is reflected in the idea of an anniver-sary. As an individual's life is remembered annually on his or her "birth-day," so the life of a relationship is remembered annually on its birthday—the moment of being married.[1]

Presenting one's self, attempting to understand the other, working to understand the relationship, discussing topics outside the identities of the partners and their relationship, asking questions, arguing, agreeing, joking, playing, supporting, destroying, beginning, ending, creating are the "ing" processural acts of two people conversing. Further, the process of what the two are doing together is created not just in their verbal exchange but also in their paralinguistic interaction. Therefore, *how* the exchange of words occurs in tandem with the actual words exchanged shapes the activity of relating. That the life of the couple has a present, built on the ongoing "nows" of their interaction, means that their intimacy is alive; it keeps shaping and creating itself with the continuousness of time, consciousness, and talk. When a narrative displays the discourse of a partnership, it inter-rupts the single perspective of the voice telling the story. It insists on a scene of the collective where two consciousnesses create together what it means to be the couple, and what it means to be in/tell their story.

Cavell suggests that the films of remarriage comedy demonstrate what a conversation is, "what it does, what talk means. . . . In these films talking together is fully and plainly being together, a mode of association, a form of life. . . . The central pair are learning to speak the same language . . . to hear, to listen" (*Pursuits* 88). As has been noted, Gadamer, like Cavell, asserts the possibility of "speaking the same language" when he says conversation "presuppos[es] . . . a common language, or better creates a common language . . . reaching an understanding on the subject matter of a conversation necessarily means that a common language must first be worked out in the conversation" (378–79). Kierkegaard, in thinking about the distinctiveness of the family, writes, "I for one am revolted by all this separatistic odious practice in families that deliberately starts right off to show how exclusive everything is with them, which sometimes goes so far that the family speaks its own private language or speaks in such mysterious allusions that one cannot make heads or tails out of them" (*E/O II* 82). The possibility of speaking as a couple implies the possibility of creating a new semiprivate language, opaque to outsiders. "We speak the same linguini" is an assertion of an intimacy derived from the exclusion of others who do not, and of a union forged between partners who speak together in a way that only "we" understand. The "we" is predicated on having "a same language" to share and on understanding that "we" understand each other, something that "they" may not be able to do.

However, if language is about the activity of making possible collective, public communication, how can it be used as a means of asserting private communication, even a private language created and shared between two? Wittgenstein reflects on the possibility of a private language created by a solitary individual when he writes:

> But could we also imagine a language in which a person could write down or give vocal expression to his inner experiences—his feelings, moods, and the rest—for his private use?—Well, can't we do so in our ordinary language?—But that is not what I mean. The individual words of this language are to refer to what can only be known to the person speaking; to his immediate private sensations. So another person cannot understand the language. (88e(243))

However, he adds:

> Why can't my right hand give my left hand money?—My right hand can put it into my left hand. My right hand can write a deed of gift and my left hand a receipt.—But further practical consequences would not be those of a gift. When the left hand has taken the money from the right, etc., we shall ask: "Well, and what of it?" And the

same could be asked if a person had given himself a private definition of a word. (94e(248))

Wittgenstein can imagine creating a language in which only the individual
doing the creating knows what the words name of his "private sensations."
He casts this into the framework of a private language of an individual's
interior life, unavailable to any other. What is at issue for Wittgenstein is
not the difficulty of inventing a private language; that can be imagined.
Rather, it is the difficulty, even impossibility, of solving a metaphysical
question in language that guides Wittgenstein's discussion of the useful-
ness of a private language. Finding the words that will meaningfully convey private sensations that only "I" can know is not for Wittgenstein what
language can usefully do because it is a communication about qualia no
one else can know.

Why is it that Wittgenstein does not take up the possibility of a couple's
creation and sharing of "their" private language? About this too his question still stands, "Well, and what of it?" Can words refer to "semi" private
events or moments not experienced by a public but just by "we two"? In
considering why Wittgenstein does not take up this shared language of the
couple, I would assert it is because the language of the couple functions
like the private language of the individual.[2] The possibility of the invention of a language by an "I," or by a couple, exists within the parameters
of what language can do—that private language can be understood. However, difficulty arises when a metaphysical problem is posed, as when the
couple desire through the use of language to enable others to know the
couple's "internal" states—knowledge to which no other can have access,
a language for which there cannot, therefore, be meaning. The members
of a couple can interact with each other in a way that feels exclusionary or
private because of the privacy of their relation, something about which
only the two can know. That Cary Grant and Rosalind Russell seem to
speak a privately shared language comes not from the fact that they have
invented and speak a language which as its authors only they two can
understand. Rather, they are the sole participants who are in *position* to
understand and to further this language. The pleasure we experience at
being let in on their conversation makes it clear that this is not a language
which only the two can understand. Placed in a position to experience and
hence to be trained in their interaction (as their audience), we too can gain
knowledge of how they converse privately and what it means.

The sense of shared privacy of a language comes from altered meanings of individual words, novel ways words are put together, the tone used when they are uttered, the creation of new words, linguistic and paralinguistic activities that require each partner to know how to read what the other is doing, how to do it back, how in essence to carry on the performance between them for us of speaking the same language. When a pair share an interest in and knowledge of how to play together through language, a boundary is drawn between those who speak in their code and those who do not, those who are in on the joke and those who are not. This linguistic division separates a sphere of intimacy from a sphere of publicness. The moments in texts of a couple's speech make up the scenes of their intimacy, the location of the life of their relationship discovering itself, adjusting how it knows itself, recovering itself, even ending itself. These instances of conversation in narratives are the audience's means of overhearing or being present to that which creates, defines, and reveals the couple's intimacy.

However, Kierkegaard insists that "real" conversations between the partners of a marriage are never aesthetically represented:

It has often amazed me that no poet really portrays a married couple conversing. If they are ever portrayed—and they are meant to be a happy couple—they usually talk like a couple in love. Ordinarily they are only minor characters and so much older that they are the father and mother of the lover the poet is portraying. If a marriage is to be portrayed, it at least must be unhappy in order to be able to come under some consideration. They are viewed so differently: falling in love is supposed to be happy and have dangers outside; marriage must have its dangers within in order to be poetic. (*Stages* 127)

What is it about the nature of a "happy marriage" which resists portrayal? Why must the danger or tension of a text lie inside a marriage and outside a couple falling in love? If the life of a relationship is considered "over" with marriage, then its resuscitation can occur with problematizing the marriage. Likewise, if it reaches its pinnacle with the moment of a mutually acknowledged passion, then the road to that conversation must be problematic. If it is true that the structure of plot demands the tension of a problem, the "happy marriage" presents itself as seemingly "unplottable." Accordingly, in rare instances where a happy marriage is portrayed throughout the course of a novel, as in *The Thin Man,* its conversations are depicted not as an evolving, changeable entity, and not as the subject of the novel. Solving the murder is what drives the plot rather than solving the problem of the marriage. Nick and Nora, in conversation, exhibit the playful variations of a single mode of interaction; the murder plot capers to a close, the marriage variations play on and on.

Although instances of a narrative of a couple's ongoing, deepening happiness occupying the central frame of a novel are rare, novels can be investigated for the intimate moments of conversations of couples, and the pleasures that accompany their talk. A smothering of conversation occurs in the Victorian novel; endless pages of description and analysis empower the individual voice that is world creating. However, even within the novels that insist most on the solipsistic control of a narrator, conversations exist between couples who are in the midst of creating a history together. These moments of dualistic interaction are about the relinquishing of narrative control and the possibility of shaping an interactional account of a couple and their world.

While the novel and to a lesser degree film rarely explore the successful, enduring intimacy of a couple, a "home" for its varied portrayal is situation comedy. But why should it be that the novel, a medium whose great achievement is telling the story of private lives over time in its quantity of words, or film, a medium with the ability to bring sound and visual representations to the rendering of intimate life, leaves it to television's situation comedy to take as its fundamental subject Kierkegaard's desire to experience the portrayal of a married couple being happy in their marriage? And what would Kierkegaard think of that?

HAPPINESS

~

CHAPTER 4

Romantic Comedy and the Male/Female Comedy Team

(A hotel lobby. Piano bar music in the background.)

NICHOLS: Louise, where were you? I was going out of my mind. Darling, to be doing this terrible thing, and to be late on top of it!

MAY: I'm sorry . . . (tears) . . . please don't yell at me . . . God, what kind of a person must I be to do a thing like this?

NICHOLS: I'm sick, I'm physically sick with guilt . . . George is my best friend.

MAY: Your best friend?

NICHOLS: My best friend.

MAY: He's my husband! . . .

NICHOLS: Do you want to know how bad I feel? Listen, if I hadn't paid for that room already, I'd say forget it.

—Nichols and May, "Adultery"

A desire to talk to *this* person, a willingness to do so about things that are difficult to say, an insistence that the talk continue over time, an interest in finding new ways to speak an intimacy that is growing old—these accounts reflect some of the ways partners express a commitment to their conversation and to each other. The pleasure of a couple's intimacy often discovers and announces itself in ways other than conversation performed "straight." When partners shift into a more crooked or at least circuitous "key" of interaction, they engage in an intimacy of invention that involves giving full play to their voices and bodies. Throwing voices, playing dress-ups, dancing a routine, exchanging banter, expressing sublimated passion point to some of the ways a partnership invents itself, knows the experience of its intimacy, and encounters some of its joys—as comic.

An earlier version of this chapter first appeared as "The Male-Female Comedy Team," in *Performing Gender and Comedy: Theories, Texts and Contexts,* ed. Shannon Hengen, Studies in Humor and Gender, vol. 4 (Amsterdam: Gordon and Breach, 1998), 3–20.

Comedy about lovers means comedy about teams. Yet, the nature of team comedy—what it is that they make together—is a phenomenon for the most part undescribed by comic theorists. The presence of team comedy within a narrative raises questions like: What happens to the narrative's plot when a team is forming? or when its members are returning to each other? or when they have stayed with each other over a long time? In what locations do they find themselves? Why does "the green world" exist for them? and why the ordinary world? What do they say and do to each other? What does the presence of a male/female couple, as opposed to just a male or a team of males, do to comedy? What, in short, is male/female partnered comedy, and what does it have to do with marriage and happiness? Because the comedy of the solo clown and the distinguishing of the plot forms of Old and New Comedy have been the privileged sites of comic theory, these have not been the questions asked, but they are the object of my study. I need, therefore, to return to the idea of New Comedy to explore what it is, and to account for the relation between the team and this narrative site to which it is bound. New Comedy becomes new again, I would assert, when understood as the shared creation of its male/female team.

A Model of New Comedy

Plots and Re-plots

From Plautus to Shakespeare, Molière to Feydeau, European writers of comic drama follow the New Comedy plots of Menander, not the Old Comedy of Aristophanes. They write one version of team comedy. The Aristophanic plot tells the story of a political outsider who undoes both his society and the coherence of the plot itself through slapstick, ingenuity, and a delight in obscenity. He remains an outsider to society even in his strange hero status. The Menander plot, in contrast, tells of a transformation from within, where society returns to its "natural" state through its own act of legitimation—marriage. The plot of new "team" comedy would seem to be about the replication of the old order, as the ending in marriage seems to imply. However, as Northrop Frye has so importantly observed, the social order is remade following the usual movement of the couple into "the green world," where love, magic, and redemption can be at last experienced and then brought back to a world that must be recast in response to the couple's experiences.[1] Frye writes about the "fifth phase" of romance in *Anatomy of Criticism* as one in which "the mood is a contemplative withdrawal from or sequel to action rather than a youthful preparation for it. . . . [Romance] is . . . an erotic world, but it presents experience as comprehended and not as a mystery" (202). In his discussion of romance, Frye gets at another of the plots of romantic comedy—that of the experienced lovers' comedy team. The "mood" he defines is just that of the comic plot of the lovers who return to each other, as if their relationship is a kind of sequel to something that has come before.

The picture of romantic comedy grows much richer when we combine the three stories Frye suggests of the obstructed young lovers, the lovers in the green world, and the older lovers who engage in the act of returning to each other. What I'm interested in here is opening up the concept "romantic comedy" to mean as much as it can, which is to say not just the Menander plot Frye first describes it to be. Further, some redefining of the term needs to be done to recover New Comedy because of important critiques of its "Frye version" by various feminist writers, perhaps most poignantly that of Kathleen Rowe.[2]

Broadly speaking, we can understand Aristophanic comedy to be the original model of male solo clown, anti–mutually constructed plot comedy. The comic writing of Rabelais, Boccaccio, Cervantes, and Fielding, and the early films of sound comedy generated by the vaudeville aesthetic of, for example, the Marx Brothers, W. C. Fields, Eddie Cantor, and Mae West, have kept it alive in the face of dramatists' preference for the Menander plot.[3] Aristophanic comedy works, too, as the basis for stand-up comedy, yet it also informs the moments when the couples of romantic comedy break into routines, quite apart from the advancement of plot. Typically, romantic comedy is distinguished from Aristophanic comedy because Old Comedy's display of the uninhibited self-expression of the clown in gags and whimsical performance sequences seems set aside by romantic comedy's apparent concern for cause-effect linearity. Yet, this distinction is called into question by Brian Henderson's sense of romantic comedy's "ethos of spontaneity."[4] To understand romantic comedy as wholly plot-driven is to miss the level of play created between the couple "clowning around."

What the couple essentially clowns around about is, according to Henderson, the "sexual question," whose utterance is always forbidden.[5] Prohibited from the immediate fulfillment of desire, romantic comedies use language, physical actions, and visual puns for saying the unsayable. What results is a narrative of spontaneous outbursts that represents the translation of sexuality into something other. Henderson writes: "In romantic

comedy, it is the past sex lives of the characters and present sexual problems that constitute a referent that cannot be named directly. . . . [Y]ou
can refer to anything, but cannot speak of it" (22). For a narrative to be
built on references without direct speech requires that there be episodic
moments of spontaneous discharge as evidence of the displacement. If the
story of romantic comedy is about the "sexual dialectic" (19), its veiled
expression creates a comic mode of outburst that interrupts the narrative's
concern for linearity and cause-effect clarity—features that align romantic
comedy with its Aristophanic relative. However, that it is a sexual dialectic distinguishes romantic comedy because of its insistence on being about
partnered sex, not just the solo clown's displays of "self" in performance.

Gerald Mast revises the classically delineated Old and New Comedy
with an outline of the eight plots that most generally structure comic film.
But his delineations still break down into the two categories of those that
follow an integrated plot and those that structure themselves around the
comic bits of the solo clown—the apparent distinction of New from Old,
or romantic from anarchistic comedy. Mast's group of comic film plots includes the young lovers plot; the burlesque of some other film; the *reductio
ad absurdum* plot where some foible is magnified to absurdity; the inves-
tigative, multilevel plot that explores the workings of several social classes
within one society; the picaresque plot where the hero bounces off people
and events; the "riffing" plot of "improvised and anomalous gaggery" where
unity is achieved only through the reappearance of performers to do their
gags; the difficult-task plot where the hero risks "his" life but achieves
success; the plot of discovery where the comic figure confronts a mistake
"he's" made all "his" life (8–9).

In addition to this enumeration of the plot kinds, Mast's depiction of
the gender and number of the figures who enact their performance reveals
something about how theorists have traditionally thought about the workings of comic plots. Four of the eight plots are specifically about the comic
actions of a "hero" whom Mast takes to be male; only the "young lovers"
plot takes into account the presence of an implied woman, though here too
"she" could be a "he." This neglect to depict how *women* plot comedies has
resulted in a forgetting of the ways teams plot—the stories, for example, of
what a partnership risks and discovers by virtue of being a partnership or
by being in a situation together. Without a recognition of women as comic
agents, equal in wit, endurance, and spirit to their male counterparts, the
idea of a male/female comedy team as partners who plot is inconceivable.

Yet, such women and such partnerships do exist in comic texts. How else are we to understand the plots of the older and I would assert "comic" lovers—Hermione and Leontes, Antony and Cleopatra—whose narratives plot their journeys back to one another and whose repeated games of interaction maintain their love? How else are we to understand the young lovers who must do more in response to each other than wait until it's safe to leave the woods, as is the case with Rosalind and Orlando, or Beatrice and Benedick? While the bias that highlights the male hero is informed by the prevalence of plots constructed around him, that bias is also informed by a refusal to look at the female hero and the male/female comedy team. Northrop Frye's comment that the lovers are the less interesting characters of the plot while the obstructors of the marriage are the ones worthy of attention typifies the move to reduce what goes on between the plotting partners in love comedy. Rather than being passive recipients of what the obstructors generate, these couples are in fact agents who use the barrier makers as a means to generate their own comedy.[6]

The solo comic performances of Mae West and Fanny Brice and those of the male/female comedy teams of Burns and Allen and Hallan and Hart, among others, in vaudeville enabled the creation of female comics and comedy teams who were not confined to the obstructed lovers' plot. Instead, the non-narrative of the comic spectacle freed women to be comedians as opposed to just wits, which made men and women equal partners in physical comedy, something that the narratives of romantic comedy came to embrace. That a woman could fall down, throw a pie, or slip on a banana peel (even when she was not cross-dressed) opened up the range of possibilities for how to structure the plots of team comedy. Henry Jenkins underscores the significance of vaudeville's enabling the emergence of the woman into comedian: "The woman, by becoming the clown and by casting the patriarch in the traditional killjoy role, forces the anarchistic scenario to speak for female resistance, offering women utopian possibilities most other comedian comedies reserve for men only" (246). Which is not to say that women did not do physical comedy in narratives before vaudeville: certainly the Wife of Bath and the women in the *Decameron* perform varying comic physical feats. The difference I allude to has to do with actually seeing a "live" woman do physical comedy—not a man in drag and not a "figure" in literature. The significance of this distinction reveals itself in screwball comedy and situation comedy: a new range of romantic comedy emerges in response to our ability to witness through film this new partnering in physical comedy, a possibility that is a direct legacy of "live" vaudeville.

Playing at Being Characters

Where are the married teams in tragedy? With the exception of "the Macbeths," there are few memorable couples in tragedy who work *together* versus in opposition. The medium seems to depend on the individual suffering and struggle of the character around whom the tragedy is built. Tragedy moves as a result of the revelations brought forward from the internal workings of the tragic figure. Others represent "facts" or place-holders of a reality that the hero must confront from within, not partners in tragedy with whom the hero interacts to work through the tragic situation or revelation. If George and Martha in *Who's Afraid of Virginia Woolf?* or Vladimir and Estragon in *Waiting for Godot* represent exceptions, they do so because, in addition to living tragically, their "marriages" often work like performances by comedy teams. That tragedies are named for individual persons whereas comedies are often named for common nouns that stand for types of character or states of being reveals much about how tragedy is taken to be about the solitary self, while comedy is taken to be about a group or something taken to be common to a group, as in *The Miser* or *Much Ado about Nothing*. Henri Bergson writes: "Here it is in the work itself that the generality lies. Comedy depicts characters we have already come across and shall meet again. It makes note of similarities. It aims at placing types before our eyes" (66). Named for a type of character or a type of attitude, comic drama is about general resemblance and representativeness, and about individual repetition as well; it asserts that resemblance, representativeness, and repetition are possible.

Traditionally, comedy has relied on a representational shorthand of character types whom audiences can recognize immediately. Without having to attend to individuality, audiences can note what is produced in relation to the character—we can, in other words, attend to the jokes or to the situation. But we can also focus on the interaction between characters, which is more important to comedy than is the particular story of its individual characters: what replaces the uniqueness of Hamlet in comedy is what is generated by groups thrown together. Interaction is what is fundamental to comedy—the external display of responsiveness—as opposed to the cogitations of self-discovery. The use of types insists on this in that we expect to discover nothing to make a type be "unique," while we do expect the exchange between characters to be unique. It's as if the "character" of comedy is the interaction itself, as opposed to the individuality of any one figure.

Bakhtin, in his study of Rabelais, insists on the production of comedy between the members of a group as opposed to actions of the individual alone. Medieval and Renaissance carnival was, he claims, a universal celebration directed at everyone and including everyone. The world is seen as comic and invites a triumphant yet mocking laughter from all the people.[7] The couple of team comedy borrows the carnival spirit of the group laughing, of the group seeing the world as funny, and of the group creating among themselves a second world. Bakhtin's discussion of the intimacy of communication and gesture between two people in carnivalesque mode defines the spirit of how this second world becomes generated by the comedy team:

A new type of communication always creates new forms of speech or a new meaning given to old forms. For instance, when two persons establish friendly relations, the form of their verbal intercourse also changes abruptly; they address each other informally, abusive words are used affectionately, and mutual mocking is permitted. (In formal intercourse only a third person can be mocked.) The two friends may pat each other on the shoulder and even on the belly (a typical carnivalesque gesture). Verbal etiquette and discipline are relaxed and indecent words and expressions may be used. (16)

A new relationship creates a new mode of intimate discourse where words and gestures are exchanged. Comedy lends itself to the display of pairs in relations because of the tone of discourse that it allows—the mocking, abusing, patting, rubbing, swearing. Comedy wants to get at what goes on between people, how they "get to" one another, how they understand and misread one another, how far they can go with one another, and how they invent together.

The male/female comedy team as a romantic couple is often further defined or parodied by the presence of another couple. Renaissance comedies can display two couples (or more) at work trying to mate, as with Beatrice/Benedick and Hero/Claudio in *Much Ado about Nothing* or Rosalind/Orlando, Celia/Oliver, Phebe/Silvius in *As You Like It,* or Viola/Antonio and Olivia/Sebastian in *Twelfth Night.* In musical comedy, the more comic partnership will devote itself to the comic bits of the narrative while the more serious pair contends with the obstructions that keep them apart. Astaire and Rogers first made their appearance together as the comic sidekicks to Dolores del Rio and Gene Raymond in *Flying Down to*

Rio. A multilayered plot works in tandem with the confusion and merriment of the multiple efforts to couple, or acts of coupling, while an assertion is made about comic levels. That there is a wittier couple means that there is a more naive and serious one, or that juxtaposed to a more anarchic couple is a more conventional one. In addition to complicating the plot structure, mirroring couples work as markers of a narrative's range of comedy. Without difference, the narrative could not break up the rhythm or flow of its presentation, which would put it at risk of a monotonous pace. With difference comes the possibility of arranging a variety of jokes and sizes of laughs, and also a pace of escalation, because contrast measures.

To get at this comic difference and to give particularity to the idea of the male/female comedy team, I turn to the parallel presences in *Much Ado about Nothing* of Beatrice/Benedick and Hero/Claudio. We know each couple through their particular interactions, but also through seeing and hearing who they are not—one another. There are no laughs to be had in the company of Hero and Claudio. This has everything to do with their dependence on sight and their resistance to speech. Claudio sees Hero and loves her, woos her not with his own words but through the voice of a masked Don Pedro, believes himself to be betrayed by her through witnessing the shadowy staging of an "as if" lovemaking between Hero and Don John's servant, and loves her again when he sees her as the "revirginated" and essentially silent version of herself—call her Hero's cousin or Hero reborn.

Hero, throughout Claudio's dance of moving toward or away from her, remains essentially still, an object to be seen and not heard. Twice when she is prompted to speak, to accept her duty as a daughter to her father or to accept Claudio's proposal, Beatrice speaks for her. Hero's great moment of action which insists on the use of her voice leads instead to the negation of her presence. As a body whose chastity is writ so large upon it or with such self-evidence, Hero swoons in mock death as a bodily response to Claudio's accusations. She has no words, just the visual evidence of her body. Claudio, we imagine, would not be able to hear the words were she to speak, as he is not able to read what her body says. She stands before him as an inaccessible image to be appropriated by the ravings of his imagination; and he stands before her as an inaccessible partner, oblivious to whatever corrections she might offer. They do not, therefore, construct together who they take themselves and their love to be. Defined by seeing and the mistakes of seeing without the mediating, interactive force of speaking, their "partnership" is nonintersecting, non–mutually constructing, and noncomedic. What their noncomedy accomplishes is the advancement of plot (the plot moves in response to the dictates of seeing, in that it follows and moves according to the visions of Claudio) and the setting off of Beatrice and Benedick as those who couple in comedy.

Whereas Hero and Claudio are silent or deaf to each other, Beatrice and Benedick cannot stop speaking, hearing, responding, living to measure their voices against each other. Leonato remarks about them: "[I]f they were but a week married, they would talk themselves mad" (59). Beatrice and Benedick make a madness together out of crossfire one-liners that seek to undo the other's point, language, or mood, or out of lengthy speeches that act as performance pieces that demand the other sit in audience and attend to the fact of the performer. However, the roles soon reverse as the other responds and assumes center stage. Their language functions as "challenge talk," or as a model for gaming or for war. Before the two ever share a scene, Leonato acknowledges this when he instructs us in how to "read" their interaction: "There is a kind of merry war betwixt Signor Benedick and her; they never meet but there's a skirmish of wit between them" (38). The nonmerry war that works as a one-sided attack of Claudio against Hero that prompts a staged death becomes revised in the interactions between Benedick and Beatrice as ongoing "couplespeech" that creates a relationship in its apparent attempt to cut the other:

BEATRICE: I wonder that you still be talking, Signor Benedick; nobody marks you.
BENEDICK: What, my dear Lady Disdain! Are you yet living?
BEATRICE: Is it possible disdain should die while she hath such meet food to feed it as Signor Benedick? Courtesy itself must convert to disdain, if you come in her presence.
BENEDICK: Then is courtesy a turncoat. But it is certain I am loved of all ladies, only you excepted; and I would I could find in my heart that I had not a hard heart, for, truly, I love none. (40)

Beatrice and Benedick know how to abuse each other, which requires knowing how to hear each other, which requires, finally, knowing how to know each other. Beatrice moves the attack of being dubbed "Lady Disdain" onto "Courtesy" by making disdain Courtesy's property when in the company of Benedick. He then converts her jab into praise for himself: while Beatrice and Courtesy (the turncoat) may not love him, all other ladies do. Not only does each successfully defend him- or herself against the words of the other, each transforms the attack into the ground for self-defense or even self-praise. There is no possibility here of gazing at each other from afar, constructing an image for the other, and being devastated by the other's reconstruction of that image. Benedick and Beatrice must continuously take into account the other's words, and speak words back, a process that ongoingly revises their understandings of themselves and each other. There's no plot to be made here, just the repetition of their routines into marriage. Their words beat them down or up into an acknowledgment of love:

> BENEDICK: And I pray thee now, tell me for which of my bad parts didst thou first fall in love with me?
> BEATRICE: For them all together; which maintained so politic a state of evil that they will not admit any good part to intermingle with them. But for which of my good parts did you first suffer love for me?
> BENEDICK: Suffer love! A good epithet, I do suffer love indeed, for I love thee against my will. (116)

The partners' declaration of love is built still on mutual attack, but with a new offering—Benedick and Beatrice acknowledge their love in a humbling of themselves: "for which of my bad parts did you first fall in love with me?" and "for which of my good parts did you first suffer love for me?" Beatrice need not die nor be revirginated for Benedick to love her, and Benedick need not be forgiven for his "shortsightedness." What essentially makes them a comedy team is that no transformation need take place—what each has to offer the other is enough at the outset and more than enough by the end. It is the variations of what they make together in their talk, in their being present to each other, in their creating another entity between them that lives for as long as they exchange talk—their partnership—that enable Beatrice and Benedick to be a comedy team. And we know who they are, what they create, and why they laugh because we also know Hero and Claudio, who instruct us in why not to laugh.

Beatrice and Benedick reveal that one of comedy's fundamental features is that it depends on its characters' ability to play, which could mean responding with creativity to disaster, or making up jokes to pass the time, or breaking out into performance. Its characters, therefore, must above all be players who recognize a playground and use it as a space in which to let go of the creative energy which defines something essential about what the self can do, think, feel, or act. Playing frees, engages, makes possible a magic that D. W. Winnicott states arises in response to the precariousness of bringing together a created psychic reality with the attempted control of actual objects. When the subjectivity of the self's vision attempts to merge with reality, as in the "actual object" of another person, Winnicott writes, "[t]his is the precariousness of magic itself, magic that arises in intimacy, in a relationship that is found to be reliable" (47).

A sense of that reliability or trust emerges from the mutual understanding reached between the creative visions of self and other, where the other acknowledges the self's reality by knowing how to play back and how to initiate the next move. This is what it means to communicate, and communicating in comedy means, according to Umberto Eco, knowing how to "presuppose" the comic frame in which the partners work without uttering what that frame is. Eco writes of this in terms of the comic and the audience, but I wish to apply it to the comedy team: "What remains compulsory, in order to produce a comic effect, is the prohibition of spelling out the norm. It must be presupposed, both by the utterer and the audience. If the speaker spells it out, he is a fool or a jerk; if the audience does not know it, there is no comic effect" ("Frames" 6). The communication between the comedy team is built on the tacit understanding of a mutual knowledge of what the comic paradigm is in which they play, a knowledge that needs to be neither explained nor spoken of, and a knowledge of how to create from that given frame an appropriate discourse of play. And it is how characters play, meaning what tricks they perform, that distinguishes the range and kinds of moves possible within a comic narrative.

Comic Climate

When C. L. Barber writes of the "holiday" spirit in Shakespeare's festal comedies,[8] and Bakhtin explores the "carnival" spirit in Rabelais, their words reference comedy's drive toward revelry, spree, and whimsy, yet what they mean by that spirit separates into distinct kinds. If the comic spirit in the *Odyssey* finds its source in survival and going home, in Shakespeare's comedy it has more to do with the discovery of coincidence and the possibility of magic.[9] In Rabelais's work, carnival is a liberation from convention and an embracing of new outlooks and ways of being (Bakhtin, *Rabelais* 34). While "carnival" insists on its primordial status as fundamental to the human spirit, "holiday" is that which is sanctioned by church and state as regulated "days off." Clara Claiborne Park locates comedy's celebration in the context of a challenge; it is a response to the obstacles life constructs and it brings into play the relationship between self and partnership. "Carnival" and "holiday" arise apart from the context of daily life: carnival is a response in opposition to it and is a group event of all peoples; holiday, while also of the group, is a regulated and so "domesticated" departure from everyday life. These three modes of interaction—the contextually responsive to life (surviving through play), the contextually opposed to conventional life (carnival), or the contextually regulated "days off" from life (holiday)—generate, however differently, the shared fundamental mood of comedy, that of celebration. If the Marx Brothers create a celebration of carnival, the lovers of *As You Like It* experience that of holiday, while Cary Grant and Irene Dunne in *The Awful Truth* replicate the celebration of survival and return.

The quality of "celebration" is constructed in all three modes of comic response through feelings of release and abandon; a desire to forsake daily routine or the boredom connected with habit; the expression of a commitment to play and the imagination; an understanding of the self as a fundamentally creative being; a belief in the possibility of magic; a willingness to engage in subversion; a conclusion that affirms the world's revival and renewal; and the demonstration of an ongoing commitment to living life intensely and for the self's pleasure. Edward Galligan has asserted that "the deepest image of comedy is its image of play" (38); of all of these qualities that create the comic mood, it is the activity of playing that fundamentally separates one narrative climate from another. Playing carries with it an atmosphere of well-being, by which I don't mean simply an absence of conflict but an ability to generate alternatives and a willingness to try on different possibilities and ways of being regardless or because of however strange they may seem. Bergson writes that the ability to "detach oneself from things and yet continue to perceive images, to break away from logic and yet continue to string together ideas, is to indulge in play, or if you prefer, in *dolce far[e] niente* [sweet to do nothing]. So, comic absurdity gives us from the outset the impression of playing with ideas" (186–87).

Comedies inform us that things will work out as long as the capacity to "break away from logic" is put into practice. We, as a comedy's audience, are assured that all will be well, despite the losses, rends, twists, and shocks (in fact, because of them), because of comedy's commitment to the break from sense and our registering of the freedom and possibility born out of that break. Comedy makes a space for the senselessness of play and invites us to imagine along with it what can be experienced and learned from play. "Comedy," Galligan writes, "trusts play as a way of knowing and as a way of doing" (37), which means it trusts the activity of invention as a way of knowing and the ever changing relationship between words and objects and gestures as a way of doing.[10] If invention means "to come upon, to discover or devise for the first time,"[11] what comedies do fundamentally is to create a climate of ongoing invention, which means continual play. Why or how that invention takes place occurs, according to Maurice Charney, without purpose, just for the pleasure of it, and with a "childlike absorption and intensity" (155–60). However, while "anarchistic comedy"[12] like vaudeville presents play for the sake of play, narrative comedy depends on a climate constructed from intentional play, whether it be the intentions of the comic figures or the directing drive of the plot. The purposive play of Odysseus which brings him home, the directed chaos of Irene Dunne which brings her together with Cary Grant in *The Awful Truth,* and the planned digressions away from plot in the Marx Brothers' *Duck Soup* all make invention the source of "plotting" drive.

The mood of the romantic company, or team comedy, is that of play walked in on. Whereas "solo"-person comedy presents itself as play shared between the comedian and the audience for whom he or she performs (in which case the audience acts as the partner to the comedian), team comedy is about play shared between those to whom the audience happens to have access. The audience/readers do not have to be there for the couple's play to make sense; they perform to each other and so create the comic climate between themselves. However, when the single comedian performs, the audience contributes as a partner to that comedy's climate in its response, by appreciating the joke or not. Eric Bentley writes of the relationship between comedian and audience:

> Does he [the comic, again, as "he"] need even a joke as much as he needs a listener? Let each of us ask himself why, at a given moment, he wishes to tell a joke. It cannot be because one wishes to be amused by it, since jokes are not amusing the second time around, and one cannot tell a joke one has not already heard. . . . [I]f one's need was to hear the joke one could tell it to oneself. It is inescapable that the need is not for the joke at all: it is for the audience. (199)

To consider why the male/female comedy still needs an audience, needs to generate laughter from outside the partnership even though the presence of that audience seems superfluous, complicates the question of who the comic is playing to and what purpose outsiders to the team serve. The confessional comic is perhaps most similar to the male/female team in that his/her routine reveals something about the performer's life, as the presence of a partner reveals something about the couple's way of interacting. When team comedy is performed as stand-up, there is a self-consciousness acknowledged about the audience's being "intimately" in the room with the couple—the couple has gone public. There is a need expressed for the couple's sharing "publicly" the "private," or transforming the private to be public—a transformation that serves as the basis of the comedy.

However, when the performance of a couple's comedy occurs within a narrative, the audience functions as voyeur. If each partner of the couple acts as "open" audience/performer to the other, the hidden audience is relegated to silence for being the veiled "third wheel" who shouldn't have access to what goes on between this couple. That it does gives the audience all the pleasures and discomforts of the voyeur: experiencing this intimacy which is not its own makes the audience "know" the interaction as if it were its, and know too that it should not know what it now knows. What the audience becomes privy to, therefore, is a kind of illicit knowledge. The thrill of that experience heightens the effects of the comedy by necessitating a negotiation as to how to make the position of voyeur tolerable.[13]

What role the audience plays in relation to team versus solo comedy brings forward the relations among who laughs, the meaning of that laughter, and the production of the comic climate. We usually think of laughter as a necessary component of comedy, yet if we take seriously the idea of the *Odyssey* as a comedy, it's clear this is not a narrative designed to make us laugh. What it does portray, though, is what Bakhtin calls the early modern folk culture's representation of the terror defeated by laughter—monsters are made comical by the response they elicit, which is laughter. "Terror," he writes, "was turned into something gay and comical" (*Rabelais* 38–39). This is the comic laughter contained within the narrative which acts as the spirit that drives away fear, both the comic figure(s)' and our own; this is laughter as a Nietzschean assertion of courage and self. While the "external" display of laughter by an audience in response to a comic narrative may not be what the comedy prompts (the "test of laughter" does not always measure the sense of enjoyment created by acts of transgression, or the creation or mastery of conflict, or the making of happiness or even a joke), I do take it to be one of the chief delights of comedy that it can make us laugh. What higher praise can a member of a team comedy offer his or her partner than to laugh? Audience and performer merge in a couple's comedy around the boundary marker of laughter—an expression of understanding and deep pleasure possible in both realms.

When a narrative world informs us that everything is going to be all right, we experience as its audience a relaxation of concern, which means that we can laugh, and we can know we're in the company of a comedy. How a narrative cues us to relax has everything to do with how its climate is structured. The plot, characters, and how these are presented or not presented determine how a particular narrative reveals its comic climate and instructs us in our emotional response to it. We know that the fundamental plot pattern of New Comedy is that things fall apart and then they fall together "happily"; this is our guiding expectation as we enter its narrative world. And we know that its characters move through the vicissitudes of falling apart and falling together with the help of their ongoing, sometimes evolving routines. The routines of a couple—how they sing or banter together, steal glances at or cajole each other—carry with them our assurances that there will be a happy outcome. Even in the face of pain and the hard experiences of the change it can bring, these performances hold traces of well-being. In being audience to or readers of these comedy teams, we feel ourselves to be in the company of people who know how to play and who live in a world that makes play what it values most. The comic narrative's commitment to routines as its staging of continuity, and its willingness to join return to loss, meaning to senselessness, invention to resilience prompt us to hope and imagine the possibility of happiness. We relax and feel the pleasures associated with release and celebration.

The world romantic comedy shows us, the one after Odysseus has returned home and stayed with Penelope or then left but with her as a couple (the fantasy of that), or the one of the lovers in the midst of a world "on holiday," or the one of the lovers and clowns collectively joined in anarchistic carnival, is a world imagined between a comedy team who entertain themselves by constructing variations on who they take themselves to be. Their fundamental task, therefore, is one of ongoing reinvention which, while at times exhausting or limiting in its solipsism and range of concerns, does demonstrate a model for an experience of pleasure, a pleasure grounded in the surprise of being in the company of another and being mutually responsible for making that time enjoyable. What results is neither extraordinary nor ordinary, but a merging of the two to produce something that has the quality of the "other" worldly (the quick wittedness, the miraculous turns of fate, the perfection of the match) and the "this" worldly (the everydayness of this being a marriage or courtship, the concern with how to pass the time, how to share space, in short, with how to be together). And it is how things occur in this location somewhere between the ordinary and the extraordinary—between partners imagining new routines and reimagining old play(s)—that makes New Comedy's climate of celebration.

∿

While the narrative of romantic comedy takes as its everyday the cycle of vicissitudes that accompany being in love, its ending promises a "happily ever after." But what is the nature of that happiness? If it is about something that takes place offstage, how can we know what it is? Is it something the narrative has trained its readers/audience to recognize from within its onstage context? Is it something not able to be experienced but only to be promised? That "happily ever after," which fills an archetypal place in our cultural heritage in fairy tales, the originating stories of our childhoods, of our wishes and fears, takes on mythic status and haunts conclusions without seeming to make a full-bodied appearance. As a phrase absorbed into our consciousness for how comic narratives conclude, it does not compel us to force it into consciousness of itself. Perhaps this is because we no longer know how to look for its presence. To regain the legitimacy of happiness requires that we look back, I think, to how comedies tell of the living and the expression of their everyday pleasures. It is in those moments in New Comedy—when its couple-made-comedy-team must perform the pleasures of their self-knowledge and of their good fortune—that we experience one form of an ordinary happiness in narrative.

CHAPTER 5

All Happy Families
Are Not Alike

I Love
all
things,
not because they are
passionate
or sweet-smelling
but because,
I don't know.
because
this ocean is yours,
and mine:
these buttons
and wheels
and little
forgotten
treasures,
fans upon
whose feathers
love has scattered
its blossoms,
glasses, knives and
scissors—
all bear
the trace
of someone's fingers
on their handle or surface,
the trace of a distant hand
lost
in the depths of forgetfulness.

—Pablo Neruda, "Ode to Things"

Naming

When D. A. Miller in *Narrative and Its Discontents* defines what he takes to be the "narratable" in the novel, he focuses on what destabilizes the plot—"the instances of disequilibrium, suspense, and general insufficiency from which a given narrative seems to arise."[1] Asserting that the "quiescence" of the novel present before its opening and recovered by its close are the "nonnarratable" of the novel leads Miller to conclude that

> [t]he narrative of happiness is inevitably frustrated by the fact that only insufficiencies, defaults, deferrals can be "told." Even when a narrative "prepares for" happiness, it remains in this state of lack, which can only be liquidated along with the narrative itself. Accordingly, the narrative of happiness might be thought to exemplify the unhappiness of narrative in general. Narrative proceeds toward, or regresses from, what it seeks or seems most to prize, but it is never identical to it. To designate the presence of what is sought or prized is to signal the termination of narrative—or at least, the displacement of a narrative onto other concerns. (3)

Behind Miller's statement lies an argument which reads: desire arises in response to lack; lack in narrative is the presence of the problematic; therefore, narrative desires the problematic—the lack of happiness—in order to tell itself. That "only insufficiencies, defaults, deferrals can be 'told'" is, however, merely a claim, which Miller addresses when he differentiates what is "narratable" (what generates a story) from what is "speakable" (what can be spoken of). That happiness can be told, in Miller's sense of spoken of, gives it the possibility of presence; however, Miller chooses what is lacking, as opposed to what can be spoken of, to account for the drive to narrate. What room would there be for a story if the end to which it moved were already present, if it were already spoken of and hence known?

Yet, must an account of what compels the telling of a novel consider only the need to move through the unknown, the not yet said, the absent? Miller's claim about what generates a story versus what generates speech asks us to consider what the relationship is between ordinary speech (that on which the novel must depend as a linguistic entity) and the extraordinary act of its suppression (that which accounts for narrative desire or having a story be told, that which cannot occur if all of its elements are known). To say that the novel depends on what it can say—on ordinary speech—means that it works by naming what it means. Proper names of individual characters and settings create a particular location for a subject; they create a named world. The language that fills in the name of that world by giving it a "thickened" background, defining appearance, speech, events participated in, and evolution over time provides additional "names" for the subject by making the entity pointed at more complex, yet still a thing being named. Concretizing a world in language, making it real through the use of the written word alone, distinguishes the novel as an aesthetic practice of ordinary language. As such, it takes as its subject the ordinary, or what can be said with a language of naming and pointing. I return to Wittgenstein's words about this: "[H]earing the name calls before our mind the picture of what is named; and it also consists, among other things, in the name's being written on the thing named or pronounced when the thing is pointed at" (18e(137)). Part of the work the novel does, therefore, is to tell what it can name, or that which it is, which means that its story must at least in part be generated by the naming of the ordinary, or what can be referred to, or what is present.

We can assert, therefore, that what constitutes the "ordinary" in the novel has to do with what can be said, what the language of the text "points to," the "pictures" it makes. And as to what a novel points to, one of the primary means of distinguishing what lies on the other side of that pointing, or what is signified, reveals itself in its concern with continuity, or the connections over time between the things named. One way to think about continuity is to consider how we know in language, meaning how we come to name experience and share those names. We encounter X but make our knowledge public or publicly knowable by knowing how to call X "red." The repeated use of the word "red" to mean a like experience makes the name reliable, makes the experience of red be available to all who understand the name, and makes the knowing and speaking of red "ordinary." The calling of something demonstrates "knowing behavior," or the attempt to know or assert that one knows. The continuous calling of something is both the ordinary practice of a language (that one repeats how one means in words agreed on by speakers to mean like things) and ordinary making (that the thing named can be spoken of, can repeat, can be generally available). Therefore, in the way that ordinary language enables the publicly available and so repeated reference to an object through its shared act of naming (what it means to *have* a language), the ordinary named is that which returns, continues, and is diurnal. Whereas the extraordinary is so constituted by its "unsignifiabil-ity," or, if nameable, by its unique or original appearance, the ordinary knows itself through its insistence on return.

Like using language, which makes experience knowable and ordinary by virtue of its ability to name it, share it, recognize it as analogous or recurrent, the passing of time itself practices the ordinary and makes the ordinary in its play with continuity. This is the notion of time as not that force which designates the "past," "present," "future" and the accom-panying events or moments which stand for that isolated, stopped period. Whereas births, weddings, divorces, and deaths—life-cycle markers—stand as the datable events of arrested time which seem to represent how a life was lived, the in-betweenness of events that occur daily is what composes a life between its framed edges. Memorable because of their returns and unmemorable because of their apparent seamless integration into the fabric of a life, these moments, dateless, fluid, create a scenario of the ordinary pleasures which define the quality of "well-being" that informs a life almost unconsciously. These are the moments between the markers of plot, between, for instance, Elizabeth and Darcy's first meeting, scene of first proposal, and scene of second proposal. Stopped time—an event, contained in clear boundaries, that can be remembered as an enclosed moment, different from what came before and after it—resembles in its structure the operation of pain in that pain necessarily interrupts the on-goingness of time. Frozen, the self searches with urgency for the means to end pain in order to continue the process of living. Continuity, on the other hand, moves to encompass similar and differentiating moments which seem to stand out and then recede into the ongoing flow. While the novel that follows a linear pattern "advances" through problem states or marches toward the unnamed, it also traces circles of repeated forms of narrating (the ordinary of what composes the identifiable language of its narrative mode) and a returned-to-narrative world (its ordinary mode of presenting being). Whereas the extraordinary arrests time and seems to stand outside of time as the definable frame of a plot or a life, the ordinary defines what constructs time's dailiness, and what occurs within that outline.

If we grant, then, that a narrative depends on the "unnameable" for its forward momentum, we must say as well that it depends on what it *can* name in its approach toward or working through of the path to "the end." Whereas Miller takes "happiness" to be the extraordinary, that which the novel cannot name, the absence or presence of happiness hinges on whether or not it has a referent or location for pointing at and naming in the novel. Using the instance of marriage in *Emma*, "the perfect union," as what can be spoken of but cannot generate a story, Miller transposes the meaning of the "perfect union" to mean happiness, an act which reflects what Austen instructs us to do in the repeated equation in *Emma*: "perfect" + "union" = "perfect happiness." Could there be a referent for this description of happiness? This take on happiness echoes an assertion of Robert Nozick's in *The Examined Life* that the emotion of happiness brings with it an accompanying sense of completion, that nothing else is desired, that all needs are satisfied (108–9).

However, an understanding of happiness which works from the premise of completion, that it is an end state, precludes the possibility that happiness can be fluid and evolving, and that it can include the problematic. When recast into a story, the happiness that exists as satisfaction—as an end state—functions as a site that can be named or pointed at as the referent, "recurrent pleasure." Set next to the problem story(s) within a novel, the happy state as an end in itself acts as a source of counterpoint, but also as a safe ground of stability that holds the problems and enables them, in being held, to sort themselves out. We see the idea of a site of "complete happiness" that holds the fluid problem in the constant good humor of the Nick and Nora marriage that exists around the constantly problematic plot of detection, which Nick solves, in *The Thin Man;* or in the ongoing warm, "whole" portrait of the Garth family in *Middlemarch* that coexists with the continuously problematic states of Dorothea and Lydgate while it enables the reformation of Fred; or in the shadowy, behind the scenes presence in *Great Expectations* of Joe and Biddy, who step fully into the daylight of complete happiness (once Mrs. Joe dies) and save Pip from himself. Fixed portraits of relations that exist in stable states of pleasure and satisfaction act as recurrent "happy ends in themselves," or as referents of happiness moving through a novel in contrast to solitary figures who evolve through pain and lack. These "happy ends in themselves" embody Aristotle's notion of happiness as a state

> which is in itself worthy of pursuit more final than that which is worthy of pursuit for the sake of something else. . . .
>
> Now such a thing happiness, above all else, is held to be; for this we choose always for itself and never for the sake of something else, but honor, pleasure, reason, and every virtue we choose indeed for themselves . . . but we choose them also for the sake of happiness, judging that by means of them we shall be happy. Happiness, on the

other hand, no one chooses for the sake of these, nor, in general, for anything other than itself. (*Nicomachean Ethics* 316–17)

The "ends" of narrative satisfaction can also be thought of as miniature "happy endings," or resting points of an ongoing narrative present which need not push forward to resolve a point of narrative lack. What can be spoken of as complete, present ends can, therefore, assist in the production of narrative by providing a contrast to the problematic, or by working as comic relief from turmoil, or by placing the novel within a scene of pause in its present, as opposed to moving into its future.

To broaden the notion of happiness from the static "happy ending" state to include, as well, a condition subject to change brings happiness into the sphere of everyday life and makes its referent the everyday life or ordinary plot of the novel. But can there be such a thing? A novel makes primary the plot of evolving happiness when it replaces a structure that moves through a series of "catastrophic" problems with negotiable problems that allow the world of the novel to remain intact while changing. That the problems are worked on rescues them from positions of such fantasy and impossibility that they must take place before or after the novel, and returns them to the level of reality the novel encompasses. It is specifically the domestic novel that tells life-cycle events through a structure of catastrophe or of comedy. When catastrophic, the events of the domestic novel take on the aura of the extraordinary because they are fundamentally beyond the novel's grasp; the insurmountability of problems propels the narrative through the unpredictable and dramatic, transforming the world of the domestic into that of the tragic, or at least the melodramatic. When, however, life-cycle events function as a working/workable part of the structure of the domestic novel's daily world, so that they are lived with, or even act as a model for how daily living is to be done, then they position the domestic squarely in the ordinary and in the ordinary's "comedy."

That a plot can go on, that characters can go on with one another, that a narrative world can remain intact and yet evolve is the "narratable" of comedy. The comedy of a marriage, like the comedy of a domestic novel, discovers itself when the continuity of common nouns meets the constant arrival of new proper nouns (the not yet known or originally encountered must be called something unique, specific, to demarcate its state of difference) with a sense of possibility that is both grounded in the steady and floating in freed opportunity. The novel of adultery, however, undoes the ordinariness of marriage's repetitions and continuity by defining its "fissures, breaches and breakdowns" (D. A. Miller 3). It makes marriage a site for the possibility of the catastrophic or the extraordinary when the ability of marriage to repeat itself or to evolve is stopped, when it comes no longer to know itself. The movement in the domestic novel from the problems of courtship to marriage, where the narrative ends with the promise of a happy marriage as a nameable but ultimately "unnarratable" end, or from the repetitions of a marriage to its end-stop in adultery defines the novel as a site for the integration of the ordinary and the extraordinary. The narrative which makes its central problem how to present the ordinariness of a marriage happening, which defines marriage over time as that which grows, falters, and works without the drama of its requisite death in adultery or divorce, makes the unfolding of a marriage life-sustaining and sustaining of the narrative. Such a narrative makes the pleasures of the ordinary, its comedy, in essence its sole topic.

The great model for the modern domestic novel that writes of marriage happening, as "new comedy," between a team is the Kitty/Levin narrative of Leo Tolstoy's 1877 *Anna Karenina*. For Tolstoy, to write a narrative of domestic comedy necessitated juxtaposing it with a narrative of domestic tragedy: we come to understand the comedy, the ordinariness of the Kitty/Levin story by virtue of its being situated next to the Anna/Vronsky story. And this too is how we come to know the extraordinariness and tragedy of the novel of adultery by virtue of its position next to the novel of marriage.

Comedy of the Ordinary

Although named for the figure whose narrative of adultery ends tragically in suicide, *Anna Karenina* devotes more than half of its attention to the marriage of Kitty and Levin, a novel of domestic comedy. Split by these opposing topics, the narrative divides the number of its pages, chapters, and scenes between the two novels, revealing the title's failure to convey its "other" half. Further, while part 7 ends with Anna's suicide, the novel concludes with part 8, devoted solely to the world of Kitty and Levin; no section of the narrative gives itself over to Anna, Vronsky, and Karenin completely. The narrative as a whole resists the tragic, and its downward movement (literalized to underneath the train), by its structure of constant counterpoint between the stories and eventual insistence on the ongoingness of the Kitty/Levin story. While Tolstoy asserts in his letters that he began to write *Anna Karenina* as a novel of adultery, he came over time to put aside that portion of the text in order to add to it what he would come to call the "scaffolding" of the novel, "the story of Levin." My assertion, however, is that the Levin portion is not just Levin's, and that the scaffolding is not just the supporting framework but a co-plot as well.[2]

Those readers seduced into forgetting the Kitty/Levin story in favor of the memorability of the Anna tale, or those critics who write on Anna to the exclusion of Levin and Kitty, imitate the novel's tragic violence and elide its form of New Comedy.[3] Such acts of reading suggest that it is easier to see longing, easier to identify with romantic pain, more "interesting" to focus on illicit desire than it is to see recurring moments of satisfaction, identify with ordinary pleasures or existential pain, focus on the ongoing struggles of licit desire lost and found. In the history of aesthetics, from the Aristotelian valorization of tragedy over comedy forward, we have been trained to consider the tragic to be the more weighty, compelling, truth-containing aesthetic. Aristotle asserts in the *Poetics* that it is worth our complete attention to be in the presence of tragedy's effects of pity and fear, whereas we grow little (perhaps even grow to be less, according to Aristotle) from comedy's "ridicule" and laughter. We continue to imagine (no matter how we define these words/states) that we learn from our pain, not from our pleasure. If part of the work of culture is to regulate our longings and act as the superego to contain our drives, the aesthetic works of culture function something like an antidote to that repressive force. The romantic tragic narrative displays our forbidden longings and teaches us to fear them and accept their prohibition. We enjoy the psychic release of reading of a woman's forbidden desires and also of knowing that she is punished for them—that there is no "out" for her sexuality but suicide.

What is missed in this version of culture's regulation of enjoyment—a drama of repression released momentarily as an act of seduction and reinforced in the closing pages as punishment—is the less dramatic enjoyment born out of what conforms at least overtly to regulation. What "breaks the rules" demands attention. But what about what is made from inside the rules? Strangely, the illicit may be more predictable, knowable, and "seeable" than the licit. In our desire to see "the forbidden other" we may miss experiencing what makes itself up as something other than the negation of a boundary. The freshness and unpredictability of creative-living-within-bounds find their source of energy and "answer" not in the knowable "opposite" but instead in the freedom to explore the potential of what is present but not fully known. The shock of things coming undone seems to be more intensely present to us than the less striking creation of something new. What is being made memorable in the novel (the Anna/Vronsky narrative) is the moment of break and the danger of stepping into an apparently unknowable, empty space waiting to be filled, but which in the end is not. What is being forgotten (the Kitty/Levin narrative) is the texture of continuous making born out of a series of collisions and repairs.

It may seem strange, even "extraordinary" to be reading about the Kitty/Levin narrative in a novel called *Anna Karenina*, a novel apparently about her and her tragedy. However, what I'm working to uncover is how the ordinary story, the one we can't seem to see or remember very well, displays (once seen and given a vocabulary to) a more complex, surprising narrative account than the more visible, predictable tragic tale of rupture, rebellion, and a woman's suicide. While the two narratives on occasion intersect, what occurs primarily is that they regard each other a few chapters at a time apart. Apparently in a position of subordination to the Anna/Vronsky narrative, the Kitty/Levin plot makes a space for its recognition, its presence by virtue of its ability to make pictures from its "common noun-ness." At issue, therefore, is, what is it that the Kitty and Levin plot "common noun names" within its "nameless" structure? To bring forward the apparently "less present" Kitty/Levin narrative requires me to demonstrate how it can be part of a novel and describe the *present* as opposed to lack, and how it does this through the act of naming and the making of a comedy of mutuality—New Comedy made by a team. What I mean is to show how a novel can still be itself and depart from Miller's structure of fissure plotting, or what Peter Brooks defines as Oedipal plotting.[4]

To begin with, the Kitty/Levin plot names collections of things; this is one of its pastimes, as in:

They had just returned from Moscow and were glad of the solitude. He was in his study and sat at the writing table. She, in the dark lilac dress she had worn during the first days of her marriage and which was specially memorable and dear to him, sat with her embroidery on that same old leather-covered sofa which stood in the study through his father's and grandfather's times. As he sat thinking and writing he was all the while blissfully conscious of her presence. He had not abandoned his work on the estate, or on the book in which the foundations of a new farming system were to be explained; but as those thoughts and that work formerly appeared to him trivial and insignificant in comparison with his future prospects all bathed in the bright sunshine of happiness. (481)

Chapter 15 of part 5 opens with a pause, a description of things returned to: their home, the writing table on which he had been and continues to write his book on farming, the lilac dress she had worn in the early part of the marriage, embroidery she is in the midst of finishing, a leather sofa from the days of Levin's father and grandfather. Taken collectively, these objects constitute their world together, the objects in which their bodies reside and the objects which occupy their hands and heads. They are objects which embody history or the presence of past lives or past work. Not only are they things to which Kitty and Levin can return, but they are things that others have inhabited (houses) or used (sofas) or will look at (embroidery, books).

Kitty and Levin live in and make a world of continuity formed from the objects with which they interact—and interact they must. We first come to know Levin working the farm and Kitty tending to the sick. When they come together in marriage, Levin will continue his work on the land and Kitty will work to set up house. Tolstoy mingles moments of their conversation, visits with others (the arrivals of Varenka, Dolly, Veslovsky)—events created by the interaction between people—with descriptions of how Levin and Kitty collectively or independently mix their bodies with objects—events created by the interaction with things (the making of jam, the use of the scythe, beekeeping). Theirs is a world in which one expects the return of Dolly and the cyclical process of making and eating jam. What gets accomplished by this atmosphere of tending is a series of pictures of satisfaction: what it looks like to be filled by the activity of lifting a scythe, growing a baby in one's body, collecting bees; and what it looks like to then gaze on the result of hay, a child, honey. Kitty and Levin do object-centered comedy in that their narrative ties them to playing and creating with things, things to which they return, things that they define through their roles as "makers" and that in turn define them as what they "do," things that when taken together harmonize or create a climate of the "bright sunshine of happiness," as Levin calls it, that penetrates their lives with some regularity. The mood made by this relation to things being worked on and played with, and to people able to return to play some more, is by nature then comic, not comic in the sense that we expect jokes, but comic in that we anticipate things, and people, and the place itself to continue and to do so with a feeling of desire that it continue. We know, by contrast, that Dolly cannot return to Anna once she has made her visit, and that Vronsky cannot continue in his pursuits as landlord. Anna and Vronsky's universe can tolerate things occurring just once, which means it is not a "place" for making; indeed it composes something like an "as if" place, call it a theater for brief entrances and exits.

The place Kitty and Levin make from all of their things and pursuits is a home. And it houses—in addition to visitors, bees, and babies—misunderstandings. Levin puts words to what these misunderstandings are and why they come about when he thinks about them as "collisions," which "were often caused by each not realizing what was important to the other" (480). Significantly, in the way that Tolstoy, as narrator, has words for the "thingness" of Kitty and Levin's life, and insists that we visit it at least as much as we do the coming of visitors to their lives, Tolstoy, as Levin, can name the elements of the interactions between the couple. How they come together, its steps, are broken down and given terms to make it understandable, in essence, to give it presence.

A series of misunderstandings ensue over the course of the novel between Kitty and Levin, which follow the pattern set in their first instance. Tolstoy gives the course of the argument a full treatment in language; we read what set off the collision: "Levin had ridden over to see his new farm and returned half an hour late . . . thinking only of her" (479). This is countered by her response to his lateness and her inability to know what is in his head: "But directly she opened her mouth, words of reproach, senseless jealousy" (479). We move to Levin's response to her words, what he has learned from this conflict: "Then it was that he first clearly understood what he did not realize when leading her out of the church after the wedding: that she was not only very close to him but that he could not tell where she ended and he began. He understood this by a tormenting sensation of cleavage" (479). Something has happened by virtue of time spent together—the transformation of selves who know themselves in separation to selves who know themselves in a world of two, and the terror of possible threat to identity when one's being is no longer defined by oneself alone. Levin's words do not name a mutuality of bliss, but a recognition of marriage's power to make one vulnerable. He goes on to define his impulse to shift the "blame" for the "breach" from him to her and back, and also to put words to his pain, words that live literally as his body: "Like a man half-asleep and oppressed with pain, he wanted to tear off the aching part and cast it from him, but found on waking that the aching part was—himself" (480). These words about Levin are not spoken by him; they are neither performed as they would be in an embodied narrative or even suggested as his written dialogue. Instead, from their perspective of internal focalization, they take us from Tolstoy's narrator to inside Levin's mind. Such moments of writing are *about* Levin's feelings for or understanding of Kitty, or what it means to be married. They do not perform or even open the space for us as his readers to perform/embody his role in the couple. Instead, they narrate how Levin in this moment inhabits himself and his being in this relationship. If the novel's great contribution to narrative is the uncovering through narration of consciousness, the nondialogic language of internal focalization gives the reader a conception of who Levin is as himself and as a man in partnership.

The narration about Levin necessarily takes us away from a shared moment of interaction between Levin and Kitty; however, it creates a groundwork from which the reader can understand the words and actions Levin does "perform"/share with her. Therefore, the displays of partnering in novels distinguish themselves from those of performance media for how they take the narrative audience inside a character. We enter a separate consciousness—separate from our own, separate from the partner. However, Tolstoy's narrator does not take us only inside Levin's consciousness. Kitty will, as in the moment of Levin's jealousy over her interaction with Veslovsky, receive the narrator's attention with regard to her internal state, her understanding of their conflicts. In particular, the narrator leads us inside her to gain a sense of what's at stake in their need to live their conflict and then make up, which happens on each occasion, as in the first breach: "They made it up. Having realized that she was in the wrong, though she did not acknowledge it, she became more tender to him, and they enjoyed a new and doubled happiness in their love" (480). While the language is a summary about her vision, her behavior, and their renewed love, and so is "out there," apart from our witnessing of it, the language gives us a context from which to imagine more deeply the nature of their partnership and why their moments of performed interaction have the sound and look that they do. The novel, in its moments of narration, apart from the suggested moments of performed partnering which the presence of dialogue lends, necessarily brings readers to the nonperformance space of an individual consciousness. And yet the gathering of these spaces together, first of one partner, then of the other, enables us to understand the narration that summarizes why they act as they do when together, or to understand their moments of conversation.

What we do, then, as the readers of Kitty and Levin is to imagine them as a couple from out of the common nouns from which Tolstoy narrates them and their relation into being. Levin and Kitty come to trade who steps forward to accept more blame or to offer the first words/acts of solace. While we don't experience how they embody this interaction, we can imagine how they do so and why. We can see that this is the defining pattern of how they function, how they work as a team. As a team, what they learn their marriage has done to them—namely, that they confront each other at the site of their individual boundaries—causes each to play out elements of the routine at the imaginary line that divides and unites them. And so their routine centers on misunderstood or disagreed with behaviors which are named and worked on collectively in performances of often violently exchanged words that lead the couple to some middle ground called a new understanding of this moment, a deeper understanding of each other, a more fully understood love built on the loss of autonomy and gain of each other.

We are not located here in some transcendent realm where a partner knows as if by magic what the other thinks and values and then responds in knowing respect. Instead, in the early days of the marriage, Tolstoy has us witness a lack of delight and understanding, what Levin will call the most "humiliating and oppressive times of their lives" (480), in order to chart the process of what it means to come to know another in dailiness. This is not coupling in perpetual happiness or even ease; this is a happiness occasionally achieved through a couple at work on finding a language to make themselves present/understandable to each other. Their interactions mirror something like the structure of a joke, in how it works through bisociation, or seeing double, "it means this and also this." Kitty and Levin engage in "switch," or seeing double, when they take on each other's position in addition to their own; this is what it means to arrive at mutual understanding. While their encounters may not have the feel to them of playing around, the process of the interaction follows the course of doing joke work. So, fundamentally, the nature of their teamwork is the performance of collision play: comic in its outcome, comic often in the triviality of its beginnings, ferocious in its recognition of pain, anger, jealousy—the threats that might destroy self and partnership and that living a marriage necessarily raises from buried within the self's or partnership's unconscious.

The collisions are necessary in that they demonstrate that two people are present; this is not about the hypothetical forming of some "new being" out of the loss of self to the other. And this is not just Levin's narrative: Kitty rearranges furniture, howls in agony in childbirth, seems to flirt with Veslovsky, causes Levin to know that he is in the company of another whom, more often than not, he doesn't understand. The felt quality we have of Levin in the text is that he is perpetually surprised, caught off guard, vulnerable to the fact of her. Likewise, though we are less often inside Kitty's head, we know of her ability to take Levin in—how she sees his jealousy, sees his brief infatuation with Anna, sees his early estrangement from their child. And we are witnesses to her inability, at times, to know what to do about what she sees—how she can't quell the jealousy, or contain her rage, or make him love his son. The plot moves in their narrative from quarrel to reunion to quarrel, but in a manner that always feels like a return. We, like Levin and Kitty, come to know this is how each tends to think or feel, and this is how each tends to respond, and this is how they work through their misunderstandings, and this is the sound of their making up.

Unlike the plotting of the Anna narrative, which advances in something like a line without a tail/tale to turn back to, Levin and Kitty's narrative charts a circle. Their circle moves not from breaks with each other but from crossovers in which they must confront the fact of the other, make room for the other, and go on until the next encounter. Part of what defines Kitty and Levin's style of New Comedy, then, reveals itself in their adoption of returns. Their first narrative encounter is a scene of proposal, a scene of rejection, a scene that demands that they separate for the first half of the novel. They play out one version of how to quarrel, or one version of the consequences of a quarrel, which is the other side that always threatens their marriage routine of "making it up" to one another: permanent division. However, this moment occurs before they have formed their comedy team, before they have developed their marriage routine. It is defining in that it teaches them both what comes of not making it up (separation), and what comes with playing the same scene again (marriage). This is something that they must learn; it is not yet a part of their lives because they have not yet formed their routine: "The choice is made, and so much the better . . . a repetition is impossible" (270), Levin confides to Dolly after she prompts him to make a renewed offer. Levin and Kitty will come to form their own Cavell-like comedy of remarriage, or at least replay again of the premarriage, an act that will make returns possible for them and essential to their understanding of what is good. The original, after all, got it wrong.

Because they find each other interesting and desirable, they can collide and recover as partners. Between Anna and Vronsky, the space is dear: confrontation seems intolerable because the realm of mutual interests is tortured by, rather than encompassed in, their desire. Having room enough for two people depends on how they inhabit their space (do they live in or exist apart from a context?), and on the felt quality exhibited between the two. Kitty and Levin each contribute to the making of a world, which in turn does not just tolerate but expands from their collisions. Likewise, their ethos of tending and offering care makes an atmosphere that can absorb its ruptures. Little lies behind the passionate bursts of Anna and Vronsky but the naming of possession, and so little can be recovered following the show of difference. Vronsky and Anna have no patter together, no full-bodied team partnership to display because Anna can only tolerate the reiteration of her position, her desires, her voice. This stems ultimately, I think, from the defining instance of their union, the moment of adultery, which Tolstoy narrates with only the word "that," a kind of nonword which points, but to nothing:

> *That* which for nearly a year had been Vronsky's sole and exclusive desire, supplanting all his former desires: *that* for which Anna had been an impossible, dreadful, but all the more bewitching dream of happiness, had come to pass. Pale, with trembling lower jaw, he stood over her, entreating her to be calm, himself not knowing why or how. (148, emphasis mine)

What lies underneath the "that" is a language of violence, murder, and loss: "He felt what a murderer must feel when looking at the body he has deprived of life" (148); and "But in spite of the murderer's horror of the body of his victim, that body must be cut in pieces and hidden away, and he must make use of what he has obtained by the murder" (148); and "'It's all over,' she said. 'I have nothing but you left. Remember that'" (149). Anna asks Vronsky to re-member the pieces of her body/her self which he has cut apart. But Tolstoy gives him only the word "use" as what he can do with her pieces. And she has only the words "nothing but you left" and a haunting Hamlet's father–like refrain. Anna and Vronsky cannot make together a language in the present tense which can name what they have together; instead, their exchanges to follow will be of Vronsky's repeating back to Anna what she must hear (a remembering) and an attempt by each separately to remember what each sacrificed to the other, to remember, in essence, loss or the absence of presence.

Levin, by contrast, generates more words, in addition to his language of collision, for getting at what he loses and gains in his partnership. He defines how his marriage lives in terms of a movement from feeling disenchantment to the discovery of new enchantments (479), which means Kitty and Levin feel alive to each other enough to experience both disappointment and surprise. He uses the example in the concluding pages of the children who discover a way to cook and eat raspberries over candles and who, in doing so, "think out something of our own invention and new" (792). This is the model he proposes for how to think his way out of the depression he returns to about the meaning of existence. It is, as well, the model for how he and Kitty proceed throughout their novel by finding the capacity to go on from disenchantment and get to renewal, delight, and the sense of newness again that makes the marriage feel sustainable. Being able to return to something—Kitty, questions about existence—and consider them in new ways brings to Levin a celebration defined by relief. For the moment, at least, he finds answers: there is love, there is belief, there is goodness. These answers, we suspect, will not stick; and we know too that that is not the point. What is interesting about Levin's thinking and the marriage are their abilities to make adjustments, see things differently, take on change and chance, and discover other ways of being. Kitty and Levin understand how to respond creatively and with some flexibility to accident and fortune, and in so doing, at times, "achieve repose in the face of both joy and sorrow."[5] Comedy trusts invention as a way of knowing and as a way of being.

And this is the happy ending of this comic novel: Levin has invented some new answers about some old questions, and Kitty and Levin have continued to invent ways of being together that are individually and mutually sustaining. They have found reasons and ways to celebrate being alive amid doubt, conflict, angst, jealousy, habit. Levin, though he contemplates suicide, like a refrain, over the course of his life because of his inability to know the answer to life's meaning, need not commit suicide. Conversely, there are no new enchantments between Vronsky and Anna. She says shortly before her suicide, "And between Vronsky and myself what new feeling can I invent? Is any kind—not of happiness even, but of absence of torture—possible? No! No!" (756). What their narrative traces is what it means to use up, spend, destroy because of the lack of capacity to reinvent in a universe defined by originality and firsts and onlys. Can anything sustain in such a narrative? What is to be done when "firsts" run out but suicide? Anna's narrative is precisely that, an anti-sustaining and a forward-driving narrative. It cannot go on but must run itself out and so bring the novel toward its end as it allows the pages to run out. By contrast, the Levin/Kitty narrative sustains the novel, perpetuates it, creates a model for how an 800-page novel could never end in its series of disenchantments and re-enchantments.

The two narratives, therefore, need each other. Tolstoy uses the Anna novel to bring us close to an ending, while he uses the Kitty/Levin novel to make a possibly endless narrative, one that resists closure, or happens to stop off at a moment of grand thinking for Levin and interest in moving a washstand for Kitty. All of Levin's intellectual tossings and turnings could, we imagine, lead him elsewhere if there were more narrative. And after the moving of the washstand in preparation for Sergius Ivanich's arrival, what would come for Kitty? Beating a rug? Cajoling Levin to get over his depression about the meaning of life so as to help with the current preparations? There is more world to come for this marriage and no more world to come for Anna. Tolstoy brings these novels together in a reiteration of Lévi-Straussian social anthropology: we know/define in opposition—the raw and the cooked, the light and the dark, the good and the bad. And he reiterates the also-coupled works the *Iliad* and the *Odyssey*, which Clara Claiborne Park takes to distinguish the comic and tragic moods:

> The *Iliad* and the *Odyssey* are the fundamental narratives of Western consciousness, even for those who have not read them: two masks, two modes, two stances; minor chord and major; two primary ways of meeting experience. The *Iliad* sets the type of tragedy, as Aristotle tells us, where greatness shines amid violence, error, defeat, and mortality. The *Odyssey* celebrates survival among the world's dangers and surprises, and then homecoming, and order restored. It is the archetype of a prosperous outcome, of Comedy. (58)

Another way of saying this is that the Anna/*Iliad*/tragic narrative meets experience and writes of it as extraordinary, a world that demands sacrifice and death, while the Kitty-Levin/*Odyssey*/comic novel meets experience and writes of it as ordinary, a world that celebrates the pleasures of survival and well-being. Joined together, the whole novel knows itself in the tensions between these poles: one seems never to let the other out of its sight. Even in what seems to be a final giving way to the ordinary in the absence of the Anna narrative in part 8, Levin takes on her voice in his suicidal musings and reiterated questions about why one lives. Levin's capacity to do the extraordinary ensures that the novel can continue as itself, while his juxtaposition with Kitty in the nursery, talk of washstands, and resistance to suicide in favor of work gives the comic climate, or mood of the ordinary, the last word.

However, the Kitty/Levin novel also discovers its own relation to the extraordinary in its giving to them the presence of magic. We get a glimpse at a comic-making between Levin and Kitty which finds its source in the otherworldly, that realm which just makes all be well without work, without reason, without reality. When the couple engage in the mutual writing/understanding of codes in the scene of the second proposal, they pursue a kind of comic business called "doing magic tricks." Johan Huizinga in *Homo Ludens* explains such a moment when he thinks about what it means for two people to play together:

> The exceptional and special position of play is most tellingly illustrated by the fact that it loves to surround itself with an air of secrecy. Even in early childhood the charm of play is enhanced by making a "secret" out of it. This is for *us,* not for the "others." What the "others" do "outside" is no concern of ours at the moment. Inside the circle of the game the laws and customs of ordinary life no longer count. We are different and do things differently. (12)

When Levin and Kitty come together after their failed first proposal scene, it is around a table where they silently draw concentric circles around each other's circles. They make a secret place, charmed by the absence of words, joined together in circles, removed from all others. The others, "the laws and customs of ordinary life," are for a moment not part of their world; they engage in an extraordinary play of exchanging letters of the alphabet as signs for their exchange of vows. The moment tells them and us that they are made for each other, that each is up to being a member of this team, in much the same way that constructing a joke together reveals the appropriateness/magic of a partnership. Reading the other's mind works here as a comic device to usher their narrative into its newfound mood of promise, ingenuity, possibility. However, this is a premarriage moment: it heralds that what Kitty and Levin have between them is the *possibility* for understanding one another, which is what they will discover when they descend into the ordinary realm of having to name words to fight their way out of misunderstanding in the pursuit of a reunion based on a meeting of minds. This extraordinary instance is never to be repeated; once married, the two will have to *work* their way toward understanding. However, in the way that they come to the notion of the "return" as something they must make part of their lives and count on to sustain them and their narrative, so too do they hold onto the notion of "understanding" as a thing they have known and can know again by coming together to engage in the play of naming.

Family Happiness

Tolstoy's desire, perhaps, to diminish the power of his Kitty/Levin novel of domestic comedy reveals itself in the famous opening sentence of *Anna Karenina:* "Happy families are all alike; every unhappy family is unhappy in its own way." What does it mean that all happy families are alike? What is that single story, and can it be told? Likewise, why does unhappiness prompt particularity? That the unhappy family is different "in its own way" suggests that it must be the story of interest, the particular story worth telling. Tolstoy anticipates Miller's claim that it is unhappiness and lack that engender stories, while happiness is a state that prompts dismissal into generality, or silence. Tolstoy's choice to name his novel for the narrative of adultery, when the narrative of domestic comedy is what concludes the novel, is a gesture that privileges the tragic. However, it attends, as well, to what it is tragedies and comedies do: tragedies name the particularities of their characters, assert the individual nature of the struggling central figure, tell how a particular family is unhappy in its own way; comedies name types of character and shared states of being—what it means to be "all happy families," how that is a state of being alike between people. *Anna Karenina,* as a title and a narrative, will name Anna's particular tragedy in the absence of what can be held onto and named, and in the nameability of her particular being. The absent *Kitty/Levin* title to accompany the Kitty/Levin story underscores the absence of their particularity and makes room for the general telling of their state. However, Tolstoy might have chosen a type of character or general state-of-being title to privilege their tale.

An earlier Tolstoy novella, *Family Happiness* (1859), tells the story of a marriage in a state of romance, in the loss of that state, and in the discovery of a new and sustainable happiness in family life. The drive of the novella centers on what is lost between the man and the woman; only the final four paragraphs suggest the idea of this other joy, of parenting, but there is no sustained narrative to plot out its course. I think we can read *Anna Karenina* as the full treatment of *Family Happiness,* divided between the losses of the Anna narrative and the discoveries of the Kitty/Levin narrative. However, the Kitty/Levin story works to do more than "settle" for a happiness known only between parents and children and between partners as parents, which is the conclusion of *Family Happiness.* It works to make romance possible as a sustainable source of happiness within the frame of the family by maintaining Kitty and Levin's relation to each other as members of a sparring, interested, caring couple. They are a team who make comic routines together, and who in so doing make a narrative that sustains itself and them. To change the title from *Anna Karenina* to *Family Happiness* would mean to name Kitty and Levin's state of being, "family happiness," as a state possible for sharing and as a character type— "all happy families are all alike." Should we read the Kitty/Levin story as the presentation of a character type, all happy families, or as a state of being, being a happy family? Tolstoy suggests that we should do both by taking their narrative to tell the comic story of marriage (call that a type) and to tell a generalizable, imitable way of being/writing that can be generalized and imitated, that is, that can function as a model. Laurie Colwin pursues Tolstoy's invitation to perpetuate his model or to repeat his type by writing her variation on both, first in her story "Family Happiness," in *The Lone Pilgrim* (1981), and then in her novel *Family Happiness* (1982). Colwin follows Tolstoy's course from story to novel and continues to use both the title he came to withhold and the "Anna affair" to help her heroine find her way into a more whole story of selfhood and mutuality within the marriage/family story. She writes of new pleasures of the ordinary discovered in what began as their elision and incorporates Tolstoy's two narratives into the life of one woman, or finds space for the extraordinary in the ordinary.

Other novelists of the twentieth century have taken the novel's apparent resistance to a sustained portrayal of an ordinary happiness demonstrated in marriage to be a problem worthy of exploration and have written variations on Tolstoy's solution. Most notably, this is what the work of Virginia Woolf is about. Like Laurie Colwin, the novelists Wallace Stegner, Lynne Sharon Schwartz, Rosamunde Pilcher, and Carol Shields, among others, rely on the ordinary for the possibility that meaning can be found in the everyday and its potential for comedy. Marriage's ongoingness is literally what makes their narratives go on. These writers all focus on trying out the pleasure of marriage as a subject for storytelling and so work to revive the Western domestic "bourgeois" novel, which Tony Tanner asserts lost its power with the deterioration of marriage's status as sanctified by and sanctifying society. He writes in *Adultery in the Novel:*

> The bourgeois novelist has no choice but to engage the subject of marriage in one way or another, at no matter what extreme of celebration or contestation. He may concentrate on what makes for marriage and leads up to it, or on what threatens marriage and portends its disintegration, but his subject will be marriage. . . . As bourgeois marriage loses its absoluteness, its unquestioned finality, its "essentiality," so does the bourgeois novel. (15)

The emergence of the domestic comedy of ongoing marriage in the latter twentieth century—as opposed to the pronounced concentration of domestic comedy leading to marriage of the eighteenth century and the domestic melodrama of dissolution of the nineteenth century—occurs at a cultural moment when marriage's position of social authority is, by comparison, at its most questioned or least absolute (and perhaps too when the novel is at its least influential). Whereas the novel of adultery seems to flourish when situated in a cultural moment when marriage assumes a position of social control, the novel of domestic comedy seems to present itself when located in an age of marital instability and lost connection between marriage and the perpetuation of a social order. It becomes, therefore, almost "antiestablishment" for a contemporary novel to portray domestic comedy. How modern novelists write marriage happening as interesting, narratable, and not as a noose (as would George Eliot or Thomas Hardy) is by making its ordinariness extraordinary, as does Woolf; or by making the extraordinary negotiable (adultery becomes a working part of the marriage plot), as does Laurie Colwin; or by making it just present (the suppressed or the original can now be revealed or repeated or worked through), as does Carol Shields, that is, by making the extraordinary ordinary.[6] In essence, with marriage's "loss of power" in contemporary culture as a social force, or with its more flexible definition, has come, in the modern domestic novel's new play about what constitutes the ordinary and the extraordinary, new interest in how language and plotting define those states and interact with each other. Which is not to say that one is lost to the other: as novels, that tension still defines the narrative form. Rather, the ordinary and the extraordinary must reinvent themselves and so interact with each other differently in a modern narrative universe that can tolerate the saying and plotting of almost anything.

While Tolstoy keeps the narratives of the ordinary and the extraordinary next to each other in *Anna Karenina,* he too makes the extraordinary ordinary by making happiness be possible, grounded, present, real. Kitty and Levin do not for the most part know an untroubled, easy happiness; they work on it and in so doing make happiness one of the things they make. However, unlike Levin's beekeeping and Kitty's furniture rearranging, they must do it together because happiness is about their partnership, their acknowledgment that they live in the world together, their recognition that something about their individual well-beings depends on the fact of the other, with all of the complications that that recognition brings. In the very ordinariness of their happiness comes the possibility of its presence in the novel: Tolstoy insists that mutual happiness is a story that can be told because it can be common noun named, even if not proper noun titled.

The return to what is present, in a language that names its very presence, coupled with the advance toward the unknown and unnamed creates a dialogue between the ordinary and extraordinary in all novels, so that stories go on, establish patterns, seem to continue without end, and, as well, necessarily move to the end of a plot and end. This dialogue makes the ordinary not only "narratable" but essential to the construction of the novel's very being. And while at times the ordinary of the novel, which points to what is present, expresses desire for what it is not, namely, the extraordinary, it also takes delight in what it is, most especially in its ability to make comedy—the ordinary's great life-sustaining gift.

CHAPTER 6

Lucy and Ricky/
Nichols and May

Life in Paradise was not like following a straight line to the unknown; it
was not an adventure. It moved in a circle among known objects. Its
monotony bred happiness, not boredom.
—Milan Kundera, *The Unbearable Lightness of Being*

Comedy of Repetition

From the first situation comedy of marital happiness, the "silk pajamas
comedy" of *Mary Kay and Johnny* in 1947, to the more recent *Mad about
You,* situation comedy has made the depiction of marital love the focus of
its narrative form, even what defines it as a genre. While situation comedy
has moved between the couple, the family, the family at work or from
outer space, and the family of friends as its character-sites of study, it
understands those arrangements as constructing a world of intimate partners who remain intimate, in partnerships, and in a state of well-being
over time together. Though the numbers and arrangements change, situation comedy always puts at its center a form of "marriage" performing a
kind of "team comedy." While it is the comic partnership that defines
what situation comedy is about—the marriage which knows itself to be a
marriage—its variations, too, present themselves as responses to "happily
ever after." Granting the difficulties of such an undertaking—this representation of the other side of "happily ever after"—leads me to questions
like these: What does it mean about the narrative problem itself (specifically, the description of marital love) that situation comedy lends itself so
"easily" and generally as the chief genre of response? And how is it and
why is it that situation comedy narrates the ongoing relationship of coupling to happiness? To think about these questions, I turn to the situation
comedy that first defined and still defines its form, *I Love Lucy.*

Historical among situation comedies in its vast popularity from its first

airing October 15, 1951, to the present, and in its other list of firsts—first
to be filmed, first to be recorded before an audience, first to shoot with a
three-camera method still used—*I Love Lucy*, in its position as first, best,
or most, fills a representative if not originating position of the genre situation comedy. However, is it a comedy? If the offensiveness of a woman's
confinement in the home, role of subservience, position as the "child" in
marriage is all that is portrayed in situation comedies of the 1950s and
'60s in particular, then these narratives offer little topically beyond their
cultural representation of sexual politics before the sexual revolution. Certainly, in those terms *I Love Lucy* will not cause laughter or, therefore, a New
Comedy's catharsis. Patricia Mellencamp, writing on *The George Burns
and Gracie Allen Show* and *I Love Lucy*, states, "[T]his pleasure/provoking
cover-up/acknowledgment is not a laughing but a complex matter, posing
the problem of women's simulated liberation through comic containment"
("Situation Comedy" 95). Certainly, *I Love Lucy* is about woman's containment. Ricky tells Lucy so in the pilot episode: "I don't want a wife in
show business. I want a wife, just a wife, who will clean, and cook, and
bring me my pipe, and be the mama of my children." The comedy results
from Lucy's breaks from what Ricky apparently desires from her. But what

Lucille Ball and Vivian Vance filming *I Love Lucy*, Desilu, 1951
Courtesy UCLA Arts–Special Collections

is striking for me about *I Love Lucy* is not the fact of Lucy at home and Ricky at work, Ricky's accepted position as rule-maker and Lucy's as rule-recipient—that's the situation comedy's representation of the culture of its day as the *culture's* known situation. What becomes remarkable is how that situation is made comic, laughable, critiquable by virtue of how this couple interacts in the face of what is "understood." *I Love Lucy* is both a laughing and a complex matter because of the collapse of the apparent frame of containment in the very staging of this marriage as a partnership in comedy.

Lucy and Ricky

Fundamentally, there are three situations that perpetually interact and repeat throughout the 179 episodes that define the *I Love Lucy* "comedy of repetition": (1) The character and location worlds of Lucy and Ricky Ricardo: who they are individually, who they are together, who they are in their relationships with Fred and Ethel Mertz, and who they are in the apartment on the seventh floor, in a building owned by their friends and neighbors the Mertzes in New York City. (2) The world of Ricky's expectations with regard to the marriage: that he work in show business and that she does not, that she stay at home and tends to the domestic world and that he be part of the domestic world that receives her care. The world of Lucy's desires: that she use any means to help Ricky "make it" to have his own television show, and that she be in the show or in essentially any performance to be viewed by an audience. (3) The histories of the "real" people Lucille Ball and Desi Arnaz, their "real" marriage and their personal relations to this comedy: Lucy's position as "star," asked by CBS in 1949 to do her own television show without her Cuban husband; Desi's position as an internationally known bandleader and rejected television partner for Lucy; their partnered Mr. and Mrs. Act that they performed on the circuits of a near dead vaudeville to prove their "viability" as a comic marriage in the eyes of the American public.

I Love Lucy is a show about becoming this show, a show whose fundamental structure is built on a reality, this marriage, and two unrealities: that he is the talent/star on whom she depends for the chance that will one day lead to her "big break," and that he has no interest in her joining his act. In distinguishing the film star from the theater actor, Erwin Panofsky writes that in film a particular actor is not transformed into a character but the actor's personality is perpetuated through different films, as "Greta

Garbo" or "Charlie Chaplin" (226–31). This has to do with the primacy
in film of the image as opposed to the words of the script: whereas plays
can be read for themselves, scripts fundamentally cannot stand on their
own because they function as stage directions for the movements and
sheer presence of their stars (226). Television, like cinema, presents moving photographs to us of actors whom we come to know as that series of
images, by virtue of the number of times we see a figure being essentially
the same in a show, and the number of people watching and collectively
making an actor fill the position of a personality. The blurring that results
between "real person" and character helps to account for the phenomenon
of "Cosby," "Roseanne," "Seinfeld"—signifiers that stand for those people,
those stand-up acts, those television shows.

Lucy and Ricky/Desi are original instances of this blurring. The situation comedy instructs us to blur the distinction between the performer's
life and what defines that life in its weekly portrayal. We, as audience,
indulge in the fantasy that we know Lucy and Ricky/Desi, know this to
be their marriage, and can trust the situation comedy to help us know
something, therefore, about the lives of others and maybe too about our
own. The format of the show is built on the comic potential of weaving
together the reality of their lives with deliberate "rewrites." This seduction
into believing these scripted lives to be "real" occurs because of the repetition of characterization and location, plot design built on the recurrence
of expectation and desires, and the actual marriage playing a marriage
(which will become an actual pregnancy playing a pregnancy). Thus while
all filmed performances encourage the audience to make an identification
between who the star portrays and who he or she "is," it is the situation
comedy's format which *narrates* this crossing over between performance
and reality in its repeated representation of home life. The stand-up comic
who does confessional comedy (like Roseanne) or self-referential comedy
(like Seinfeld) is particularly ripe for this movement from the stage into
television.

The structure of *I Love Lucy* as a situation comedy is fundamentally a
gestural one in that plotted actions do not define what is most compelling
about its movement. The plot, the known frame, makes possible and holds
a world of surprises within its walls. Robyn Warhol writes in "Guilty Cravings" about the serial fiction soap opera as a plot that is understood radi-
cally differently according to the amount of "backstory" the viewer knows
when watching an episode. In the case of soap opera, knowledge of pre-
plot determines how one "reads" the present-plot of the new installment.

This is not the case with situation comedy. Essentially, there is no "back-story" to an *I Love Lucy* episode. How the viewer "reads" an episode is not determined by particular knowledge of previous episodes. *I Love Lucy* works from a premise of viewer amnesia: each week we can pretend that we didn't see/know what came before this week's show because the show makes no references to its past. The serial situation comedy pretends that it has no past; it lives in the present moment of "this week," "this episode."

As viewers, we go along with the pretense because the medium allows us to let go of the demand of the memory line of narrative, that is, the demand that we remember this and then this and then this if we are to make sense of the narrative of the whole series. Freed from the need to remember everything, we can attend more closely to what is performed in the moment. However, we do know that *I Love Lucy* will most likely return next week and most likely was on last week. And we know too that the large structures of this episode's plot—how it unfolds, who enacts it, and where it unfolds—are repetitions of what came before and model what will follow. That knowledge of serial return and structural repetition (even with the particulars of past-plots, or backstory, forgotten) creates in the viewer a narrative desire much like that of the "devotee" of the soap opera, who, Warhol writes, "[I]s less interested in a story's resolution or closure than in its indefinite open-endedness: climax and resolution are not the goal . . . instead, the long-term soap opera viewer experiences narrative climax after narrative climax as the multiple story lines continue, deferring forever the story's ultimate end" (353). While the "successful" registering of the comedy of each episode of *I Love Lucy* does depend on an interest in seeing how the untied plot becomes retied—on the climax, the place where the untied gets tied—an engaged audience to situation comedy also resists the desire to experience "the" climax, that which brings the whole series to "the end." The open-ended space in situation comedy grows out of the repetitions of the plot's frame: the repeated situation prompts the audience to attend more closely to what emerges in between the known structures. And that open-ended space is Lucy.

Lucy could do something other than act the part of the obstructed lover, the shrew, the "cuckolder," or even the plot-turning wit—the traditional parts for the woman of narrative-driven romantic comedy.[1] The non-narrative of the comic spectacle frees her to be a clown. If Carole Lombard was the first beauty of screwball comedy to take and give a slug, Lucille Ball was the first beauty of situation comedy to be frozen, starched, drenched, covered in clay, and set on fire. While the premise of the show

may be built on Lucy's confinement at home as wife, a confinement justi-
fied by the "fact" of her gender, its comedy finds its source in the breaking
up of that fact, which here means Lucy's and the situation's messing around
with her body, her body as the site determining her gender. And Lucy's
body seems capable of almost anything. She can "do" men: Superman, for
instance, and scale buildings; or Charlie Chaplin, and handle chocolates
with the same alacrity with which he tightened bolts on the conveyor belt
in *Modern Times;* or Harpo, and mirror his gestures without a sound. She
can "do" women: Carmen Miranda, and sing while almost balancing fruit
on her head; or the roles of "vamp," or "pregnant wife." And she can be
"Lucy," which means this particular body gliding into three dozen eggs, or
fighting and bathing in grapes, or wrestling in mud, or dismembering a
television. Lucy's clown can be male, female, or both. In performing as a
body to which almost anything was done and which seemed game to try
almost anything, Lucy became unrecognizable as the cultural position
"wife at home." She became something dangerous, multigendered, impro-
visatory, courageous, insane, unstoppable, in short, unconfinable.

   She fills a presence in this situation comedy in much the same way,
according to Bakhtin, the carnival body fills the comedy of Rabelais.
Transgressing the limits of realism, unaffected by social convention, Lucy's
body performs a kind of carnival past in her willingness to don all forms
of costume, place her body in any situation that will enable her to perform
before an audience, mock the conventions dictating how a woman should
look and act, and interact with the world with a pretechnological abandon
(as much as Lucy wants to be on television or any recorded medium, in a
studio she destroys all machines at hand). Finally, Lucy's pregnant body
literalizes the embodiment of extremities: her protruding belly, the physical maneuverings she must generate to continue to pursue stardom, the
growing realization that hers is an "unfinished" body, and the willingness
to make farce with her child-making/bearing body define Lucy's body
as a celebrant of carnival. She undoes convention while embracing life,
refuses social definitions as she gives herself over to the cycles and moods
of nature.[2]

   Lucy's clowning, however, does not happen in a vacuum. Without the
presence of Ricky as comic antagonist, the one who makes the rules or
who generates deadlock, Lucy would have no cause to metamorphose into
the clown who engages in riot to unhinge the structure that binds her.
Further, Lucy's antics grow larger in the presence of Ethel, who acts the
sidekick. It is in the interaction between Lucy and Ricky, Lucy and Ethel,

Lucy and Ricky and Fred and Ethel that the comedy emerges. What it means to be "Lucy" has everything to do with what it means for her to be in company, otherwise she would be a solo clown, a vaudevillian who, for apparently unmotivated reasons, just falls down, sprays water from a corsage, or rides a miniature bicycle. Lucy's acts are responses to rules and perceived about-to-be missed opportunities. The comedy emerges out of a series of snowballing responses, from rule, to idea to break the rule, to performing the break, to hugging on top of the wreckage. It's not, therefore, that the stable order of the beginning has been reinscribed at the end (the plot structure New Comedy is so often taken to impose), but rather that the rule is broken and the couples are reunited in the face of what's been undone.[3]

One of the few instances in which the original order is expressly desired by all at the end is the episode "Job Switching," aired September 15, 1952. A mutual dare is taken up by both couples: the men agree to stay home and keep house while the women go out into the world "to make a buck" in order to see who really performs the harder job. What results are scenes

Vivian Vance and Lucille Ball in "Job Switching," Desilu, 1952
Courtesy Academy of Motion Pictures Arts and Sciences

of Ricky and Fred in aprons beating back steamed rice pouring down from the stove, and Lucy and Ethel grabbing chocolates off a speeding conveyor belt and stuffing them down any available orifice. The reversal leads to farce, and it leads to a reenactment of the Renaissance penchant for additional couples set alongside the central pair. The ongoing presence of both Fred and Ethel with Ricky and Lucy, separated from one's marriage partner and reformulated with new partners as "the girls" and "the boys," works as a revision of the heterosexual double-coupling of New Comedy. If Shakespeare used Hero and Claudio to make a space for an almost-tragic telling of the obstructed lovers' plot and to highlight the comic genius of Benedick and Beatrice, the format of *I Love Lucy* adds the "also-already-married" neighbors to create a means of keeping the marriages intact while separating them into new partnerships, and of making the comedy of the already-married grow exponentially by virtue of its mirrored enactment by yet another couple. Further, the also talented, though less attractive Fred and Ethel make Ricky that much more charming and Lucy that much more of an apparent paradox (why does this beautiful redhead choose to engage in these unbeautiful antics?). The writers of *I Love Lucy,* Jess Oppenheimer, Madelyn Pugh, and Robert Carroll Jr., claim that they created Fred and Ethel because they needed the Ricardos to have neighbors to talk to.[4] But these neighbors do more than just open up the dialogue of each sketch. The also-marrieds underscore in their less attractive, less zany way that it is marriage which makes this comedy, marriage which leads partners to try on new ways of being, marriage which draws each partner back, marriage which necessitates the desire to break out and to return—but as what?

In "Job Switching" each of the four declares that s/he wants to return to the way things were, to have his/her old job back. Each has discovered nothing in the other's world to prompt the desire for change. This is, however, a bizarre end because Lucy never does let go of her desire for Ricky's world. Generally each episode closes with a shared recognition by Lucy and Ricky of what she has undone or created or endured or masterminded to break into his world. And generally while all has collapsed under the force of her staged riot, Lucy has made it to the other side of her performance, and Ricky embraces her (for it, for her, both?). They may be the only ones left standing, but Lucy and Ricky are in a new world. There is no new world to be created in "Job Switching," just the entrance into what is most banal about the places "housework" or "assembly line work." And those spaces are never the ones desired on *I Love Lucy;* instead, they are

places no one in this situation comedy inhabits. Lucy does not do housework and Ricky does not work in a factory. They return, therefore, to
the original order because they acknowledge those origins—Ricky's club,
Lucy's living room—as sites for creating, for disrupting, and for playing.
Having stepped backward or downward into some version of the other's
life that defines itself as being anti-play, call it the work part of their work
worlds, each chooses his/her own starting point because from those opening, fertile positions can come the making of a new world, call that a world
of costumes and music and dance and slapstick—an aesthetic world they
will come to together: their marriage.

If Ricky is considered only the comic antagonist, then it is difficult to
understand how they as a team create this new comic order together. Even
when the women are paired in riot, the men never disappear offstage only
to appear at the end to restore order. They too become engaged in some
form of creative destruction, or they learn of the women's plot and play
with it by fueling its twists and turns until all four must come to resolve
the plot through discovery. When Lucy and Ricky are paired alone, she
is not left to clown alone. To dismiss Ricky's role as "straight man" is to
miss the essence of their partnership.[5] Against his presence, she can go
"crooked," and in her company he can go "straight": the all-American girl
can be crazy, and the Cuban male with the funny accent can assume a
position of authority.

A great instance of this form of their pairing occurs in "Lucy Does a
TV Commercial," aired May 5, 1952. The reiterated format announces
itself: this is Ricky's chance to audition his show before television sponsors;
this is Lucy's chance to do the commercial for his show. For both, it's "the
big break"; therefore, each must audition, each must perform, each must
carry some part of the show which is their show together. Lucy *plots* her
way into getting the "Vitameatavegamin girl" slot. While Ricky has *earned*
his audition to be the bandleader on television, has come to it "straight,"
Lucy has come to her position through "crooked" means—she lied.[6]
Ricky's denying Lucy the part from the outset prompts her cunning: it is
the rigidity, the undefilability of the order he imposes, the rules themselves
that lead Lucy toward a comedy that most often begins from a position
of deception. The situation as defined by the patriarchal order, Ricky's,
makes Lucy be the crafty Odysseus who creates a climate of celebration
through her ability to meet experience and transform it. Theirs is not an
ideal universe: she understands that and knows how to respond to it in
appropriate terms.

Lucy performs her shtick—the clown drunk on the 24 percent alcohol "pepper-upper" after multiple takes and spoonfuls before the camera; Ricky performs his gig—the Spanish balladeer in tuxedo. They at last intersect before the camera when Ricky plays a singing matador and Lucy winds her way on stage as the drunken bull. Their dance together, his attempts to hide her and her restagings in front waving hello to Fred and Ethel, makes it unclear who is winning this contest, or what Gerard Jones calls their "theater of battle" (71). While not here "giving in" to Lucy, in the sense of laughing with her or gesturing back to her in kind, Ricky's decision to stay within his comic frame by attempting to block her out and then finally to ban her, carrying her offstage, keeps their positions defined and separate. And yet, necessarily, there is a crossing over between them by virtue of the competition between their bodies and voices, her mimicking of his "Olés," his newfound clumsiness. The bull and matador exit with neither dead; together, Lucy and Ricky forge a performance that is what this show Ricky hosts before the camera is proclaimed to be, "Your Saturday Night Varieties." The variety is what each has brought to the other; while remaining

Lucille Ball in "Lucy Does a TV Commercial," Desilu, 1952

Courtesy of Movie Star News

individually Lucy and Ricky doing the performances they each do best, together they become an amalgam of parts, separate and choral. They make a Mr. and Mrs. Act.[7]

The doing of a Mr. and Mrs. Act is the premise on which *I Love Lucy* is built. This is the act Lucille Ball and Desi Arnaz took on the vaudeville circuits, and this is the defining frame of the pilot they made independently and sold to CBS in 1951. The pilot lays bare the structure of the situation and its comedy to follow: a world of home (where Lucy is to stay and tend a nest) and the club (where each will perform, one legitimately and one through guile), a world essentially absent of children (though children are born into it and then essentially vanish), a world on holiday (where the possibility exists to break the rules, but also where the rules still have the possibility of standing), a world of physical comedy (people fall down, or sit inside television sets), and a world centered on a performing clown and a comic antagonist who happen to be married. What the pilot further highlights is how well Lucy and Ricky work together, not just in antagonism, but in the constructing of a shared routine. The premise of the opening sounds remarkably familiar: Ricky auditions his act at the club for television sponsors, and Lucy makes her way on stage as the final act. She replaces the scheduled performer Pepito, solo male clown of vaudeville, as Lucito.

What we see in full realization is who Lucy will become in metaphor in the sketches to follow: an oversized man's suit, tie and bowler hat framing her red curls and fine features, Lucy is the man/woman clown, a Charlie Chaplin/Lucille Ball. And Ricky, rather than attempting to expel Lucy from his world, welcomes her as a partner in cooperation. Such an embracing reveals itself in how he greets her: it is Ricky who names her and presents her to the audience as "Lucito." The act of naming insists on a kind of acceptance and even assertion of mutual creation. They then proceed through the sketch together; he offers the set-up lines, and she builds them to their finish, as in his presentation to her of the "saxiphonitrombonovitch" and the guarantee that if she can play it she will have a place in the band, and her dropping to her knees like a seal to play "How dry I am . . ." The bit closes with Ricky's offering fish to her from a bucket near by. No disapproval reveals itself when a sketch is collectively built through a process of turn-taking. And Ricky takes his last turn by closing the routine with a sight gag. The male solo clown of vaudeville is replaced here by a hermaphrodite clown and her Cuban husband, by their oddly natural partnership.

In the midst of the sketch, Lucy satirizes Ricky's English through improvisation. He says, pointing to her cello, "Do you play that thin?'" She says,
"What 'thin'?" He says over muffled laughter, "Never mind making fun of
my English." She responds, "That was English?" Ricky, in his laughter,
prompted we suspect by surprise, is caught off guard by this exchange.
The "aliveness" of the moment reveals itself: these are two comics performing live before an audience, in addition to this being a taped film.
Lucy and Ricky are alive to each other, to the moment. Their intimacy as
a couple and as a comic couple makes itself felt in how they slip in and out
of the expected and unexpected. They enjoy working together enough
that they are still audience to each other, able to laugh at and play to each
other. In the universe of Lucy and Ricky, the timing of how bodies interact and move in relation to objects makes comedy. While language plays
a part in the cracking of, for the most part, very easy, very big jokes, language works primarily in *I Love Lucy* as the other straight man. It prompts
or sets up the ideas which the bodies will enact, with the abandon and
grace necessary for the making of great farce. Language does not function
here, as Brian Henderson would have it, as that which fills the place
between desire and its fulfillment (22); the bodies *do* in fact tell the whole
sexual cycle.

Nichols and May

To think from a different direction about how situation comedy works
and to consider briefly the other model of situation comedy, the language-
based one, leads me not, however, straight to it. *I Love Lucy*'s limitations
with regard to language-driven partnered comedy prompt me to take up
another kind of partnered comedy, namely, team improvisation, in order to
consider some linguistic features of what situation comedy can and cannot
do. Mike Nichols and Elaine May were offered a contract from the Desilu
studios in the early 1960s to do a situation comedy, to do as a situation
what they did better than any other male/female team—improvisation—
and they walked away from the offer. The moment of Lucy and Ricky
breaking from their script to make a joke about his English, the surprise
of that break, the freshness, informed all the work of Nichols and May. As
their manager, Jack Rollins, defines it, they wrote comedy on their feet, and
then like sculptors took what they liked of the piece and built on it.[8] However, what's so essential to the mystery of their team comedy is that they
spoke their comedy on their feet, like storytelling partners of a preliterate

Lucille Ball and Desi Arnaz in "The Pilot Show," Desilu, 1951
Courtesy of Movie Star News

world. If we are stunned by the notion of a solitary bard who sings an epic, we can know something of that experience from the making of these coupled sketches out of the air between them. The situation comedy works from a repeated format of the known scene rubbing up against an unknown element; yet, taken together, it is all still scripted, rehearsed, taped. Team improvisation works from a suggested first and last line, or the assuming of characters or types and the point to which those characters want to arrive; it is not scripted, and not necessarily rehearsed or taped. What Nichols and May couldn't do, it seems, is tie their work down to one situation, or perhaps even to a script. However, what their interactions and the structure of those interactions reveal is how verbal situation comedy creates its comedy around the *felt improvisation* of these characters coming to these words in this scene together. Improv comes prior to situation comedy, as does the spoken before the written word. And situation comedy does to improvisation what the written word does to the spoken: it narrows its range of movement by freezing it into one form, call that the situation, and it makes there be a "the" language which its performers will perpetually use.

Nichols and May make improvisations from their voices, their language. Often set to music, their routines make words interact to perform melodies. They perform not by reading and then acting, but by playing it by ear: Nichols and May listen to the sounds of the other and perform words back to build a musical composition of language. They tell us in their comedy that language is music. Separated from their bodies and yet most often about their bodies, their language functions as a shared narrative-maker, sung between them, even when they're performing in a club or at the Golden Theater on Broadway. Lucy and Ricky play with objects: a stool, a plunger, a bow. Nichols and May's humor is so essentially immaterial that there are no bits with objects, bits that would require us to see the gag. We may wonder, will she take off her shirt? or, how sexual will they get? but they prompt that wondering in our imaginations not because of what they make us see. Theirs is conversation as music, conversation as sex, conversation as team comedy.

Their bodies, while constantly referred to and made present as the objects of desire of these voices, exist for their audience under sheets. In "Bach to Bach," as their voices echo in rhythm and tone the sounds of an adapted Bach piece, we learn in offhanded asides of their location on a bed, a seemingly besides-the-fact fact which is very much before us and kept hidden beneath the surging waves of their vocal delivery. Or, in

Mike Nichols and Elaine May
Courtesy Wisconsin Center for Film and Theater Research

"Physical" we hear that Nichols literally lies underneath a sheet, naked, in response to which May must attempt to perform a physical examination as his doctor. We hear the sheet torn in his struggle to keep himself covered and hers to see the ailing body. The "physical" becomes physical when their voices act out her "examination" of his body; the use of double entendre creates the sexual space of the scene with no bodies present. The language plays with itself and tells us that we're located inside and underneath the professional world/words:

MAY: Does this hurt?

NICHOLS: (With relief and a warm, relaxed tone.) No, not at all.

MAY: Fine. There?

NICHOLS: (Responsive to her touch, as if a massage.) Doesn't hurt.

MAY: Breathe in. You've got quite a chest expansion (little laugh). Do you go to the gym much? . . . Umm. Excellent physical condition. How old did you say you were? . . . I can't seem to find anything wrong. I do have a suggestion, and that is I think you should go to bed around 8:30, 9. Try to avoid any social activity for the present. I would suggest rest.

NICHOLS: Rest.

MAY: A lot of rest. Come in and I'll check you again in about, an hour.

May has spoken earlier in the routine about the consequences of keeping someone in bed too long as a method of recovery. The consequences play themselves out here: he responds to her touch and she responds to his body. Under the guise of the "lady doctor" and the male patient with the bad stomach, they use the professional scene and its accompanying language to get at what lies underneath the sterile, white sheet—a knowledge of his body (and availability) and her touch. The situation in narrative and in reality that Lucy's and Ricky/Desi's bodies are married bodies helps to account for the physicalness of their comedy. Without the tension of the illicit or unknown, their situation comedy displays their sexuality freely, even innocently, without reference to it, as physical clowning. Nichols and May occupy no such "situation." Their routines ooze with a directness in language about sexual desire and fulfillment made wholly indirect through the absence of their bodies' interaction: they share with the bourgeois families they trash in "Bach to Bach" "proximity, but no relating." What Nichols and May make, then, is a comedy built on the joke that doubles their frame of reference, in their play between the stated and the implied scene they create. Always, their language and the world they construct from it, between them, mean multiple things, "this" and also "that."

Their language finds its doubling impulse, as well, in how Nichols and May swap words to play with accents, tones, inflections, rhythms of the types stepped inside for the course of the sketch. They make together a language of impersonation or "doubling" that insists on pushing Mike Nichols and Elaine May elsewhere, offstage. Nichols has said in a *New York Times* interview, "When we were improvising at our best, we actually did disappear." How this happened had everything to do with their standing before each other, caught up in the moment of playing together this language game of, what shall we make up/perform next? Nichols continues, "When you see that wild light in the other person's eyes, and you realize that you don't know how you got there, it's thrilling and sort of shocking. . . . You had to stop thinking instead of start thinking. You can't plan; you can steer toward conflict or seduction, but you have to give yourself to it."[9] If the script of situation comedy took away much of the shock Nichols describes that came from originating the comedy, the performance of the comedy *as a company* in *I Love Lucy* carries with it some of the same sense of surprise that comes from the interactions of this moment of performance between "us." While the words and movements may be anticipated, what comes out and how and what is prompted as a result make for the situation comedy's ability to share in improv's thrill in making comedy. Both partnered and company comedies insist on a turning of oneself over to the other(s), although improv's turning must go so deep that what's being wandered into isn't knowable until one's there, unlike situation comedy, which relies on anticipation.

I Love Lucy, with its series of physical gags and making of farce, depends on the choreography of a script, the tightness necessary to designing a physical joke constructed by a group. Nichols and May could afford to play with words because their bodies were not at stake. She didn't have to know he would be there to catch her. However, she did have to know he would be there to catch her *tone,* the direction of her plotting, the sense of what was at stake in the making of a moment as a thing that could only happen between them. Without that intensity of listening to the other, the scene couldn't be made. This is about a leave-taking that happens between two performers when they disappear inside what they're creating, and when we as audience give ourselves up to believing what they make. It has everything to do with how their language moves as a collective force, with a conviction and tightness like the most scripted physical jokes of *I Love Lucy,* or like the most verbal of situation comedies, *M*A*S*H* or *Frasier.* In "Bach to Bach," Nichols whistles their invented score, and then their improvised conversation-as-lyrics follows:

> MAY: You know it very well.
>
> NICHOLS: Better than myself in some ways. . . .
>
> MAY: It's serene. It has a kind of mathematical certainty that's almost sensual to me.
>
> NICHOLS: Yes, yes. An order. A finality, finally . . . Can you move over a little. I'm falling off the bed. . . .
>
> MAY: There is always another dimension to music. And, it's apart from life. I can never believe that Bartok died on Central Park West.
>
> NICHOLS: Isn't that ugly?
>
> MAY: Ugly, ugly, ugly.
>
> NICHOLS: Ya got enough room?
>
> MAY: Yah, I do now. Thanks . . . Oh, I love this part.
>
> NICHOLS: Yes, here, here. It almost hurts.
>
> MAY: Yes, beauty often does.
>
> NICHOLS: What a shock when I discovered Nietzsche. He said that in a way.
>
> MAY: In many ways when I read *Thus Spake Zarathustra,* a whole world opened for me.
>
> NICHOLS: I know *exactly* what you mean.
>
> MAY: Do you know what I mean?
>
> NICHOLS: I know exactly what you mean.
>
> MAY: I had never known such things existed.
>
> NICHOLS: Yes, yes, yes. A door opening.
>
> MAY: Got a cigarette?

This is Nichols and May doing pillow talk to "their" Bach. The clarity, the certainty of the piano in its rhythm and lightness of touch make it sound as if it is responding to a metronome. Here, though, the metronome has been replaced by the two voices that rise and fall with the music, that step back to allow the music to "speak," that time their phrases to each other and to the phrases of the piano as if they are part of this pseudo-Bach score. The repetition of "I know *exactly* what you mean" merges with the building climax of the music, whereas the words "a whole world opened for me" mark off the moment when the climax begins. The precise matching of tones becomes, as well, a matching in rhythm. Short phrases woven together with a constant beat, a quickness without a sense of rushing: the music frames their language and their words score the music. Not only could Nichols and May do impersonations of types, which require playing by ear the sounds that compose the verbal makeup of characters, they had timing. They shift from following the surges and falls of the music, which they narrate with the high tones of intellectualese, to undertoned references to the scene, as if in audience to themselves and the music. These undertoned references are the moments like "Can you move over a little. I'm falling off the bed," and "Got a cigarette?" The juxtaposition of these "Bachs"—the piano, the classical commentary—becomes the juxtaposition of these backs, side-by-side, in bed, smoking cigarettes, after sex. Both juxtapositions happen by virtue of timing. Music to words to bodies: we hear them because of the variations in their interactions, variations in when each is brought forward as if standing on its own, or held back from being present, or set side-by-side with the others. The timing of the in-bed references as withheld and then briefly dipped into marks off that part of the routine as what's unroutine here, as what's underneath "Bach to Bach."

When situation comedy makes its comedy from the play of voices, it patterns itself on the sounds of what Nichols and May improvised. The team's "thrown together" mixes of accents, tones, languages of professions or types or scenes, and rhythms appropriate to the conversations to match those scenes become *recipes* in the hands of situation comedy's comedy of repetition. In the perpetuated scene of sitcom, *this* is the rhythm of these characters, *this* is the tone they use, *this* is the language they generate. The variety that Nichols and May offer cannot be what situation comedy offers; however, the perpetual remake of the situation or variations on the scene are what the verbally driven situation comedy does provide, though rarely with the same "kind of mathematical certainty," even beauty.

How Happily Ever After?

The world of situation comedy defines a problematic happiness, problematic in its static nature, problematic in the types of characters or situations it defines, problematic even in what it takes happiness to be. And what happiness is taken to be is something like the equation, the same couple or friendship or family or small community equals happiness. What we see in situation comedy is returning, returning to stably defined characters and settings. What enables this return and this stability is the very structure that defines situation comedy's mode of performance: its weekly, thirty-minute, televised broadcast. But the returns stem as well from New Comedy's commitment to the possibility, even at times necessity, of working through contingency, accident, emergency, or just events demanding response, in ways that enable continuity. Events do not shatter or promote enduring change; instead, they underscore both the creativity/flexibility of the situation, which comes to understand how to play with, incorporate, or expel the unknown element, and also its stability, in that the situation endures. Does this make the situation smothering or antiprogressive? The amnesia that situation comedy indulges in in its desire most often to forget what happened the week before bespeaks a resistance to the progress that is defined by change through the integration of an accumulated response to the past. However, situation comedy offers its own logic of discrete progression: within each thirty-minute segment the whole force of New Comedy's plotting drive, from stability to chaos to stability, will have been felt. So that while what defines the situation at large—this marriage (however broadly defined)—will not have changed in the sense of having a discernible past and a movement toward a different future, its present moments (which are what situation comedy has: this thirty-minute sequence and this thirty-minute sequence, and so on) will have undergone radical change.

Marriage and situation-based narrative share the premise of the return and of stability: the same two or more characters carry on together in the face of ongoing challenges to their world, which may be smothering in the perpetual return of the same characters, setting, and range of conflicts/challenges—the same world. However, because that world defines itself as happy, it does not take itself to be smothering. What "happy" means in situation comedy is that this way of carrying on is chosen, desired, sought after as preferable to the disbanding of the partnership/situation or the reconfiguration of its makeup. Marriage works as the primary situation of situation comedy in the 1950s and '60s (and then in the decades to follow, mirroring the social changes of the times with some "as if" replacements—the workplace as the scene of marriage, life at home with aliens as the marriage, friends as the marriage) because it defines in its structures what the narrative frame most desires: the embodiment of intimate continuity. Further, if comedy requires a happy ending, then situation comedy as New Comedy insists that its marriages achieve states resembling happiness by their weekly close. And to get there, marriage must be taken to be essentially comic—not just comic in its restoration of order by the day's end, but potentially comic along the way. The presence of the laugh track is a nod toward situation comedy's nervousness about this premise. We find ourselves in the presence of invisible other viewers who understand the comedy and laugh and prompt us to see its comedy as well. These disembodied laughers also make it possible for us to laugh out loud because we're in their company, laughter being something hard, it seems, to do alone.

Given the lack of range of what constitutes these marriages or these situations, or given their ability to hold back the forces of change, it may be too difficult to consider these marriages and situations comic. However, part of what's at stake in these narratives' success in making comedy and happiness has to do with what is created, in addition to what is denied. *I Love Lucy* works particularly well as a model for what situation comedy attempts to achieve in its comfort with indeterminacy. As fixed as the world of Lucy and Ricky and their marriage seems to be, over the course of their exchanges, the place of order from which they began is not the one asserted by the end. Their interactions are about getting to a new world of sorts. The creation of that world emerges from Lucy's movement out of the living room into Ricky's club. Other ways of being are actively chosen, ways of being that involve hats, a certain amount of running, moments of deception, and the courageous presentation of one's body to the public. The places Lucy and Ricky start from resemble the closets that contain rags and bones of their past which when seen again, invested with a narrative of reinvention, become magic objects. Together, Ricky and Lucy transform their space into a playground, until the game stops, the set shatters, and everyone has to go home. However, we never truly know what that home is: what is the norm against which Lucy defines herself? and where are we at the end of an *I Love Lucy* episode?

After Lucy performs her "Lucito" gig at the club, we return to the apartment and Lucy still dressed in clown suit but wearing an apron and holding a broom. And this is what the interplay with Ricky has produced: the housewife and clown, the husband and straight man. Their comic play together, their marriage act together, prompts her to inhabit some other realm—that of the male/female, the at home/at theater occupant, the cleaner and creator of order/the maker of dirt and disorder—and, by contrast, makes him inhabit only the spaces they create together. Ricky doesn't get the job; he doesn't have the "chance" to leave their mutually derived playground for what is a mythical space in *I Love Lucy*, the television studio, a space apparently reserved for him alone but at some remove called "the future." In a switch that defines both the real background to the episode and how the situation comedy will create the precarious ground of mixed desires underlying a partnership, it is Lucy who is offered the television contract. "What are you going to do?" he asks. Her response sets us squarely inside the world they have come over the course of the episode to devise: avoiding a direct answer, Lucy refers to his expectations that she cook for him, clean, be the mama of his children. "About that . . ." We, like Ricky, are left to think that what she has to tell him will "resolve" everything, that she will stay at home with a child. However, the "about that" isn't "that" but "this," a pie. A pie, not a baby, is Lucy's offering.[10] While the episode ends with an object, it is not an innocent one, but one that carries with it the slapstick tradition. Will Ricky end the show with pie on his face, or will he eat this American pie (I'm imagining it's apple) from the hands of this American mama? Even though Lucy intends by her supplicating presentation of the pie the latter, we've learned that things go screwy in her hands. Lucy's response, therefore, is to undo Ricky's and our expectation, and to tell us that what she will do is reinvent "wife/mama" to be "clown," born out of the materials of their shared world.

That space we have entered, which is not just Lucy's alone but Lucy's and Ricky's, is some other setting called New Comedy. It is not a place of lost opportunities (a refused contract), or of confining walls (a living room), or of men only (a club with a performing band of Latin men). All of these settings will be broken up and made into something other by virtue of Lucy's and Ricky's, and sometimes Fred's and Ethel's, interaction within them. What would it mean in the world of *I Love Lucy* for Lucy to accept the television contract without Ricky? Essentially, such a consideration can have no meaning in the situation they create together; therefore, it gets no direct reply, only a joke.[11]

The indeterminacy of comedy's space, specifically of partnered comedy, is possible because of the stability of the marriage it uses as the groundwork from which to unmake and create. Team comedy, therefore, depends not just on the presence of rules and order so that they can be undone but also on the materials, the imaginations, and the desires to make something else, which must be negotiated between players. This is why a "green world" exists in Shakespeare's comedies and not in his tragedies. Part of what is so tragic about tragedy has to do with the absence of alternatives, which reflects as much a lack of imagination (given that usually only one person is doing the thinking) as it does a lack of real possibilities. Lucy and Ricky and situation comedy at their best work when they make possibilities out of revisited materials. Freud says about this in *Jokes and Their Relation to the Unconscious* that "[i]n a second group of technical methods used in jokes . . . we can single out as their common characteristic the fact that in each of them something familiar is rediscovered, where we might have expected something new. This rediscovery of what is familiar is pleasurable"—call that pleasure the "quiet sense of comfort" that familiarity brings.[12] Yet, what has been made or tried on from out of the familiar may be no longer wholly known; definition and clarity may not have asserted themselves to be triumphant by the end. Situation comedy, it seems, wants to take us somewhere else outside of itself and yet still in reference to itself. The marriage works because of its metamorphosing capabilities: tonight the marriage performs a clown sketch; next week the team may be playing Adam and Eve, the first Mr. and Mrs. Act. Situation comedy asserts that the known can be flexible and creative, and that a partnership can generate more ways of being by virtue of its numbers.

So that while the happiness situation comedy defines finds its source in stability, recurrence, and resistance to change, it also makes happiness out of almost anything, meaning out of its discovery that almost anything or anyone, no matter how well known, can be reinvented (with perhaps a redhead and a set of bongo drums), and played with, and so returned to. And it is that understanding of *being* which makes marriage possible, because it makes it creative, and it is that understanding of *marriage* which makes situation comedy possible, because it makes it comic. While at first glance we may want to dismiss the narrative problem of how to design the happiness of coupling because of its exploration by situation comedy, both the problem and its medium of greatest development suggest the unexpected—"green worlds" to call their own.

Claudette Colbert and Joel McCrea in *The Palm Beach Story*, Paramount, 1942
Courtesy Academy of Motion Pictures Arts and Sciences

CHAPTER 7

What It Means to Be
Nick and Nora

Joel McCrea: I mean sex didn't even enter into it?
Claudette Colbert: Oh, but of course it did, darling . . . Sex *always* has
something to do with it.

— *The Palm Beach Story,* 1942

This New Woman/This New Man

Preston Sturges opens *The Palm Beach Story* with a series of silent shots:
a hysterical, fainting maid, a minister kept waiting at the altar, a groom
being dressed by the best man in a taxi, two Claudette Colberts (one
locked, tied, and gagged in a closet, and one in full bridal regalia leaping
over the body of the maid and running outside), and the union of bride
and groom as they meet each other in mid-flight down the aisle, accom-
panied by the *William Tell* Overture mixed with Mendelssohn's bridal
march. As the finale of the prologue, the camera zooms back from the
couple joined at the altar and two doilies come into view, reading first "and
they lived happily ever after," followed by "or did they?" Credits and background complete, the acted present of the film begins five years after the
wedding with the wife walking out on the husband.

The orchestrated, frenetic pantomime of the opening does more than
pay homage to the silent film era: it plays an intertextual joke with yet
another, earlier image of Claudette Colbert. She has worn the same veil
and had the wind at her heels before. As the bride who laboriously dresses
for her impending marriage to King Wesley and reluctantly walks down
the aisle to join him in marriage, Colbert in *It Happened One Night*

An earlier version of this chapter first appeared as "Hollywood, 1934: 'Inventing' Romantic Comedy," in *Look Who's Laughing: Gender and Comedy,* ed. Gail Finney, Studies in
Humor and Gender, vol. 1 (Amsterdam: Gordon and Breach, 1994), 257–74.

suddenly bolts. In running from this marriage and choosing the real King, Clark Gable's Peter Warne, Colbert/Ellie Andrews jumps into a marriage that the narrative of *It Happened One Night* suggests (in the course of their previous interaction together) is a model of living "happily ever after." Elizabeth Kendall's provocative study *The Runaway Bride* focuses on this moment of the Capra film and this image as a way to locate the beginnings of a genre of Hollywood filmmaking—the romantic comedy—and with it a new conceptualization of America. However, if the 1934 *It Happened One Night* closes with a leap into the suggested possibility of a new form of comedy, the 1942 *The Palm Beach Story* opens with a leap into its closure. Kendall's recognition of the "runaway bride" locates the woman as the primary site of wonder of these comedies—she problematizes marriage by risking running away from and toward it; she discovers and expresses a sense of self-determination and freedom in this act of running toward and away from her object of desire.[1] Yet, what the woman comes to risk—both her self-discovery and her self-protection—find themselves matched in her partner's responses to her in these films. If this new woman runs, this new man stands still wearing an apron. Brought together by a shared talent for play and a shared desire for each other, the coupling partners of these films discover more of who each is by virtue of sometimes keeping and sometimes running away from the company of the other. It is, I would suggest, the display of a partnership that allows for strong, independent selves joined with the mutual desire to couple and to work at trying to understand what that means which makes these films romantic comedies and which makes them remarkable.

From 1934 to 1945, Hollywood invented narratives that did more than distract the country through the worst of the Depression years and World War II. While dramas, melodramas, westerns, musicals, adventure tales, science fiction, and comedies of solo and male teams had been portrayed in silent and then "talking" films, comedies that found their energy in the interactions of a romantic couple did not appear until the 1930s. They then dominated Hollywood for a decade. Frank Capra's *It Happened One Night*, Woody Van Dyke's *The Thin Man*, Howard Hawks's *Twentieth Century*, and Mark Sandrich's *The Gay Divorcee* opened in 1934 and collectively transformed how the narrative of movies constructed the intimacy of romance—through a comedy that invented itself before it knew what it was.[2] Shot in a scant four weeks, *It Happened One Night* was taken neither by its creators nor by reviewers to be a watershed work in the evolution of Hollywood filmmaking. However, within a month of its release audiences were flocking to it, the Greyhound Bus Company came back to life after near bankruptcy, and the makers of men's undershirts lost substantial business thanks to Gable's revealing himself to be bare chested when he scared Colbert to her side of "the walls of Jericho" (Sikov, *Screwball* 84). What the "It" was that happened was what the studios sought to reproduce, the "It" that enabled the transformation of Carole Lombard from the "Orchid Lady" of weeper films to "the first beautiful woman comic" (Kendall 138–39), and that prompted a national desire to see repeated portrayals of the marriage of Nick and Nora and the marriage in movement of Fred Astaire and Ginger Rogers.

With the institutionalization in Hollywood in 1934 of the Production Code (a response within the industry to a growing desire among the clergy to censor and control the "unhealthy" influence of films), which subjected all movies to a considerable fine if released without the Code's stamp of approval, the sultry, libidinous presence of Mae West, Jean Harlow, and Marlene Dietrich went underground. The platinum blonde seductress languishing in satin in the bedroom of the 1920s and early '30s was replaced by the working woman, or by the independent heiress whose common sense or need to break free from her dominating father or crazy family leads her to flee home. With restrictions placed on the explicit expression of desire, desire reinscribed its presence in the 1930s comedy through allusion or sublimation. If sex was to become aggression, then the sexual partners would become physical and verbal combatants; and if sex was to be couched in metaphor and humor, then it required a partnership where the joke could be shared.

What the presence of the Production Code encouraged, therefore, was that women become active players in their portrayals, that their words and actions be as vibrant and playful as their male partners'. Rather than being the vamp whose seductive powers overwhelm a necessarily diminished male, or the passive woman against whom a male acts and from whom he gains his assertion of self in the denial of hers, the woman of these 1930s comedies is set squarely in the position of equal in wit, energy, and resourcefulness to her male partner. Yet, the surprise of these films comes not just from their notions of what it means to be a woman but also from what occurs while the couple is in the midst of going at it with each other: each attains a deepened understanding of his- or herself, and a more complicated appreciation of the other, as a result of being in this partnership. Molly Haskell writes of the couples in these films: "[T]here is an equalization of obstacles and a matching of temperaments. A man and a woman seem to prickle and blossom at each others' touch, seem to rub each other with and against the grain simultaneously, and, in the friction, in the light of each others' eyes, to know themselves for the first time" (*From Reverence* 126–27).

If the presence of the Production Code helped to take the woman out of the bedroom as her primary place of residence, get her a career (or if she is an heiress locate her on the road), and put her into a partnership with the man, the Depression made her the representative of a beleaguered, yet determined, even madcap possibility of America. The women stars who were surviving the Depression offered a sense of endurance, skepticism, wit, and common sense. Claudette Colbert, Barbara Stanwyck, Ginger Rogers, Rosalind Russell, Jean Arthur, Myrna Loy, Carole Lombard, Katharine Hepburn, and Irene Dunne portrayed varying roles from the "party girl" who endures anything to survive to the heiress who tries anything to find meaning, even if that just means learning how to dunk doughnuts. Cary Grant, Clark Gable, Gary Cooper, William Powell, Fred Astaire, Jimmy Stewart, Spencer Tracy, Robert Montgomery, Joel McCrea, and Henry Fonda display an energy equal to their costars but most often act as the ones in the partnership to whom things are done. They learn what it means to be the "dupes" of the woman's jokes, and in so doing discover their own vulnerability.[3] Dressed in women's robes, cooking breakfast, tongue-tied, playing the servant, befuddled, disastrously clumsy, these men find themselves unhinged by the sheer presence of these women and discover their own desire for irreverence and screwiness by being in relation to them.

Although vaudeville from the 1890s on had introduced the male/female comedy team to America as a "domesticated" humor in response to the growing numbers of women in the audience, never did it portray the couple as equals in the ability to jest, and never did the woman gain a comedic role as wise-cracking, sexual, and strong. When the Palace could no longer support vaudeville because its audiences had migrated to movie theaters by 1932, vaudeville's departing image of the woman in male/female comedy was of the character Gracie—an illogical, childlike figure in her own world, a world into which the audience could peer with husband George and wonder knowingly, how she could be so idiotic.[4] The model of the woman comic as "dumb" was not the one followed in these films of New Comedy: Carole Lombard in *My Man Godfrey* and Katharine Hepburn in *Bringing Up Baby* may be "screwy," but they are not without the ability to discern how to use a situation to their own best advantage.

The women of the films of romantic comedy rely on the quickness of their wits to bring their partners to the recognition that they have met at least their equals and can at best hope for a draw.

Where vaudeville left off in its initiation of the male/female comedy team, these films pressed forward in their reinvention of coupling as the shared site for the mutual production of comedy. Superficially, what emerged was a reversing of roles: a seeming "feminization" of the man and a "masculinization" of the woman. But more provocatively, the woman offered the Depression audience a catharsis that the man could not, and the woman and the man teamed together worked through what neither could address alone.[5] If the Depression emasculated the man by removing his traditional sites of status and power—his work and his body (where could he assert himself economically and against whom could he vent his rage?)—it invented in the woman an emotional and intellectual resourcefulness. Further, in softening his edges and defining hers more, the Depression reinvented the couple as the site for expressing rage/passion and for redefining the self in relation to the self's partner. Coupling, therefore, became an arena which not only endured the Depression but flourished as the "entity" that defined another New Comedy: marriage found a narrative for its expression.

George Meredith's "An Essay on Comedy" provides a theoretical frame which suggests that Capra's adaptation of Samuel Hopkins Adams's "Night Bus" as *It Happened One Night* reveals comedy's highest form. In Meredith's model, comedy depends upon the freedom and equality of the woman in relation to the man. His description of the evolved woman of comedy and the comedy which emerges as a result of this evolution stands as a working definition of the form that Hollywood's romantic comedies of the 1930s takes:

The heroines of comedy are like women of the world, not necessarily heartless from being clear-sighted; they seem so to the sentimentally reared, only for the reason that they use their wits, and are not wandering vessels crying for a captain or pilot. Comedy is an exhibition of their battle with men, and that of men with them; and as the two, however, divergent, both look on one object, namely, life, the gradual similarity of their impressions must bring them to some resemblance. The comic poet dares to show us men and women coming to this mutual likeness; he is for saying that when they draw together in social life their minds grow liker; just as the philosopher

discerns the similarity of boy and girl, until the girl is marched away
to the nursery. Philosopher and comic poet are of a cousinship in the
eye they cast on life. (15)

Frank Capra (*It Happened One Night, Mr. Deeds Goes to Town, Mr. Smith
Goes to Washington, You Can't Take It With You*), Leo McCarey (*The Awful
Truth, Love Affair*), George Stevens (*Alice Adams, Swing Time, Penny Ser-
enade*), Gregory La Cava (*My Man Godfrey, Stage Door, Fifth Avenue Girl*),
Howard Hawks (*Twentieth Century, Bringing Up Baby, His Girl Friday*),
George Cukor (*Holiday, The Philadelphia Story*), and Preston Sturges (*The
Lady Eve, The Palm Beach Story*) are Meredith's comic poets. The directors,
working in collaboration with the screenwriters and the stars themselves,
created narratives that re-create the partners of a marriage. As childless
couples (though often with a dog: William Powell and Myrna Loy's Asta,
Cary Grant and Irene Dunne's Mr. Smith, Cary Grant and Katharine
Hepburn's George—all played by the same wirehaired terrier) freed from
domestic drudgery, these partners are liberated to assert themselves as
individuals, discover the other, and experience a passion that translates not
into a blissful harmony but rather into a kind of struggle between giving
oneself over to the other and resisting the offer. While there is no woman
among the directors of this genre (which is more, I think, a comment on
the impossibility of being a woman director at the time than a reflection
on the genre's resistance to female direction), different women writers—
Vina Delmar for *The Awful Truth,* Gladys Lehman for *There's Always a
Woman, Good Girls Go to Paris, Hired Wife,* Dorothy Parker (with Alan
Campbell) for *The Moon's Our Home, Woman Chases Man, Weekend for
Three,* Bella Spewack (with Samuel Spewack) for *My Favorite Wife,* and
Virginia Van Upp for *Café Society, Honeymoon in Bali*—made names for
themselves scripting these films and brought their felt presence to the
shaping of the language of the films. If the focus of the comedy relied
on what happened between the starring couple, Capra, Stevens, La Cava,
McCarey, and Sturges entered into creative partnerships with their women
stars. Informal collaborations emerged between them which helped to
enable the film's vision of these women to be not just constructions of male
fantasy but companions, co-creators of their own comedy and their own
visions of themselves.[6]

The activity of "inventing" by naming a genre insists on recognition of
a new form of narrative. That the coinage of the phrase "screwball comedy"
has been traced to Paramount Studios (in their efforts to make identifiable

and therefore to sell their new productions) and to a reviewer of or publicist for *My Man Godfrey* (1936)[7] makes apparent the consciousness of those connected with the films of their radical difference and how that difference needed to be accounted for by name. And yet that difference was to be marked by a word borrowed from baseball—"screwball."[8] Here was a distinctly American genre making itself up. Mark Winokur asserts in *American Laughter* that what is so American about this genre's invention of itself has to do not with baseball but with assimilation, the assimilation of "two ex-ethnics" (for example, Powell in his persona prior to *The Thin Man* as Italian villain, and Loy in the former role of oriental siren) into the Anglo, romantic couple (225–26). The source of their screwiness is not in the way they talk or look (in fact, quite the opposite, given the beauty of these couples and their mid-Atlantic speech), but that they say and do ridiculous things to each other, in a manner that excludes others from their world and insists on mutual acceptance between them: this is who we are, and this is why we're nuts for each other. For Winokur, screwball comedies work as narratives both about the exclusion of others outside the couple and about the inclusion of the idiosyncratic selves who make up this marriage, in short, as "fantasy account[s] of immigrant assimilation."[9] As suggestive as Winokur's claim is, it requires a willingness to substitute "assimilation" for "marriage" as a way of reading what these films are about.

What these films give us most self-evidently about themselves, what they define as the chief feature of their "screwiness," is their language: they are thick with voices. Rapid exchanges abound where dialogue overlaps and produces, as if chemically from an attraction of opposites, responsive sparks and memorable one-liners, whereas extended, uninterrupted speeches are absent. Prolonged tracking shots without words are rare. Verbal intercourse is the primary distinguishing feature of this new form—conversations work as performances of vibrant, uncontrolled, interactive, sublimated sexuality. Slapstick, cross-dressing, fetishizing of body parts, are additional markers of the form that, like the frenetic outpouring of language, fall into the narrative not from requirements of logical plotting but from the sexual energy of coupling. And while courtship proves to be a time of ordeal, the ordeal is not resolved in marriage. Topically, marriage is a state that screwball comedy depicts as frequently as courtship, but without acknowledging victors of or solutions to conflict. Instead, these films understand marriage as a condition of discord and of passion, which does not lead to marriage's end but rather to its continued return. Hence, Stanley Cavell, in *Pursuits of Happiness,* defines the comedy of remarriage to be a genre within screwball;[10] in *Bringing Up Baby* (along with *The Lady Eve, It Happened One Night, The Philadelphia Story, His Girl Friday, Adam's Rib,* and *The Awful Truth*),

> the validity of marriage takes a willingness for repetition, the willingness for remarriage. The task of the conclusion is to get the pair back into a particular moment of their past lives together. No new vow is required, merely the picking up of an action which has been, as it were, interrupted; not starting over, but starting again, finding and picking up the thread. Put a bit more metaphysically: only those can genuinely marry who are already married. It is as though you know you are married when you come to see that you cannot divorce, that is, when you find your lives simply will not disentangle. If your love is lucky, this knowledge will be greeted with laughter.[11]

If comedy is fundamentally a festival of renewal, then the marriage actively chosen and desired over time works as a site for comedy's display in being about the willing renewal of itself. The clown comedy of Chaplin, Keaton, Lloyd, and Langdon sets off the male comic as alone in and victimized by an indifferent, at times malevolent world where accident forces him to submit to the beatings of a universe over which he has little control.[12] Rising again after suffering stinging pratfalls and physical humiliations, the clown comics display the renewal of endurance and reciprocation—they stand up and return to others the blows that were delivered to them. The talking comedy of a pair of lovers borrows the physical blows and pranks, but pares them down to the size of jest between domestic partners and adds to them the verbal games that make each speaker dependent on the presence of the other to talk back.[13] After the technological advances of the 1927 *The Jazz Singer,* in which sound is synchronized with image, the talkers of these films defined what it means to be a "talkie," namely, a movie about talking. The choice by these partners to continue to play together, to construct together a world which they make with the interaction of their voices, hands, and bodies, then destroy and remake again, fashions their marriage as a shared, alive creation, more their own than a child, more renewable because changeable than the repertoire of acts of a solitary figure facing the world alone. Yet, if the silent male comic is set loose in a world that works as a backdrop against which he can showcase his comedy, the comic couple is by no means set off in isolation, much as they may at times desire it. The world, whether it be a neutral ground like the road, the sea, or Connecticut, or places of attachment and identification like the home, place of work, or New York City, functions as the setting for these marriages, which are not confined to a home or private space. With at least one partner wealthy enough not to worry about a steady income (or if they work, it functions as another setting for marriage), the boundary between public and private blurs, enabling the marriage to spill into unexpected locations. The life of the marriage fills the narrative with itself.

Why is it, though, that these marriages justify or enable these films? Morse Peckham's comment that comedy "celebrates the sense of adequacy" (140) leads me to wonder, What makes these marriages adequate? What precludes the narrative's following through on abandoning the old partnership for the unknown possibility of the new? What creates in these films a sense that this comedy is good enough?

Comedy of Performance

As a way into considering what makes screwball comedy "adequate," which is another way of asking what makes its marriages adequate, I turn to the openings of two of its films to bring us closer to the particularity of screwball's comedy. In the way that novels cue us to attend differently to the first conversations of couples by distinguishing their talk to be exceptional, and subsequently reveal how their opening exchanges set the pattern for their speech and the relationships that follow, how screwball films portray the couple's introductions to each other and to us, their initial looks and sounds and what they do when first together, defines the pattern of their comedy.

I return to the opening conversation of Nick and Nora, filmed as Woody Van Dyke's *The Thin Man*, in order to reconsider it as an instance of screwball comedy. The "translation" of the conversations in Hammett's novel into the comic cross-fire routines of the Thin Man films reveals the adaptability of the Nick and Nora "structure," that structure's shared presence in fiction and film. Further, it declares Nick and Nora to be both representative of the couples who "perform happiness" in narrative and distinctive in their flexibility and appeal.[14] Woody Van Dyke's *The Thin Man* (1934) and Mark Sandrich's *Top Hat* (1935), with Fred Astaire and Ginger Rogers, helped not just to define a genre of comic narrative but also to define partnerships that, like the teaming of Hepburn and Tracy, created marriages on film through multiple films over many years. Subsequent to

Fred Astaire and
Ginger Rogers in
Top Hat, RKO, 1935

Courtesy Academy of
Motion Pictures Arts
and Sciences

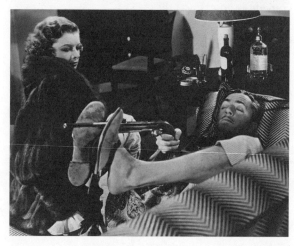

William Powell and
Myrna Loy in
The Thin Man,
MGM, 1934

Courtesy Academy of
Motion Pictures Arts
and Sciences

The Thin Man, William Powell and Myrna Loy would star together in thirteen films, including five more in the Thin Man series; likewise, in response to the audience's excitement at their dancing of the carioca in *Flying Down to Rio,* Fred Astaire and Ginger Rogers would do ten movie musicals together. These performers' early appearances in *The Thin Man* and *Top Hat,* respectively, established their images as couples on film: Powell and Loy are sophisticated, wealthy, and bemused together in the face of a surrounding world of corruption; Astaire's arch theatricality is tempered by Rogers's version of American pragmatism and lack of pretension. But while solving crimes or performing in shows, they are primarily couples who play together. And it is how they play, their different forms of team performance in the midst of how they work, which transforms their world and lives together to be comic, to insist on their marriages' renewal, to reveal models for how to see and differentiate their form of New Comedy and its romance.

Jokes require a verbal or visual feedline to set them up and a punchline to "punch out" their resolution or reveal the joke (Josefsberg 1). There is a kind of violent energy required in joking if it is to "knock" us as its over-hearers into the recognition that this is play. William Powell and Myrna Loy perform such a knocking in their separate joke entrances to *The Thin Man*. The camera removes Nick and Nora from the linear plot-telling of the film by introducing each from the back. Powell's three bartenders, who mirror us as his audience (though we only get to see his back), watch and listen as he provides the punchline to his own joke:

> WILLIAM POWELL: You see, Vic, the importance is in the rhythm. You should always have rhythm to your shaking. A Manhattan you shake to foxtrot, a Bronx to two-step, a dry martini you always shake to waltz time.

Delivering a monologue, Powell shakes and pontificates on dancing rhythms (the punchline), not to dance (as is everyone else around him— the feedline) but to drink. Rituals complete—shaking, giving the drink to the waiter, being given the drink by the waiter—he at last drinks. Sur-rounded by shouting hotel attendants dropping packages, led by Asta, Myrna Loy's entrance to us and to Powell presents her from back to front, but in a reversal of roles. While there were no great slapstick female comics like Chaplin, or teams like Laurel and Hardy, Loy when at last filmed from the front falls forward, drops packages (the feedline), and brushes herself off with "Women and children first, boys" (the punchline). Singly, each is capable of telling his or her own joke; each, therefore, is a comic, which makes one an appropriate match for the other. Yet, neither is as funny alone as they are together. The elegant Loy collapses while the equally elegant Powell gazes on, and offers neither to assist her nor to disown her. The delay of their full frontal appearances suggests that these two will turn their backs on this plot, that the detective plot is not ulti-mately the one that most interests them; and that it is coming into the presence of the other that prompts or merits the full "frontal" attention of each, which means the offering of a joke.

With the arrival of a worthy partner, a dialogue can begin. Nick is

Myrna Loy, Maureen O'Sullivan, William Powell, and Asta in *The Thin Man*, MGM, 1934
Courtesy Wisconsin Center for Film and Theater Research

ultimately alone when in the company of fawning bartenders and sweet ingenues; Nora has no need of hotel men gathering around her as if, like a child, she needed assistance. His response, "Say, what is the score?" reveals that he is the one in the room who knows what to say and do, which makes him her partner. Nick does not act the part of the husband who insists on the fragility of his wife, and Nora insists that her fall act as the feedline to their ensuing joke which they construct together:

MYRNA LOY: Oh, so it was you he was after.
WILLIAM POWELL: Hello, sugah.
MYRNA LOY: He dragged me into every gin mill on the block.
WILLIAM POWELL: I had him out this morning.

Using the terse rhythm of almost uniformly monosyllabic vaudeville patter, the two construct a kind of song out of their bantering in which gaining information is not the object of their speech. Rather, it is the pleasure each takes in knowing how to respond and in hearing the other's response that drives the conversation, gives it the ring of private delight which the voices of Powell and Loy make so evident in their delivery as the ones who have the good fortune to be the players of this comedy team. The pleasure of hearing their verbal juggling comes from its marked difference to the ordinarily slow, irregular exchanges of words in a conversation, from the sense of excitement that brevity and a fast pace generate. Whereas a slow rhythm creates a thoughtful, plaintive adagio and sonata, quicker tempos inspire sprightly allegros—the musical display of comedy. The rapid, rhythmic beat of Powell's and Loy's speech sharpens the comedy of their words' meanings with a comedy of sound.

Finding puns, jesting at jealousy, using the other's body as a mirror of their own, the two continue their routine after the departure of the ingenue who has brought with her to the table the problems of the plot, which they immediately dismiss in the fast, edged dialogue introduced in Dashiell Hammett's novel and developed further in the film's remaking of the couple into a team:

MYRNA LOY: Pretty girl.
WILLIAM POWELL: Very nice type.
MYRNA LOY: You got types?
WILLIAM POWELL: Only you darling. Lanky brunettes with wicked jaws.

MYRNA LOY: Who is she?

WILLIAM POWELL: Oh darling, I was hoping I wouldn't have to answer that.

MYRNA LOY: Go on.

WILLIAM POWELL: Dorothy is really my daughter. You see it was spring in Venice, and I really didn't know what I was doing. We're all like that on my father's side.

MYRNA LOY: By the way, how is your father's side?

WILLIAM POWELL: Oh, it's much better, thanks, and yours?

MYRNA LOY: Say, how many drinks have you had?

WILLIAM POWELL: This will make six martinis.

MYRNA LOY: All right. Will you bring me five more martinis, Leo, and line them up right here.

WILLIAM POWELL: Hmmm.

Dismissing along with the detective plot of the film the sexual threat of a "pretty girl," the two reduce her to an old joke ("Dorothy is really my daughter") and then to a pun ("How is your father's side?"); the gendered roles of "jealous wife" and "duplicitous husband" are undone. This is not about a threatened marriage, but it is about playing with the elements of a context, working them over to discover what games can be constructed from them. Without their mutual presence as a team, there could be no play about the "sexual threat" of a third interrupting their partnering; similarly, punning requires two voices to work the transformation from one meaning of a word to another with the repetition of the word in a different context. Loy plays the "straight man" who questions here, and allows Powell the verbal freedom to design his own fun in response; she is also the partner who through finding the pun turns the joke over to her benefit. They both therefore "score," and their making of comedy is an ongoing game where the role of "winner" repeatedly changes and shifts.

If the language game of joking between two people necessarily places one in the position of laying the groundwork for the context and topic of the joke, and the other in the position of making the joke out of those elements, then the joke must work as a shared production, like a conversation. Yet, it also works as a physical creation designed between the team who must present their bodies to each other as other elements of the joke. When Loy and Powell face each other to speak the above lines, the camera films them from the side and watches their mirroring acts of first leaning their heads into their hands and then lowering their hands to signal the end of the fantasized reverie. Their play insists that one's physical identity be brought into line with the other's, that that much care be paid to recognizing the motions of the other as a way to signal how completely the joke is understood, how mutually constructed it is. Loy's act of lining up the five martinis to equal Powell's brings an embodied closure to this scene about their balancing act of wit in words, gesture, and inebriation, a scene that finds itself mimicked and redesigned (though less powerfully because more soberly) throughout the five films to follow.

The gestures of Powell and Loy suggest a way in which a joke works as a mutually derived, physical construction in the mirroring of bodies. The films of Fred Astaire and Ginger Rogers bring that element of team comedy to its full flowering. In *Top Hat*, the opening scene of this couple together, what the movie will mean by their being together is revealed when they dance together for the first time to Irving Berlin's "Isn't It a Lovely Day." They perform a "routine"—an elaborately staged joke built from a sketch about an idea that gets repeated in varying guises as "their" routine. Its repetition makes it routine (Astaire and Rogers's routine is, of course, the wooing of the woman in dance), as does its being a dance (something that must be staged, learned from repeated practice), but what could feel *less* routine, less like the everyday than the experience of watching a couple break into dance? There is a magic to this routine that stems from its un-routineness. Whereas the aura of Powell and Loy's unroutine routine comes from their ability to trade remarks and the delight they take in doing so, Rogers and Astaire offer instead the trade they make between their bodies. Their feet sound their wit, creativity, and talent. Powell and Loy's quick, abbreviated rhythm of exchanged speech becomes with Astaire and Rogers the bantering of taps, which at a faster, more intensified, more athletic pace translate the voice swapping of a talking comedy team into the tap swapping of a dancing comedy team.

Tap dancing, above all forms of Western dance partnering, insists on a noisy, talkative interaction of bodies in which gendered movements (like that of a woman performing on toe or a man leaping) are bypassed for the androgynous noisemaking and motions of the taps. Wearing the same shoes and equally free to explore the same moves, both partners challenge one another to see how far the taps of the other will lead each to perform. Tap finds its great era of expression in films of the 1930s, thanks to the "talkies" that highlight its sound, the depth of talent of tappers available from vaudeville and Broadway, and the desire of contemporaries to see this fashionable, American invention of dancers "having it out" romantically in tap. Astaire and Rogers, using the choreography of Hermes Pan, appropriate this as their form of expression, their way of making New Comedy.

In the Rogers and Astaire routine, repetition is a fundamental device that joins the two into a couple. First Rogers whistles the second stanza of "Isn't It a Lovely Day" after Astaire has finished whistling the first stanza. When he saunters away from her to trace a circle before her, an act beckoning her to join him, she does so behind him, putting first one hand in her pocket to match his and then the other, as he does so. The repetition of the joke "Walk this way" (uttered by the butler whom guests follow imitating the butler's gait) becomes an unspoken jest here. It is not a trope of deprecation of the imitated Astaire, but the signal that what he does she can do, that she is there not to be passively entertained but to join him as his partner in this act of play. Imitation in step acts like the rhyming of a song. There's a kind of giddiness that accompanies rhyming words and rhyming feet, something madcap that gets at the nature of play, its desire for the screwy.

We can think of their dances, which engage not in dueling acts of escalating destruction but in competing feats of art, as the other side of slapstick—the nonviolent comedic choreographing of bodies interacting. Prompted by the number of taps, the degree of difficulty of tapping at the toe or heel in relation to the position of the body, the intermingling of tapping to turning, the speed of execution, Astaire and Rogers throughout their routine modify their individual motions according to what the other is doing. They trade off who leads a step and who follows, whether to initiate a new move or to imitate what the other has done. Staging the opening bars of "Isn't It a Lovely Day" as a dialogue in imitation and in one-upmanship, the two circle around each other but resist touching. This activity of challenge tapping is a variation of doing a play on words, where the sounds of words themselves, their double meanings, their foreignness, become the grounds for generating a routine out of confusion, as in Abbott and Costello's "Who's on first?" or out of private understanding, as in Sid Caesar's imitation Japanese and its comprehension by Imogene Coca. A play on words works here as a play on the sounds of shoes through replication and transformation, games that challenge one pair of shoes first to understand the other's delivery and then to do the same or better. The two only break into unison movements, which face front to the camera, side by side to each other, when the music escalates into a crescendo, as if this is where the music/their moving has been leading—a collapsing of the dialogue into a monologue of sounds.

Fred Astaire and Ginger Rogers sing and dance to
"Isn't It a Lovely Day" in *Top Hat*, RKO, 1935
Courtesy Movie Star News

With claps of thunder and the music's arrival at its fastest tempo and
most intense, complete execution of its melody, the dancers at last touch
with a fury that sets them swinging in dance position across the stage.
Compared to his partnering with Rita Hayworth, Audrey Hepburn, Leslie
Caron, or even Cyd Charisse, there is a fullness to the force Astaire uses
in his partnering with Rogers. This is as much about copartnered sex as
it is about strength. Katharine Hepburn's often quoted remark, "Astaire
gave her elegance, and Rogers gave him sex appeal," highlights what differentiates Rogers from Astaire's other partners: her presence as a sexual
force prompts him to meet her as a fully engaged sexual partner—this is
her doing.[15] About the relation between the woman, sex, and comedy,
Kathleen Rowe writes:

> The very centrality of sex to comedy and the comedic agenda of
> renewing life open up space for the presence of women that does
> not exist in the more masculine world of tragedy. Because sex is to
> comedy what death is to tragedy, the heterosexual couple that is the
> mainstay of Hollywood narrative film is also one of comedy's most
> fundamental conventions. In comedy, sex is not a means toward

knowledge or transcendence of self, as in tragedy, but social. Sex is part of comedy's overall attack on repression and a celebration of bodily pleasure. ("Comedy, Melodrama" 45)

What Rogers and Astaire dance together is an interactive, shared "bodily pleasure." He throws her around him and she sturdily continues; what they create between them is not about modifying energy or treating the other as less than one's equal in force, presence, or passion. Toward the close of the dance, Rogers even lifts Astaire in a knee-high turn as he has done to her. Their ability to mime each other in unison dancing, their responsive motions back and forth, their delayed repetitions of each other make their bodies seem tied to a string, tied to each other. What we see is their understanding of their own and each other's body. This understanding is not just about how another body looks or feels against one's own but about how it moves, how it takes shape in the world, joined through a deep connection within to knowing how to match one's own body with it to create a third body in motion composed out of the two, a sexualized body in dance.

The sound humor of the taps merges with the sight humor of the bodies discovering themselves and each other to create, like Powell and Loy, a comedy that is mutually constructed and embodied in contrasting visual and aural forms. And like Powell and Loy, Astaire and Roger's mutual knowledge of how the other plays and their well-matched talent for being able to run with the joke enable them to create a shared comedy constructed from their equalizing talent and desire. With whom would each member of the team more want to be than the partner who challenges and forces a deeper discovery of him- or herself by virtue of being in the other's presence? When Astaire and Rogers shake hands as the final act of their dance, they introduce themselves to each other, congratulate each other on their performances, and contract themselves to a binding relationship—a marriage in dance.

The movies take these opening encounters between Powell and Loy, Astaire and Rogers as models for what their marriages are, and then recast them by discovering variations of how they play. Each film's comedy finds its source in the couple's interactive creation and re-creation of this repartee; the film's romance asserts itself in its wonder that these two have found each other, and that they are able to do so easily what no one else in their narrative universes can even attempt, let alone see in the case of Astaire and Rogers or hear in that of Loy and Powell. What these couples do together is private. Whether it be the athleticism of Hepburn and Grant, the desire to con and be conned of Fonda and Stanwyck, the talent for slapstick and for laughter of Grant and Dunne, the ability to argue of Tracy and Hepburn, the delight in banter of Powell and Loy, the pleasure of making a dance between Rogers and Astaire—these couples separate themselves from the others of their worlds by virtue of their gifts for what they can do together, and out of a desire to be alone with each other. Apart from each other they are not what they are together, and together they are not only adequate as a marriage/comedy act but unmatched, which is to say, perfectly matched.

The Marriage Act

What the films of screwball comedy want to tell, the drive of their narratives, is of marriage spilling out frenetically into all locations, making all spaces available for its playing out, as in Hitchcock's *Mr. and Mrs. Smith;* of marriage incorporating public events into its privacy and working itself out between the bedroom and the courtroom, as in Cukor's revival of the form in *Adam's Rib;* of marriage over cocktails and witty repartee set against a world of crime, as in W. S. Van Dyke's *The Thin Man;* and of marriage on the dance floor working through the miscommunications by word in dance, as in Mark Sandrich's *Top Hat.* The films find their narratives of marriage of continuous interest: marriage either constitutes the plot's focus, or the text repeatedly returns to the marriage regardless of its connection to the plot. Letting go of the desire for a linear progression of storytelling—where the known is left behind, the novel is sought, and the energy of the narrative is sustained in a movement of "progress" by the individual—screwball comedies create a desire for circles of familiarity. Figuring the woman and the man as a community of two set against or within a larger community, this version of New Comedy joins highly defined and differentiated individuals in an interactive relation of sexual opposition and attraction. This charged interaction of the woman and man creates an ongoing sense of energy, surprise, and movement in the narrative from the couple's continuous playing out of themselves when set side by side. As the team performs its interaction, something gets worked through without the movement ending; where one cycle ends another begins as the marriage explores itself and the partners explore themselves in a middle realm somewhere between beginnings and ends.

When a narrative allows repetitions and returns, it reveals a distinctive form of narrative desire, the wish for more, the pleasure of that more; the screwball comedy discovers happiness in an intimacy found pleasurable and returned to. Taking delight in marriage, the screwball film portrays the pleasure found in the performances of married people, in their play together as a couple and as individuals in response to one another, and in the sustaining power of that delight. That it took an economy of privilege and of focus in these films to enable the luxury of exploring marriage without financial worry, without children—that such luxury was in fact possible because of these exclusions—makes this exploration a site of privilege, not of the everyday. And yet marriage defines itself to be a site of the everyday; Kierkegaard asserts this when he asks in *Stages on Life's Way,* "What is as plain and everyday as marriage?" (118). Extraordinary times— the Depression, the coming into being of the talkies, and the instituting of the Production Code in the film industry—collaborated to make marriage a location of the fantasy of filmmaking, transforming it from a story so ordinary it could not be told to an everyday story laced with the possibility of the remarkable. "You see, every once in a while I find myself dancing," Fred Astaire tells Ginger Rogers when they first meet in *Top Hat*—an ordinary feeling made extraordinary in the performance of a couple at play.

Conclusions

To conceive of happiness as not just an "end" but as a series of makings, or as a series of interactions with life's happenings, or as what can accompany the process of play rescues it from a position of being the chief virtue of those who cannot tolerate pain, or as so idealized that it can never be attained. To be a maker of ordinary happiness means to know how to create and re-create attachment to the object world, to know continuity and endurance over time, to embrace accident and fortune, to "achieve repose in the face of both joy and sorrow" (Schaar 236), to find in repetition the possibility for creation, to desire what is present, to discover spaces in the day for performance, and perhaps most profoundly to have the capacity to be startled by, as Vicki Hearne calls it, "the simple and astounding knowledge that others exist" (xvi). While that recognition can prompt a sense of threat—this is the Robinson Crusoe response to seeing a footprint after twenty-five years of solitude—it can also lead to the desire to work out what it means to be together and still be oneself. It can even on a good day lead to a sense of elation: I can know myself more deeply in relation to others; I need not know my life only in the context of myself alone. One of the finest challenges that can grow from the sensation of being in a partnership is finding play—our play—how we create together our ways of imagining ourselves, the world, us. And I take happiness to be a creation that results from this creativity.

What drives my work is the desire to name and be present to the nature and manifestations of a couple's pleasures in narrative: the pleasures of coming to shared knowledge, and the demonstrations of that knowledge in speech; the pleasures of interactive invention and of recognition (that we had the good luck to find each other), and the performances of that invention and recognition in making team comedy. The challenge of the team "who make together," which means who are alive to the moment and to the formation of being in relation, is to discover just what they do together and how. And that is the necessity, even the urgency, of partnering: to make these discoveries that come from two people being present to each other, that cannot be made otherwise. Without these discoveries, the fact of another becomes the Crusoe burden/threat; and with them comes an ordinary happiness made from what a partnership likes about itself, finds surprising about itself. How a narrative displays what the partnership finds pleasurable reveals itself in the couple's routines (what the narrative will return to again and again), or in their performance of a unique piece (what the narrative will highlight as spectacle). And I take those refrains and spectacles to be at their heart comic.

Throughout this book I've considered what constitutes a partnership of mutuality, why that way of being is chosen, and how narratives display its formation. Informing this concern has been a central, if unstated, tension between charting a path toward knowing oneself as a member of a community and achieving individuation through separation. I take that to be a central polarity in most social thought, one which leads Freud, for instance, to theories of attachment to and separation from the breast, or of the conflict between Eros and Aggression; and Darwin to a theory of natural selection; and by contrast, Kropotkin to an evolutionary theory of mutual assistance. While narratives more easily tell stories of the individual consciousness struggling with the fact of others, and with feelings of threat to the individual ego which interaction brings, narratives also have strategies for displaying the drive toward community-defined selves. If there is truth to Winnicott's assertion that it is in play that we discover the self and the other, then we must attend to the traces in life and in narrative that reveal play happening; otherwise, our vision of what constitutes the self will be limited at best. Narratives, as cultural artifacts, reflect not just the individual pursuit of happiness but the cultural pursuit of happiness as well, which includes the notion of community happiness.

Freud imagines lovers as a community apart from all others and as part of the larger community of culture, and they must continuously negotiate the boundaries between the two. He writes, for instance, "When a love-relationship is at its height there is no room left for any interest in environment; a pair of lovers are sufficient to themselves, and do not even need the child they have in common to make them happy" (*Civilization* 65). And, "This rift between them [love and civilization] seems unavoidable. . . .

It expresses itself at first as a conflict between the family and the larger community to which the individual belongs" (58). *Civilization and Its Discontents* opens our eyes to the oppositions between lovers and culture that arise from lovers' resistance to integration and culture's demand for integration. We take this model of boundary skirmish to be what sets these communities in blind or hostile relation to one another. However, what I'm suggesting is that the lovers who come to know themselves as a community of two or who come to negotiate what it means to move between the boundaries of ego, partnership, and culture need not just be understood as occupying a position of "rift" from the larger community that holds them. The small community of lovers and the large community of culture always stand in relation to one another, whether acknowledged or not.

To consider how lovers in their pursuits of happiness serve as a model for a culture's pursuit of happiness requires a shift of imagination. Lovers in narratives "at the height" of being in a world apart grant us a remarkable look at their happiness-making because of their distance from the larger world that holds them. We peer in at them and wonder what it might feel like to be them, act like them, know what they know because of how we know them in their separation from us. Set apart from all else, engrossed in their play, these narrative couples display with an intense clarity, even purity, a small-community model of how people, through acts of performance, discover the pleasures of being in relation. And we can learn from the focus of their intersubjectivity, stripped bare of all else, about the possibilities of what might happen when, for a moment at least, one is wholly present to oneself and another. The lovers who know the struggles of integration (in resistance or acceptance), who must negotiate the complex pulls of being members of many worlds, mirror for us the being-in-the-world difficulty of straddling different boundaries. Through them we experience an intersubjectivity that is more crowded, more dispersed, more distracted, probably more like our own. From studying the narrative couples who always know themselves to be part of another community and to be apart from it, we can learn about why the movement between boundaries feels threatening, or enlivening, and about the process of navigating conflicting or just multiple affiliations. These couples find one another and lose one another, find worlds and lose them, find their selves and lose them, again and again. All of this finding and losing and recovering and discovering between the self, the other, and the world model for us experiences of resilience and hope—knowledge that may be the groundwork of community happiness. One way then to imagine community happiness is to conceive of it in terms of pairs, and to consider it through close attention to how a community of two makes itself happy.

Perhaps then we can begin to work toward a notion of cultural happiness based not just on how a culture obstructs or enables the fulfillment of the needs of the individual but on how the couple/community play together, build a joke, do a time step, return to one another over time with renewed interest and deepened knowledge, experience an optimism that things can work, and that they can and should go on. However, to know these things requires an awakening to how aesthetic works of culture make models of ordinary pleasure, the ordinary pleasures of, for instance, a couple who perform as comedy what it means in their narrative world to share reciprocal knowledge, mutual satisfaction, and good luck.

To read for the presence of happiness in narrative means not, I think, to look for some distant utopia, but rather to see the possibilities for invention, play, and pleasure that lie before our eyes, and within our reach, here and now.

Notes

Introduction

1. One volume that does explore depictions of the happiness of the self alone is *Solitary Pleasures: The Historical, Literary, and Artistic Discourses of Autoeroticism,* ed. Paula Bennett and Vernon A. Rosario II (New York: Routledge, 1995). See, in particular, Roger Celestin's essay, "Can Robinson Crusoe Find Happiness (Alone)?: Beyond the Genitals and History on the Island of Hope." Celestin analyzes Michel Tournier's *Friday*—how the 1967 novel revises what it means for Robinson Crusoe to desire the Island of Hope (Speranza) and not Home, how Crusoe incorporates Friday into his sexual practices with the Island (the vegetal woman he fecundates), and how, with the loss of Friday (who seeks out the new world while Crusoe stays alone on the Island), Crusoe knows happiness being alone. Celestin writes, "Perhaps in giving us a happy Robinson, Tournier has also given us a new myth: the possibility of happiness" (246). Tournier's novel and Celestin's account of it are versions of a happiness I'm not taking up, that of the pleasures of solitude.

2. For a more detailed discussion of the terms *story* and *discourse,* see Gerald Prince's *Dictionary of Narratology;* Gérard Genette's *Narrative Discourse;* Shlomith Rimmon-Kenan's *Narrative Fiction: Contemporary Poetics;* Seymour Chatman's *Story and Discourse: Narrative Structure in Fiction and Film.*

3. See in particular his chapter "Mood" in *Narrative Discourse.* Genette, unlike Chatman, implies that what divides drama from narrative is its capacity to show: "[I]n contrast to dramatic representation, no narrative can 'show' or 'imitate' the story it tells. All it can do is tell it in a manner which is detailed, precise, 'alive,' and in that way give more or less the *illusion of mimesis*—which is the only narrative mimesis, for this single and sufficient reason: that narration, oral or written, is a fact of language, and language signifies without imitating" (164). Genette's "narrative discourse" is a language that is not performed or "acted out" as an imitation of the thing it represents. Chatman's "narrative discourse" includes performed language and visual imagery. I am using Chatman's broader conception of narrative discourse because its more capacious vision and scope help support my inclusion of what I consider to be various forms of couples' narratives.

4. Of course the chief exception to this is "voice-over," which has a strangeness to it that finds its source in its reference back to the presence of a storyteller, the very oral

communicator a film denies in its replacement of human presence with simulated reality. Voice-over, not so curiously, often accompanies novels made into films: the novel's insistence that there be a narrator's voice finds its transcription in the simulation of a voice reading the novel that it is "telling."

5. I'm borrowing this word "usual" from Harvey Sacks, whose lecture "On Doing 'Being Ordinary,'" in *Structures of Social Action,* 413–29, asserts that what we do when we talk is to be ordinary, by which he means to learn what the ordinary structures are of any context and define ourselves—that is, the stories we have to tell about ourselves—in accordance with those contexts so as to tell a story in the way anybody would tell it. In the way that situations prompt certain rules that regulate what constitutes a usual response versus an unusual response, I'm asserting that narratives generate structures that determine what constitutes their usual process of storytelling and what constitutes extraordinary telling.

6. Of course others have explored the significance of the narrative sites "beginning" and "ending" as well. For instance, Richard Neupert's *The End: Narration and Closure in Cinema* takes up how endings function in relation to different forms of film. In his introduction, Neupert cites at length works of literary analysis that consider the question of the literary ending, including Barbara Herrnstein Smith's *Poetic Closure,* David Richter's *Fable's End,* John Gerlach's *Toward the End,* Elizabeth MacArthur's *Extravagant Narratives,* Armine Kotin Mortimer's *La Clôture narrative,* Marianna Torgovnick's *Closure in the Novel,* and Rachel Blau Du Plessis's *Writing beyond the Ending.* Neupert's is the first book-length study, however, on the specific functions of endings in film and how they inform cinematic narration (12–13). More work has been done on openings in film, which has to do, Neupert asserts, with the perception of the beginning as the privileged site of the narrative in how it addresses its audience with credits, music, and a world-initiating first scene (12). He cites as examples Thierry Kuntzel's "Le Travail du film" and "Le Travail du Film, 2," Michel Marie's *Histoire d'une récherche,* Marc Vernet's "The Filmic Transaction: On the Openings of Film Noirs" and *Aesthetics of Film,* and David Bordwell's and Kristin Thompson's *Film Art* (193). Neupert's bibliography makes evident that the bounded spaces of the opening and the closing of narratives continue to draw attention from critics for how they signal their readers that they are the grounds of the narratives that must be attended to, for how they draw us inside them and for how they leave us. At issue then for the study of narrative is, how do we/should we attend to its middles?

Chapter 1

1. Many writers in the humanist tradition engaged the dialogue as their "mode" of writing. The ancients Plato, Xenophon, Lucian, Cicero, and Horace created a range of models for the moderns Hume, Berkeley, and Kierkegaard, for instance, to consider. My highlighting of Plato's version of the Socratic dialogue is meant to explore its mode (the one we tend to consider *the* ancient example), not to suggest that it is the only mode. For a discussion of the variety of ancient models, see K. J. H. Berland's "Dialectic, Catecheticall, or Obstetricious?: Socrates and the Eighteenth-Century Dialogue"; on Hume and Berkeley's dialogues, see Pheroze Wadia's "Philosophy as Literature: The Case of Hume's Dialogues."

2. I relate this remark to Wittgenstein's "sense of a sentence" in the *Philosophical Investigations.* He writes, "One would like to say—may, of course, leave this or that open, but the sentence must nevertheless have *a* definite sense. An indefinite sense—that would really

not be a sense *at all* (45e(99)). Wittgenstein implicitly questions the idea of making a sentence have only one "definite sense" when he characterizes this goal as a desire and as something "one would like to say." Gadamer, in contrast, wholly endorses the singularity of meaning, of *a* sense, of *a* direction. In light of Gadamer's notion of "sense" and Wittgenstein's of "a sense," it makes sense that Gadamer takes the language of Socrates as the model for how one engages in dialogue and why Wittgenstein never makes such a claim.

3. And yet such a notion of conversation, as a mutually derived arrival at the truth, seems wrong to Jürgen Habermas, who instead privileges the concept of argumentation in his *The Theory of Communicative Action.* Whereas Gadamer asserts that the "truth" of conversational subjects can be found if the topic is left to lead its discussants, Habermas asserts that there is no longer a "truth" to be distinguished in the modern age of reason. In response to Weber's recognition of the "iron cage" of reason's demythologizing of the spiritual and so too of a universal sense of meaning, Habermas proposes that individuals of the modern age achieve a sense of meaning in the use of reason to engage discussants in rational communication to bring about "assent" that one idea is better than another, "agreement" as consensus among participants of a discussion, and "redemption" of a particular claim as valid because of the recognition of its intrinsic reasonableness. At the heart of his theory is the concept of argumentation. If communication leads to disagreement because no universal system of meaning exists to navigate disputes toward the "truth," communicative rationality in the form of argumentation offers itself as the means for discussants to discover meaning and avoid the use of force.

Defining the structure of argumentation, Habermas characterizes it as "the problematic utterance for which a certain validity claim is raised (conclusion) and of the reason (ground) through which the claim is to be established" (25–26). Stating a problem, drawing a conclusion, offering reasons in support, work as the means by which disputants weigh their opposing positions and come to a collective agreement as to which argument is superior because of the force of its reasonableness. However, Habermas understands his to be an idealized description of argumentation and agreement. Writing of the norm of everyday communication, he describes it as "diffuse, fragile, continuously revised and only momentarily successful communication in which participants rely on problematic and unclarified presuppositions and feel their way from one occasional commonality to the next" (100–101). If Habermas's theory of argumentation can be understood as an alternative to Gadamer's model of conversation, it is a self-declared idealization that in actuality offers only the hope of momentary successes.

4. See Genette's *Narrative Discourse,* 109–12.

5. See Richard E. Vatz's discussion of the "rhetorical situation" in "The Myth of the Rhetorical Situation."

6. If the Socratic dialogue works as one model of philosophic discourse, Hume's *Dialogues Concerning Natural Religion* work, by contrast, according to Wadia, as a "dialectical work in which the views of each of the main protagonists is unfolded in stages under the impact of criticism leveled against him by the other" (50). Coming to "knowledge," in Hume's writing, is dependent on the mutual work of its explorers who are engaged in a joint venture to find/make it. Their arguments wrap around, modify, adjust, and clarify one another. It is in the social scene of minds and language mutually, equally interacting that forms of knowing for Hume emerge.

7. See, for instance, the work of Carl F. Graumann, Klaus Foppa, Mechthild

Papoušek, Harold G. Walbott, John J. Gumperz, Robert M. Krauss, Susan R. Fussell, Yih-siu Chen, Per Linell, Ivana Markovà, and S. Collins in *Mutualities in Dialogue,* ed. Ivana Markovà, Carl Graumann, and Klaus Foppa (Cambridge: Cambridge University Press, 1995).

8. While the naming and categorizing of the conversational devices are Tannen's (*That's Not* 33–48), the elaboration of how they are derived and the additional categories of "claiming" and "relaying information" are my own.

9. The originator of "frame theory," Erving Goffman, offers a full-bodied discussion of his concept in *Frame Analysis.* In particular, his penultimate chapter, "The Frame Analysis of Talk," is useful in its depiction of the role of frames in conversation.

10. Tannen in *You Just Don't Understand* asserts a gendered distinction in how men and women view and conduct conversations. While men, she claims, prioritize the linguistic or information level of the conversation, women look to the paralinguistic, or the unstated level of "how are we relating?" True to her claim, she writes on *how* partners of a conversation interact, while Gadamer, Grice, and Wittgenstein model their theories on *what* is said, and in so doing exclude the dynamic of how conversants relate extralinguistically.

Chapter 2

1. My claim that "first-time" conversations between particular lovers model their particular future relations and are, therefore, rarely generic or repeatable doesn't hold true in all cases. Texts that follow a formula for romance—Harlequin romances, soap operas, teen movies—work from predictability. The formula romance narrative works from the fundamental premise that the romance of its genre is formulaic, so the conversations of its lovers must be the stuff of repetition and of a generalizable kind.

2. This "business" of getting married connects itself to the emphasis of the text on "worth," an economic term used to measure both the esteeming of character and the estimating of net worth, the vision and revision of who are matched appropriately according to the weight of character to income. Darcy's strange role as matchmaker—he arranges behind the scenes the marriage of Lydia and Wickham and urges against and then for the nuptials of Bingley and Jane—enables his own marriage to Elizabeth.

3. Consider as well Jane's "undoing" of the marriage ceremony in her repetition of its rhetoric couched in a context of negation in chapter 27. Jane retreats from her depiction of Rochester as idol: he is *not* husband; this is *not* "I will be yours," but rather "I will not." Repeating "I do" three times in response to his question posed three times about whether she means for them to go their own way, Jane declares that she cannot "obey" Rochester and hopes that they meet someday in heaven, as opposed to being blessed by God in their relationship on earth.

4. Wittgenstein writes that the relation of the name to the thing named consists "[a]mong other things in the fact that hearing the name calls before our mind the picture of what is named; and it also consists, among other things, in the name's being pronounced when the thing is pointed at" (18e(37)).

5. With the advent of the videocassette recorder and bringing a film of choice into the home comes the ability to screen multiple times. Necessarily, the impact of film on viewers must change with repeated viewings, as rereading changes a novel, or as reattending a production changes a play. To return to a novel, play, or film requires that there be features of it which we want to be with again, as opposed to features that compel us by their

ability to surprise. I wonder what differences are transpiring in cinematic production as films move from "knowing" the audience will leave them in the theater, perhaps never to see them again, to now knowing that an audience may see them repeatedly in their homes.

6. I am grateful to James Phelan for his reading of this moment, that it's about Rhett's loss of feeling for Scarlett, for what that alternative reading offers. It's an interesting way both to conceive of the moment and to make sense of why Scarlett feels so poignantly the shift in her desires. Whether he's gone "dead" to her or not, Scarlett feels the loss of him, which reignites her feelings of desire for him or moves the locus of who desires from him to her.

7. That desire left unattached led to the ill-fated writing by another author of the novel's sequel, *Scarlett*, and its film. However, even here "the end" of the conversation could not occur because no sequel could respond on an equal footing to the conclusion of *Gone with the Wind*. Therefore, while desire left unattached spawned new life, its life expired because the real power of this desire resides in its primary feature—that it float, not be answered, just beckon for answers, and remain to charge this couple and this narrative.

8. Significantly, both films are of the pre-VCR era.

9. One way to read *Casablanca*, with its repeated structure of the public world (Renault/Sam/Victor) poised on the edge of the private (Rick/Ilsa/Victor), is as a beckoning to a 1941 America to fully join the war, to abandon its isolationist desires in order to enter the public fray. In essence, *Casablanca* invites America to become Victor—the figure who bridges the private and the public.

Chapter 3

1. See Gregory Bateson's *Steps to an Ecology of Mind*, 68.

2. See René Girard's *Deceit, Desire, and the Novel.*

3. Charles Musser redefines this genre of the remarriage comedy to mean, not just the return of the same couple back to each other, but the fact of a couple divorcing and then choosing to remarry, though not necessarily to one another. See his "Divorce, DeMille and the Comedy of Remarriage." However, because my interest here lies in the conversations of a couple who return to one another after some declared ending, I am drawing only on Cavell's description of the genre.

4. Whereas Cavell sees fundamentally a transformation occurring in the woman of these films, as her experience of education, I see instead the couple metamorphose. What it means to be the woman and the man of these marriages shifts for each by virtue of what happens out of their still-shared company and their still-in-play "talkiness," as each works (knowingly or not) toward remarriage. Chap. 7 is my working through of this idea.

Conclusion to Intimacy

1. I am grateful to Steve Duck for our conversation about the idea of intimacy as a process and for sharing with me his articles "Friends Romans Countrymen, Lend Me Your Retrospections: Rhetoric and Reality in Personal Relationships" (with Kris Pond), "Intimacy as the Proverbial Elephant" (with Linda K. Acitelli), and "Relationships as Unfinished Business: Out of the Frying Pan and into the 1990s."

2. Perhaps it would be better to say I will consider what Wittgenstein might have

suggested had he taken up the shared language of a couple. It may be asserted that Wittgenstein did not take up the problem of the shared language of the couple because it simply did not interest him.

Chapter 4

1. T. G. A. Nelson, *Comedy: An Introduction to Comedy in Literature, Drama, and Cinema*, 31. Nelson's is a good introductory guide to comic elements, themes, and forms.

2. See Kathleen Rowe's "Comedy, Melodrama and Gender: Theorizing the Genres of Laughter," and her *The Unruly Woman*. In both works she examines how Frye and other comic theorists have essentially forgotten the woman's presence in the comic narrative, except as the object of desire. What of her desires? What of her capacities to make comedy? What of her abilities to turn the social order of her narrative upside down so that she ends up "on top"? These are some of the questions Rowe addresses. Her essay on comedy and melodrama is particularly powerful in its redefining of those genres.

3. About the "vaudeville aesthetic" and its influence on early sound film comedy, see Henry Jenkins's fine *What Made Pistachio Nuts?*

4. See Jenkins on the plot dependence of romantic comedy (220–21), and Brian Henderson's revision of that position in "Romantic Comedy Today: Semi-Tough or Impossible."

5. Henderson, 21. This unsayability of the "sexual question" may *help* account for the rise of the male buddy movies and the absence of heterosexual romantic comedies of the 1960s and '70s when the "sexual question" becomes the fundamental topic of the movies. It might also help explain Tom Hanks and Meg Ryan's not meeting until the final scene of *Sleepless in Seattle*. The coming of the sexual revolution has brought something close to the demise of romantic comedy.

6. Frye, *Anatomy of Criticism*, 167. I'm thinking, for example, of *Much Ado about Nothing* or *It Happened One Night*, where the text insists that we sit up in attention to the lovers who fall in love through the comedy of their resistance to each other, rather than to the paternal forces of authority who stand as placeholders for what keeps them apart. Leonato and Don Pedro encourage the union between Benedick and Beatrice; Ellie Andrews's father arranges for the getaway car to enable the eloping of Ellie/Claudette Colbert and Peter/Clark Gable.

7. Mikhail Bakhtin, *Rabelais and His World*, 12. Bakhtin's opening chapter on the history of laughter's perceptions defines its evolution from the Renaissance vision of laughter as an essential form of truth, a chief attribute distinguishing that which is human, to the seventeenth-century notion of laughter as the "simply amusing," the "gay," the "recreational." It is a powerful piece that charts not only a period of transformations in Western culture's notions of laughter but also the implications of those transformations.

8. See C. L. Barber's *Shakespeare's Festive Comedy*.

9. Clara Claiborne Park, "No Time for Comedy," 61. Park's essay brings forward in fresh and surprising ways the relation between comedy, magic, and the ordinary.

10. Fred Miller Robinson, *Comic Moments*, 25–26.

11. Robinson, 29. Robinson is particularly interested in comedy's desire and ability to invent: even if the materials or the game is old, comedy transforms the known so that it suddenly feels unknown in its capacity to reveal what was not previously seen.

12. Jenkins defines "anarchistic comedy" as comedy that moves away from linearity and causality in its celebration of the impulsive, creative, and nonregulated. See in particular 22–25.

13. If the culture of confession, discussed by Foucault in *The History of Sexuality* and so much a part of contemporary American life, has erased the discomfort of voyeurism, then it has as well diminished the power of team comedy's impact on its audience.

Chapter 5

1. Miller's title links his sense of what drives a narrative, a life, a creative act inextricably to Freud's—namely, the aggressive, hostile impulses of the self-in-separation sublimated at the end of the novel into marriage—a sanitized state of what Freud defines as "cleanliness," "beauty," and "order." The drives of the individual set him or her in opposition to the culture, a scene of union. Freud writes in *Civilization and Its Discontents,* "[T]he two urges, the one towards personal happiness and the other towards union with other human beings must struggle with each other in every individual; and so, also, the two processes of individual and cultural development must stand in hostile opposition to each other and mutually dispute the ground" (99). In Freud's likeness Miller's theory of narrative precludes the possibility of happiness in marriage as a narratable plot: the aggression, individuation of the self drives the text in its opposition to union. D. A. Miller, *Narrative and Its Discontents,* ix.

2. Priscilla Meyer's "*Anna Karenina*: Tolstoy's Polemic with *Madame Bovary*" narrates briefly the order in which Tolstoy wrote the novel and his sense of the significance of the portions (252). However, the primary work of the Levin section of Meyer's article is to set it in relation to Rousseau's Émile. Much of the critical work on *Anna Karenina* since its publication has been devoted to a discussion of the "unity"/"disunity" question of the novel, meaning explorations that consider how the "Anna"/"Levin" stories work separately to create or not an integrated whole. For instance, Joan Delaney Grossman's "Tolstoy's Portrait of Anna: Keystone in the Arch" reads the one scene where Levin and Anna meet in order to discern why this should be the instance of the narratives' intersection, how the "intricate meeting of past and future . . . constitutes the meeting of Anna and Levin" (14). There are the named unity articles, like E. B. Greenwood's or Gary R. Jahn's, both called "The Unity of *Anna Karenina*," which use a thematic approach to discern how the "Anna" and "Levin" narratives work in tandem. And there are the structural books, like Elisabeth Stenbock-Fermor's *The Architecture of "Anna Karenina"* or Sydney Schultze's *The Structure of "Anna Karenina."*

What runs throughout these readings is the sense that two consciousnesses predominate, Anna's and Levin's, and that their stories are theirs individually. While Vronsky, Karenin, and Kitty are players in the two narrative's worlds, they assume secondary importance to the two primary consciousnesses, who "use" them in the working through of their particular stories. Oblonsky (again this cannot be Dolly's narrative too), while not ignored, is usually framed for the counterpointing he supplies between the two tales, not extreme enough for death, not good enough for happiness. What gets lost in this contrapuntal delineation of just two lives are the ways in which the novel navigates how to tell of the making that goes on between couples, how the languages and structures of the novel pursue ways of being in addition to the telling/mirroring of an individual consciousness.

A book that declares itself to be on the topic of "family happiness" must take on narrative modes of "familyness" which necessitate forms of community-telling.

3. See, for instance, Amy Mandelker's *Framing "Anna Karenina": Tolstoy, the Woman Question, and the Victorian Novel*. Mandelker's stated topic is a revision of Tolstoy as a feminist and of *Anna Karenina* as a novel that uses art and visual representation to reimagine an aesthetics without gender or class discrimination. She pursues this thesis almost entirely through an examination of how Tolstoy "frames" Anna, mostly to the exclusion of Kitty and Levin. Likewise, Judith Armstrong's *The Unsaid "Anna Karenina,"* while interested in the way Kitty and Levin define a happiness that is different from the Scherbatskys or the Sviazhkys (26), declares that without the Anna story there would be only the Levin story, "a very unlikely bestseller" (71). Richard Hare describes the Levin sections as "relaxation" and "anticlimax" (cited in Greenwood, 126). Further, there is the genre of "suicide of women" criticism which, when it takes up *Anna Karenina*, must focus on the Anna story to the exclusion of Kitty and Levin by virtue of its stated purpose. Included in this genre are Barbara T. Gates's *Victorian Suicide: Mad Crimes and Sad Histories;* Margaret Higonnet's "Speaking Silences: Women's Suicide"; Nicole Loraux's *Tragic Ways of Killing a Woman;* Tony Tanner's *Adultery in the Novel: Contract and Transgression.* It is difficult to conceive of a contrapuntal body of writing which would work to address the Kitty story, as in "lives of women often content" criticism. The topic of women and suicide has drawn critics to it and hence led to more thought on the "Anna story," whereas the absence of dramatic pitch in the Kitty-Levin narrative has made it vulnerable to less attention, more neglect, even to being forgotten.

4. I take Peter Brooks's *Reading for the Plot* to be another version of Miller's central claim about the novel, though Brooks frames it in terms of the Oedipal story (the structure of it). The plot proceeds by virtue of the movement between secrets until they are solved at their extraordinary ends.

5. These words are John H. Schaar's in ". . . And the Pursuit of Happiness." Schaar examines the root of happiness—*hap*—as in happening and happenstance, and asserts, "Happiness originates in a thing of the moment and reaches the lot that befalls one in life—a sardonic etymology, suggesting that our happiness owes less to our deliberate efforts than to accident and fortune" (232). This points to the notion of happiness as that which cannot be achieved as a goal, as that which is subject to the whimsy of circumstance. To embrace chance has to do with a willingness to turn one's life over to designs shaped by forces other than one's will. Couples at play must excel at such a willingness. Further, in his thoughts on the relation of the pursuit of happiness to America's sense of itself, Schaar brings the Puritan desire for or work toward the achieving of "eternal felicity" together with the later Yankee delight in "worldly joy or gain." He concludes, "To choose either exclusively is to lose the best of both. A noble culture and religion must find a view of life profound enough to understand both the joys and the burdens which attend a regard for our responsibilities, and to *achieve a repose in the face of both joy and sorrow.* That repose is simultaneously less and more than what most men have meant by happiness" (236, emphasis mine). For me, Schaar's comments suggest questions like, how does one live well (in the sense of learn from or be comfortable with) the presence of pain and pleasure? To know how to do so suggests a kind of ease with living that seems fundamental to the concept of living happily. And I take this to be most of all what Levin and Kitty attempt.

6. What Woolf, Colwin, and Shields do is give the extraordinary "presence" in their

novels by giving it a language and names, and thereby make it ordinary, which in a sense removes the very possibility of the extraordinary. This urge may be an attempt to recover the feeling of the extraordinary by giving it an ordinary construction in what might be thought of as the modern novel's/world's absence of the extraordinary. Throughout *To the Lighthouse,* for instance, Woolf moves between a doing of the ordinary (having conversations, having dinner together, having a look at the water or the sky) and experiencing piercing revelations prompted by those ordinary moments, revelations that work to destroy or highlight what is so meaningful about those ordinary moments. Such a moment occurs when Mrs. Ramsay sits alone and Mr. Ramsay watches her. Their actions, made poignant by the pitch of Woolf's language, reveal how they know how to read each other. We are to see the intensity of this flash of mutuality as extraordinary:

> He would let her be, and he passed her without a word, though it hurt him that she should look so distant, and he could not reach her, he could do nothing to help her. And again he would have passed her without a word had she not, at that very moment, given him of her own free will what she knew he would never ask, and called to him and taken the green shawl off the picture frame, and gone to him. For he wished, she knew, to protect her. (65)

In *Another Marvelous Thing,* Laurie Colwin writes of how Billy can love her husband, fall in love with another, and maintain love relationships with both until the difficulties of pursuing both loves/lives becomes too exhausting. Not only does Colwin make it possible to "choose" the marriage, but she makes the affair something that can be incorporated into Billy's life, even as an element of the marriage, on which the marriage stands:

> Parting had been the sensible thing to do. A love affair could be compared to a cellar hole. Old Mrs. Stern's property had several such holes, remnants of eighteenth-century households. After a long while, without a map of the property, it was impossible to tell where they were. Standing on a road kissing your husband, taking the car to be serviced, letters, meals, telephone calls, arrangements, and errands filled up the hole of a love affair so well that after a while it would be possible to stand comfortably on top of it. (86)

Though she ends the affair and goes on to experience a passionate relationship with motherhood, she continues to maintain a love for her lover. Billy finds that the ordinary frame of her domestic world tolerates the coming into it of "another marvelous thing"— the entrance of multiple loves, loves which she pursues and holds onto as parts of herself. Colwin writes narratives that acknowledge the presence of the extraordinary, which for her means feeling what she calls in another story "magic emotion." Her heroines learn what it means to come upon magic emotion, and what it takes to bring extraordinary feeling to their ordinary emotional worlds. Colwin's modern heroines have both the right and the complexity to experience their full emotional selves, and they exist in worlds that encourage that exploration.

    Carol Shields writes of the presence of magic within the domestic, not as something over which to pause, or wonder if it can be tolerated, or analyze how it came to be, but just as a part of the way things are. The extraordinary for Shields has its place, happens, because it defines in the Shields universe the nature of things. As a result, in *The Stone Diaries* the narrator witnesses her own birth and death, a man cuts a stone model of a pyramid, a woman gives birth to a fully formed baby not having known she was pregnant, and a man discovers a sexual love with his wife that changes him so "that the very substance of his body seemed altered." He experiences something like "the men of medieval times [who] were put to bed with a disease called lovesickness, which was nothing more than a metaphysical assault too strange and too powerful to be absorbed by simple flesh" (34). These things are present, possible in a world that deadens with routine or misses a layer of explanation or prompts embarrassment or just makes one forget. Both the ordinary and the extraordinary live inextricably and deeply together in Shields's novels. This man, for instance, Cuyler Goodwill, so metamorphosed by the sheer touch of his first wife's corpulence, makes her ordinary enough to be forgotten, yet still present in remembering her absent body:

> But what was her name? What was her name? His first wife's name? A suppressed rapture. There is something careless about this kind of forgetting, something unpardonable. His dear one. His sweetheart. Her face had the quality of a blurred photograph, yet he knew her body, every inch, and remembers how he woke one night to the loudness of the rain with his arm across her breast. All that was good, that soft breast. (275)

Chapter 6

1. This is not to say, however, that *I Love Lucy* functions without a tightly designed narrative structure. On the contrary, Jess Oppenheimer, the creator of the show and head writer, insists in his *Laughs, Luck . . . and Lucy* that each script had to move from an opening premise to its logical end, logical in that how the end undoes the opening grows out of a sequence of causally linked, believable connections. Thus he defines how situation comedy works as a narrative display of a joke: the punchline is reached at the end of a thirty-minute feedline that twists its way seemingly irrevocably to that end. Oppenheimer's definition of the structure of situation comedy in his chapter "Anatomy of a Script" parallels in essence Aristotle's structural definition of tragedy. While the narrative structure creates the backbone of the comedy, we attend to the background only enough to lose ourselves through the aid of "plausibility" to the comic shtick of its performers. This lack of attention to plot has everything to do with the repeated form it takes as "the situation."

2. Kathleen Rowe draws on Bakhtin's formulation of the carnivalesque to define a particular "type" of female clown—"the unruly woman." She asserts that Lucy, like the other unruly women Roseanne and Miss Piggy, fares better on television than on film because of the possibility of being the matriarch of the domestic situation. And as to what it means for Lucy to be an "unruly woman," Rowe describes her as characteristically involved in

> a special kind of excess differing from that of the femme fatale (the daughters of Eve and Helen) or the madonna (the daughters of Mary), whose laughter, if it ever occurred, no longer rings in the myths still circulating around them. Like Medusa, the unruly woman laughs. Like Roseanne Arnold, she is not a "nice girl." She *is* willing to offend and be offensive. . . . Associated with both beauty and monstrosity, the

unruly woman dwells close to the grotesque. But while mythology taints and dooms Medusa, the unruly woman often enjoys a reprieve from those fates that so often seem inevitable to women under patriarchy, because her home is comedy and the carnivalesque, the realm of inversion and fantasy where, for a time at least, the ordinary world can be stood on its head. (*Unruly Woman* 10–11)

3. Jackie Gleason's Ralph Kramden in *The Honeymooners* appears to clown in a strikingly similar way and situation to Lucy's. Married to Alice, friend to Ed Norton and Trixie, who live in the same apartment building in New York City in the mid 1950s, Ralph creates comedy out of an almost parallel domestic situation. And yet certain facts divide their situations across the lines of gender (Ralph is a man), class (Ralph is working class), and profession (Ralph is a bus driver). Most important, Ralph's comedy requires the presence of a comic antagonist, a marriage partner, who acts the foil to Ralph's larger than life bursts of rage, surprise, hope, and despair. And that partner is Ed Norton. Lucy's comedy escalates in relation to Ethel, who mirrors Lucy in a kind of "less than" likeness; Ethel remains always in the role of girlfriend—like Lucy, yet a little more reasonable, a little more scared, a little less inventive. Ricky stays squarely in the position of comic antagonist/marriage partner. He is the "other" as the "he," the rule maker, i.e., the "straight man." And as straight man, he contributes to Lucy's comedy by creating the boundaries up against which she rubs and with which she creates a comic world.

But while Ralph has a marriage partner in Alice, who spends each show negating Ralph's desires until the end, when she concedes or reveals that she always did take his position, he avoids engaging in interactions with her antagonism. In a way she's like the "senex" figure of comic dramas who makes the rules at the outset against which the lovers rebel until the senex alters those rules at the end, or fate takes a hand and makes it possible for everyone to have their way. In her position as static, essentially forgotten-until-the-end boundary, Alice frames what follows. Ed Norton seems at first to be the mirroring friend, like Ethel. However, in appearance, manner, way of being in the world, Norton is the "other" to Ralph. Almost all of the comic interaction happens between the two men. Ralph's large, emotional presence as the figure who dreams and meets endlessly with disappointment, and Norton's lanky, laconic, unfocused presence as the foil who essentially never longs but just is and who often doesn't make sense to anyone but himself, create together a comic team and universe.

While all four members of the *I Love Lucy* world have important roles to fill in the ongoing making of their world together, the women of *The Honeymooners* are not the ones on the honeymoon—they exist in this world as placeholders or boundary markers. Much like Laurel and Hardy, however, the two men explore what it means to be the ones "newly wed" in the sense of trying to understand the other to whom each is bound, namely, each other. They constitute this world of the honeymoon—a comic universe characterized by an inability to understand the other coupled with an endless desire to be with the other in the mess/happiness of misunderstanding.

The Honeymooners stands in a striking relation to *I Love Lucy* as something like a mirror image upside down or inside out. The similar domestic situation turns when the woman clown becomes a man, when the comfortable, middle-class wife becomes an uncomfortable working-class husband, and when the positions "friend" and "marriage partner" collapse and metamorphose. *I Love Lucy* finds marriage between a man and a woman to be of ongoing interest, and (along with the exploration of same-sex friendship and couple's friendship) to be the stuff from which the making of a comic world comes. And it's this desire to stay with the ordinary, given relationships, and move inside them, and see what they create that makes *I Love Lucy* remarkable.

4. This comment comes from an interview with two of the show's writers, Madelyn Pugh and Robert Carroll Jr., aired following the pilot's first broadcast on April 30, 1990 (the pilot was never shown in 1951).

5. A writer from the *Hollywood Reporter,* reviewing the first episode (October 1951), described Ball and Arnaz as comic partners: "Half a step behind her comes her husband, Desi Arnaz, the perfect foil for her screwball antics and possessing comic abilities of his own more than sufficient to make this a genuine comedy team rather than the one woman tour de force it almost becomes" (quoted in Oppenheimer 162). From the outset, Lucy and Ricky were understood to be making comedy together.

6. Lying is one of Lucy's character traits: so automatic is it a form of communicating and functioning for her that the episode "Lucy Tells the Truth" is devoted to the wager that she cannot go twenty-four hours without lying (Oppenheimer 32). Brooks Robards writes in *Situation Comedy and the Structure of Television* that it is Lucy's "worse than average" character that makes *I Love Lucy* a comedy in Aristotelian terms, in that she is worthy of ridicule. And yet, it is Lucy's tendency toward deceit, competitiveness, obsessive desire of the material, and scheming, merged with her naïveté, vulnerability, and desire to promote Ricky, that make her, out of their mix, competent, self-protective, ingenious, and loyal in a world that steps on the vulnerable and rewards the "streetwise" self-promoter (56–58). Molly Haskell says of Lucy's contradictions and how they contribute to her comedy: "She risks not being lovable: there's a klutzy, unappealing, low-brow, Ugly-American side to her woman on the move. . . . Yet she *is* ordinary—a back-fence gossip, an onlooker—in a way Chaplin wasn't . . . she becomes a champion, an angel of ordinariness, a woman of blinkered credulity capable of flights of beauty" (*Holding My Own,* 106). And Darrell Hamamoto in *Nervous Laughter* writes of Lucy's simultaneous, extreme states of power-fulness and powerlessness: "No matter how often she failed to subvert [Ricky's] authority, Lucy always seemed ready for a new challenge that would establish her self-worth. . . . Lucy often tried to work her way into Ricky's acts, which would invariably result in her humiliation. Failing this, Lucy went to extremes in placing herself near greatness, whether it be Cornel Wilde, John Wayne, Orson Welles" (28). What writers on *Lucy* agree on, then, is that she is a mass of contradictions (though they differ on their nature), and that her comedy comes from their dissonant juxtaposition.

7. In an alternate point of view, with her interest in Lucy very much apart from Ricky, Frances Gray in *Women and Laughter* asserts that we wait for Ricky to leave so that Lucy can make the comedy happen. Further, that when the two are paired, that pairing takes a father/daughter form (46–52). Gray understands Ricky's role to be that of imposing narra-tive on Lucy's slapstick outbursts: his law and order reigns in her atmosphere of sponta-neous, wild, dangerous chaos.

8. Jack Rollins spoke about the team in an interview for the PBS American Masters documentary "Nichols and May: Take Two," aired May 22, 1996.

9. These quotations are from Peter Marks's "The Brief, Brilliant Run of Nichols and May."

10. Lucy, during the filming of the pilot, was in fact pregnant with their first child. Part

of the impetus behind her baggy, "male" dress was to cover this fact—a fact she will come to use to make comedy from out of its roots in carnival with her second pregnancy. Curiously, therefore, at this moment, thick with references to Ricky's desire to have Lucy be the mama of his children, Lucy again fulfills and denies that desire. She manages somehow to be just "a little pregnant."

11. The shows to follow, which feature Lucy paired with Vivian Vance or Gale Gordon after her divorce from Desi, work as possible answers to that question. And yet, those shows are not *I Love Lucy.*

12. Sigmund Freud, *Jokes and Their Relation to the Unconscious,* 148. The second category of jokes to which Freud refers include "unification, similarity of sound, multiple use, modification of familiar phrases, allusions to quotations." That the rediscovery of the familiar is pleasurable stems, Freud says, from the "quiet sense of comfort" that familiarity brings. Further, it is a "pleasure in economy" and "economy in psychical expenditure" in that the mind does not have to generate new ways of thinking in order to come to terms with the familiar, as it must with the unfamiliar. There is pleasure to be had then, Freud asserts, in being able to draw on known ways of processing experience.

Chapter 7

1. These running brides on film connect themselves to earlier women in narratives— to Jane Eyre for one, whose ultimate act of self-expression is to walk as a bride away or toward a home and a husband as her assertion of the right to choose where or if she will place herself sexually and as whose partner. Emma Bovary runs away from marriage when she tosses her bridal bouquet into the fire and runs outdoors toward her first lover with whom she discovers sexual freedom, an act from which she can never return her to her husband. However, it is Jane Eyre's running back to Rochester to choose to be his bride, as she has come to understand what that means, which presages something of the story these films tell, of the woman who reframes marriage as a grounds for her freedom, sexuality, and self-expression.

2. For a more extensive reading of these four films and the cultural moment in which they arose, see James Harvey's *Romantic Comedy,* in particular chap. 6, "1934: Turning Point," 107–39. Virginia Wright Wexman, in *Creating the Couple: Love, Marriage, and Hollywood Performance,* mixes textual reading with social history to explain how Hollywood (films, acting techniques, stars) has informed our sense of what constitutes the self in relation to love and coupling, and likewise how social desires and conventions have dictated what Hollywood produces. Curiously, she basically passes over a discussion of screwball comedy, an elision I attribute to the degree to which these films subvert the convention/ stereotype-making of Hollywood Wexman wishes to critique (though they do fit her model in their advocacy finally of "the couple").

3. Rowe in *The Unruly Woman* calls the play with sexual identity in screwball comedy "ambivalence":

Such actresses as Barbara Stanwyck, Carole Lombard, Irene Dunne, and Jean Arthur bring together in the characters they play the extremes that Sylvia negotiates. While not as explicitly androgynous as Hepburn in this film [*Sylvia Scarlett*], they convey a kind of femininity that is decidedly more active, more aggressive, more physical, and indeed more masculine than anything modeled on Mae West would allow. Yet they avoid the threat of catastration embodied in more mature, masculine stars such as Bette Davis and Joan Crawford. . . . The lingering sense of the boyish about the unruly virgins these romantic heroines play enables the masculine superstars of their era, from Clark Gable to Gary Cooper, to explore with them their own sexual ambivalence. (143–44)

It follows from Rowe's argument that "castrating" women are reserved for melodrama, whereas "unruly"/masculine-ish virgins romp in screwball comedy. Likewise, I must conclude, Paul Henreid, Charles Boyer, and Louis Jourdan are the ones earmarked for castration—i.e., the men of melodrama "must" be French or "almost" (or at least not cowboy material)—whereas the American man of screwball comedy retains his sexual organ but comes perhaps to wonder just what to do with it.

4. The development of the male/female comedy team in vaudeville from the 1890s to 1932 charts a course from the immigrant humor of ethnic marriage routines of, for example, John and Maggie Fielding doing sketch acts like "The Tipperary Couple," to the enactment in song and dance of courtship in elegant evening clothes by Hallan and Hart (like those to be featured by Ziegfeld), to the carping, shrewish wife and defenseless husband in the "talking acts" of Melville and Higgins, to the routines of Ryan and Lee, which first featured the woman's "stupidity" as the primary force of the couple's comedy. The dividing of "straight man" from comic in the team always made the humor be at one partner's expense; vaudeville did not produce a couple who shared the ability for "smart" talk and for being the butt or creator of the joke. Shirley Staples's *Male-Female Comedy Teams in American Vaudeville, 1865–1932* provides a sweeping overview of the evolution and decline of the male/female comedy team in vaudeville.

5. For an extended discussion on how the woman of these films embodied an image for the American audience of endurance and hope in the Depression, see Kendall's chap. 3, "Romantic Comedy Settles In," 50–65. Wes Gehring is interested primarily in the male protagonist in screwball comedies, whom he calls the "anti-hero," a figure he associates with the form of screwball comedy itself, which he calls "anti-heroic." He takes screwball comedy and its male protagonist to be such because of their presentations of "abundant leisure time, childlike nature[s], [locations in] urban setting[s], [pursuit of only] nonpolitical activity, and frustration" (in the sense of inability to understand and interact with machines and women). See *Screwball Comedy: Defining a Film Genre*, 17–18, or more extensively, *Screwball Comedy: A Genre of Madcap Romance*.

6. It is one of Kendall's primary narratives to tell how this collaboration was achieved between the central directors and the women stars of these films.

7. See Duane Byrge and Robert Milton Miller, *The Screwball Comedy Films*, 8; Gehring, *Screwball Comedy: A Genre of Madcap Romance*, 7; and Kendall, 88.

8. Fittingly it was in 1934 that Carl Hubbell, a pitcher for the New York Giants, struck out Babe Ruth, Lou Gehrig, Jimmie Foxx, Al Simmons, and Joe Cronin, all future members of the Baseball Hall of Fame, relying on a pitch he called the "screwball." Ed Sikov, *Laughing Hysterically*, 19. Kristine Brunovska Karnick provides a good overview of the varying definitions film theorists have offered over the years of the term in her "Commitment and Reaffirmation in Hollywood Romantic Comedy." She performs a "morphology" of screwball comedy and discerns two fundamental stories of the genre: the comedy of

commitment and the comedy of reaffirmation. Both stories, she asserts, tell one paradigm: sexual confrontation and courtship (though one tells of its establishment and the other of its return) (131). Tina Olsin Lent, in the same collection of essays as Karnick's article, asserts that what fundamentally defines the films of screwball comedy is their depiction of "love-companionship," or love/friendship, and that they do so to a degree that is this style of love's "most in-depth exposition on the Hollywood screen" (314). She builds her argument on an analysis of how screwball comedy took up "a redefined image of woman" (the flapper), "a redefined view of marriage" (as a romantic-sexual union), and "a redefined idea of cinematic comedy" (the romantic leads were also the comic leads). See "Romantic Love and Friendship: The Redefinition of Gender Relations in Screwball Comedy."

9. For a fuller account of Winokur's argument, see in particular chap. 4, "Unlikely Ethnic Heroes: William Powell, Myrna Loy, and the Fantasy of Assimilation," in *American Laughter*, 179–234.

10. Cavell's collection of films, which he groups together under a genre he names "remarriage comedy," a subgenre of screwball comedy, may at first glance seem strange given that in two of the films the couples don't marry, even for the first time, until the end of the film, as is the case in *Bringing Up Baby* and *It Happened One Night*. Cavell accounts for this by claiming that these couples engage in what it means for them as couples to be "married" throughout their technically unmarried interactions with one another. Katharine Hepburn and Cary Grant, Claudette Colbert and Clark Gable are far more "married" to each other (in the sense of mutually entangled, immersed, ineluctably joined) than they are married to their "actual" partners (Grant's "Alice" and Colbert's "King Wesley"). For Cavell, the work of these films is to display the nature of their "marriages," and then what necessarily follows their separations—"remarriage"—technically, the first marriage.

11. Cavell, *Pursuits of Happiness*, 126–27. Musser, in "Divorce, DeMille and the Comedy of Remarriage," historicizes Cavell's philosophically conceived genre of remarriage comedy, and in so doing redefines what it means, from a small collection of films from the 1930s that are about a couple's return to each other and their notion of what constitutes the self and the other who are doing the returning, and their marriage itself, to an expanding of the genre's temporal conception (about 1910–45) and of its meaning (that a couple divorces and at least one of the partners marries again but not necessarily to the original other partner). Musser must let go of what's essentially at stake for Cavell in these films—the work they do on acknowledgment, reconciliation, forgiveness, mutual life entanglement—in order to "broaden" Cavell's category. The historical argument he offers gives a social account of why it is that the Hollywood film between the world wars took on the topic of divorce (he looks at rising divorce statistics during these years, the coming of women's suffrage, and a growing body of evidence on shifts in attitudes about the need for marriage to be essentially companionate in nature and attend to sexual gratification).

While Musser's historical explanation answers something like "why" films of the day took up the topic of divorce, his work misses, I think, the point of reading how they mean and what they mean as particular films or as aesthetic texts, beyond functioning as just more evidence for what ideas preoccupied America from 1910 to 1945.

12. Leland A. Poague, *The Cinema of Frank Capra: An Approach to Film Comedy*, 34. Poague has interesting things to say about the clown comedy of Aristophanes and its reappearance in silent film comedy, and the plot comedy of Shakespeare and its reformulation in the cinema of Frank Capra, in his chapter "Capra and the Comic Tradition."

13. It is significant that Mae West is the only model of the solo female "clown" from the early films of Hollywood, and that her routine was about talking sex. West works as the bridge between these eras of comedy to suggest how the woman could be brought into comedy, as a sexual presence and as dangerous and wonderful in speech as the male clown had been in visual jest. Similarly, the absence of female comedy teams in vaudeville and early film, with the exception of Hal Roach's "creation" of the female Laurel and Hardy in Thelma Todd and Zasu Pitts (Pitts was later replaced by Patsy Kelly; see Leonard Maltin's *Movie Comedy Teams* for a more detailed account of this female movie comedy team), reveals how the role of the woman comic revolved around her sexual interaction with the real or imagined presence of a male partner. Screwball comedy uses and moves past this sexualized partnering by giving the woman and the man the freedom both to exploit and to dispense with a sexually determined rendering of their comic roles.

14. So central are Nick and Nora to my understanding of the "couple function" in narrative that early on in this project I considered naming the book something like *Nick and Nora, and Narrative,* or just *Nick and Nora.*

15. While with Hayworth, Hepburn, and Caron, Astaire is careful, or with Charisse he watches, matches her erect or sinuous lines, or just reacts by being stunned, when dancing with Rogers a youthful exuberance explodes between them that seems to demand loud tapping, big sets, and the throwing of themselves at each other for the sake of bodily happiness, which is the dancing couple's version of making a sex comedy. And I take this difference to be not just a function of his age or the era of filmmaking in the 1930s and early '40s (though these contribute) but a response to Rogers's sexiness.

Bibliography

Adelman, Gary. "*Anna Karenina*": *The Bitterness of Ecstasy.* Boston: Twayne Publishers, G. K. Hall, 1990.

Alexandrov, Vladimir E. "Relative Time in *Anna Karenina.*" *Russian Review* 41.2 (1982): 159–68.

Annas, Julia. *The Morality of Happiness.* New York: Oxford UP, 1993.

Aristotle. *The Nicomachean Ethics. Introduction to Aristotle.* Ed. Richard McKeon. New York: Random House, 1947. 308–546.

———. *Poetics. Introduction to Aristotle.* Ed. Richard McKeon. New York: Random House, 1947. 624–67.

Armstrong, Judith. *The Unsaid "Anna Karenina."* New York: St. Martin's, 1988.

Attallah, Paul. "Situation Comedy and 'The Beverly Hillbillies': The Unworthy Discourse." Ph.D. diss., McGill University, 1983.

Austen, Jane. *Northanger Abbey.* Harmondsworth, England: Penguin, 1996.

———. *Pride and Prejudice.* Harmondsworth, England: Penguin, 1972.

Austin, J. L. *How to Do Things with Words.* Cambridge, Mass.: Harvard UP, 1975.

Babington, Bruce, and Peter William Evans. *Affairs to Remember: The Hollywood Comedy of the Sexes.* Manchester: Manchester UP, 1989.

Bailblé, Claude, Michel Marie, and Marie-Claire Ropars. *Muriel: Histoire d'une recherche.* Paris: Galilée, 1975.

Bakhtin, M. M. *The Dialogic Imagination.* Trans. Caryl Emerson and Michael Holquist. Ed. Michael Holquist. Austin: U of Texas P, 1981.

———. *Rabelais and His World.* Trans. Hélène Iswolsky. Bloomington: Indiana UP, 1978.

———. "The Problem of Speech Genres." *Speech Genres and Other Late Essays.* Trans. Vern W. McGee. Ed. Caryl Emerson and Michael Holquist. Austin: U of Texas P, 1986. 60–102.

Barber, C. L. *Shakespeare's Festive Comedy.* New York: Meridian, 1962.

Barreca, Regina, ed. *Last Laughs: Perspectives on Women and Comedy.* New York: Gordon and Breach, 1988.

———. *New Perspectives on Women and Comedy.* Philadelphia: Gordon and Breach, 1992.

Barthes, Roland. *The Pleasure of the Text.* Trans. Richard Miller. New York: Hill and Wang, 1975.

Bateson, Gregory. *Steps to an Ecology of Mind.* New York: Ballantine, 1972.

Bellah, Robert, Richard Madsen, William M. Sullivan, Ann Swidler, and Steve M. Tipton. *Habits of the Heart.* New York: Harper and Row, 1985.

Bentley, Eric. "Farce." *Comedy: Meaning and Form.* Ed. Robert Corrigan. New York: Harper and Row, 1981.

Bergson, Henri. *Laughter. Comedy.* Ed. Wylie Sypher. Baltimore: Johns Hopkins UP, 1986.

Berland, K. J. H. "Didactic, Catecheticall, or Obstetricious?: Socrates and Eighteenth-Century Dialogue." *Compendious Conversations: The Method of Dialogue in the Early Enlightenment.* Ed. Kevin L. Cope. Frankfurt: Peter Lang, 1992. 93–103.

Bordwell, David, and Kristin Thompson. *Film Art: An Introduction.* New York: McGraw Hill, 1993.

Brontë, Charlotte. *Jane Eyre.* New York: New American Library, 1982.

Brooks, Peter. *Reading for the Plot.* New York: Random House, 1985.

Busi, Frederick. "Emma Bovary and the Pursuit of Happiness." *Dalhousie French Studies* 30 (1995): 55–63.

Butsch, Richard. "Class and Gender in Four Decades of Television Situation Comedy: Plus Ça Change . . ." *Critical Studies in Mass Communication* 9.4 (1995): 387–99.

Byrge, Duane, and Robert Milton Miller. *The Screwball Comedy Films.* Jefferson, N.C.: McFarland, 1991.

Casablanca. Dir. Michael Curtiz. With Humphrey Bogart, Ingrid Bergman, Paul Henreid, Claude Rains, Peter Lorre, Sydney Greenstreet. Screenplay Julius J. Epstein, Philip G. Epstein, and Howard Koch. Warner Bros., 1942.

Cave, Terence. *Recognitions: A Study in Poetics.* Oxford: Clarendon, 1988.

Cavell, Stanley. "The Fact of Television." *Themes Out of School.* San Francisco: North Point, 1984. 235–36.

———. *In Quest of the Ordinary.* Chicago: U of Chicago P, 1988.

———. *Must We Mean What We Say?: A Book of Essays.* Cambridge: Cambridge UP, 1976.

———. *Pursuits of Happiness: The Hollywood Comedy of Remarriage.* Cambridge, Mass.: Harvard UP, 1981.

———. *The World Viewed.* Cambridge, Mass.: Harvard UP, 1979.

Celestin, Roger. "Can Robinson Crusoe Find Happiness (Alone)?: Beyond the Genitals and History on the Island of Hope." *Solitary Pleasures: The Historical, Literary, and Artistic Discourses of Autoeroticism.* Ed. Paula Bennett and Vernon A. Rosario II. New York: Routledge, 1995. 233–48.

Chambers, Ross. "Narrative and Other Triangles." *Journal of Narrative Technique* 20.1 (1989): 31–48.

Charney, Maurice. *Comedy High and Low.* New York: Oxford UP, 1978.

Chatman, Seymour. *Coming to Terms: The Rhetoric of Narrative in Fiction and Film.* Ithaca: Cornell UP, 1990.

———. *Story and Discourse: Narrative Structure in Fiction and Film.* Ithaca: Cornell UP, 1978.

Clover, Carol. "Her Body, Himself: Gender in the Slasher Film." *Representations* 20 (1987): 187–228.

Colwin, Laurie. *Another Marvelous Thing.* New York: Penguin, 1986.

———. "Family Happiness." *The Lone Pilgrim.* New York: Harper and Row, 1981. 189–211.

———. *Family Happiness.* New York: Fawcett Crest, 1982.

————. *Happy All the Time*. New York: Penguin, 1978.

Combs, James E., and Dan Nimmo. *The Comedy of Democracy.* Westport, Conn.: Praeger, 1996.

Cope, Kevin L., ed. *Compendious Conversations: The Method of Dialogue in the Early Enlightenment*. Frankfurt: Peter Lang, 1992.

Corngold, Stanley. *Complex Pleasure: Forms of Feeling in German Literature*. Stanford: Stanford UP, 1998.

De Beauvoir, Simone. *The Second Sex.* Trans. H. M. Parshley. New York: Random House, 1974.

Descartes, René. *Meditations on First Philosophy.* Trans. Donald A. Cress. Indianapolis: Hackett, 1979.

Doody, Margaret Anne. *The True Story of the Novel.* New Brunswick: Rutgers UP, 1996.

Dreyfus, Hubert, and Paul Rabinow. *Michel Foucault: Beyond Structuralism and Hermeneutics.* 2nd ed. Chicago: U of Chicago P, 1983.

Duck, Steve. "Relationships as Unfinished Business: Out of the Frying Pan and into the 1990s." *Journal of Social and Personal Relationships* 7 (1990): 5–28.

Duck, Steve, and Linda K. Acitelli. "Intimacy as the Proverbial Elephant." *Intimate Relationships: Development, Dynamics, and Deterioration.* Ed. Daniel Perlman and Steve Duck. Sage Focus Editions, vol. 80. Beverly Hills, Calif.: Sage, 1987.

Duck, Steve, and Kris Pond. "Friends Romans Countrymen, Lend Me Your Retrospections: Rhetoric and Reality in Personal Relationships." *Close Relationships.* Ed. Clyde Hendrick. Review of Personality and Social Psychology, vol. 10. Newbury Park, Calif.: Sage, 1989.

DuPlessis, Rachel Blau. *Writing beyond the Ending: Narrative Strategies of Twentieth-Century Women Writers.* Bloomington: Indiana UP, 1985.

Eco, Umberto. "The Frames of Comic Freedom." *Carnival!* Ed. Thomas A. Sebeok. New York: Mouton, 1984. 1–9.

————. *The Limits of Interpretation.* Bloomington: Indiana UP, 1990.

————. *The Name of the Rose.* Trans. William Weaver. New York: Harcourt Brace Jovanovich, 1983.

Eliade, Mircea. *The Myth of the Eternal Return.* Trans. Willard R. Trask. Princeton: Princeton UP, 1965.

Evans, Mary. *Reflecting on "Anna Karenina."* London: Routledge, 1989.

Fielding, Henry. *Joseph Andrews.* Boston: Houghton Mifflin, 1961.

Foucault, Michel. *The Care of the Self.* Vol. 3 of *The History of Sexuality.* Trans. Robert Hurley. New York: Random House, 1988.

————. *Discipline and Punish.* Trans. Alan Sheridan. New York: Random House, 1979.

————. *The Use of Pleasure.* Vol. 2 of *The History of Sexuality.* Trans. Robert Hurley. New York: Random House, 1986.

Frazer, Timothy C. "'Father Knows Best' and 'The Cosby Show': Nostalgia and the Sitcom Tradition." *Journal of Popular Culture* 27.3 (1993): 163–72.

Freeman, Lewis. "Social Mobility in Television Comedies." *Critical Studies in Mass Communications* 9.4 (1992): 400–406.

Freud, Sigmund. *Beyond the Pleasure Principle.* Trans. James Strachey. New York: Norton, 1961.

————. *Civilization and Its Discontents.* Trans. James Strachey. New York: Norton, 1961.

———. *Jokes and Their Relation to the Unconscious*. Trans. James Strachey. New York: Norton, 1989.

Frye, Northrop. *Anatomy of Criticism*. Princeton: Princeton UP, 1957.

Gadamer, Hans-Georg. *Truth and Method*. 2nd rev. ed. Trans. rev. Joel Weinsheimer and Donald G. Marshall. New York: Crossroad, 1989.

Galligan, Edward. *The Comic Vision in Literature*. Athens: U of Georgia P, 1984.

Gates, Barbara T. *Victorian Suicide: Mad Crimes and Sad Histories*. Princeton: Princeton UP, 1988.

Gehring, Wes D. *Screwball Comedy: Defining a Film Genre*. Ball State Monograph, no. 31. Muncie, Ind.: Ball State U, 1983.

———. *Screwball Comedy: A Genre of Madcap Romance*. Westport, Conn.: Greenwood, 1986.

Genette, Gérard. *Narrative Discourse*. Trans. Jane E. Lewin. Ithaca: Cornell UP, 1985.

Gerlach, John. *Toward the End: Closure and Structure in the American Short Story*. Birmingham: U of Alabama P, 1985.

Gilliatt, Penelope. *To Wit*. London: Weidenfeld and Nicolson, 1990.

Girard, René. *Deceit, Desire, and the Novel: Self and Other in Literary Structure*. Trans. Yvonne Freccero. Baltimore: Johns Hopkins UP, 1988.

Goffman, Erving. *Frame Analysis*. Boston: Northeastern UP, 1986.

Gone with the Wind. Dir. Victor Fleming. With Vivien Leigh, Clark Gable, Leslie Howard, and Olivia de Havilland. Screenplay Sydney Howard. Based on the novel by Margaret Mitchell. MGM, 1939.

Gray, Frances. *Women and Laughter*. Charlottesville: UP of Virginia, 1994.

Greenwood, E. B. "The Unity of *Anna Karenina*." *Landfall* 15 (1961): 124–34.

Grice, Paul. *Studies in the Way of Words*. Cambridge, Mass.: Harvard UP, 1989.

Grossman, Joan Delaney. "Tolstoy's Portrait of Anna: Keystone in the Arch." *Criticism* 18.1 (1976): 1–14.

Grotjahn, Martin. "Beyond Laughter." *Theories of Comedy*. Ed. Paul Lauter. New York: Anchor Books/Doubleday, 1964. 523–29.

Gurewitch, Morton. *The Ironic Temper and the Comic Imagination*. Detroit: Wayne State UP, 1994.

Habermas, Jürgen. *Reason and the Rationalization of Society*. Vol. 1 of *The Theory of Communicative Action*. Trans. Thomas McCarthy. Boston: Beacon, 1984.

Hall, Stephen, Larry Keeter, and Jennifer Williamson, eds. "Toward an Understanding of Humor as Popular Culture in American Society." *Journal of American Culture* 16.2 (1993): 1–75.

Hamamoto, Darrell Y. *Nervous Laughter: Television Situation Comedy and Liberal Democratic Ideology*. New York: Praeger, 1989.

Hammett, Dashiell. *The Thin Man*. New York: Random House, 1972.

Harvey, James. *Romantic Comedy*. New York: Alfred A. Knopf, 1987.

Haskell, Molly. *From Reverence to Rape: The Treatment of Women in the Movies*. Chicago: U of Chicago P, 1987.

———. *Holding My Own in No Man's Land*. New York: Oxford UP, 1997.

Hearne, Vicki. *Animal Happiness*. New York: HarperCollins, 1994.

Heldt, Barbara. *Terrible Perfection: Women and Russian Literature*. Bloomington: Indiana UP, 1987.

Henderson, Brian. "Romantic Comedy Today: Semi-Tough or Impossible." *Film Quarterly* 31.4 (1978): 11–22.

Higonnet, Margaret R. "Speaking Silences: Women's Suicide." *The Female Body in Western Culture.* Ed. Susan Rubin Suleiman. Cambridge, Mass.: Harvard UP, 1986. 68–83.

Horton, Andrew, ed. *Comedy/Cinema/Theory.* Berkeley: U California P, 1991.

Huizinga, Johan. *Homo Ludens.* Boston: Beacon, 1955.

Hume, David. *Dialogues Concerning Natural Religion.* Ed. Norman Kemp Smith. Indianapolis: Bobbs-Merrill, 1947.

I Love Lucy. Dir. Mark Daniels. With Lucille Ball, Desi Arnaz, Vivian Vance, and William Frawley. Writers Jess Oppenheimer, Madelyn Pugh, and Bob Carroll Jr. Desilu Productions, 1951–61.

Irwin, Bill. "Just Clowning Around with Intellect." Interview, by Bruce Webber. *New York Times,* 3 March 1993.

It Happened One Night. Dir. Frank Capra. With Claudette Colbert, Clark Gable. Walter Connolly, Jameson Thomas. Screenplay Robert Riskin. Based on the short story "Night Bus" by Samuel Hopkins Adams. Columbia, 1934.

Jackson, Kenneth T. *Crabgrass Frontier: The Suburbanization of the United States.* New York: Oxford UP, 1985.

Jagendorf, Zvi. *The Happy End of Comedy: Jonson, Molière, and Shakespeare.* London: Associated U Presses, 1984.

Jahn, Gary R. "The Unity of *Anna Karenina.*" *Russian Review* 41.2 (1982): 144–58.

James, William. *The Varieties of Religious Experience. William James: Writings, 1902–1910.* New York: Library of America, 1987.

Jenkins, Henry. *What Made Pistachio Nuts?: Early Sound Comedy and the Vaudeville Aesthetic.* New York: Columbia UP, 1992.

Johnstone, Barbara, ed. *Repetition in Discourse.* Vol 2. Advances in Discourse Processes, vol. 48. Norwood, N.J.: Ablex, 1994.

Jones, Gerard. *Honey, I'm Home!: Sitcoms, Selling the American Dream.* New York: St. Martin's, 1992.

Josefsberg, Milt. *Comedy Writing for Television and Hollywood.* New York: Perennial Library, 1987.

Karnick, Kristine Brunovska. "Commitment and Reaffirmation in Hollywood Romantic Comedy." *Classical Hollywood Comedy.* Ed. Kristine Brunovska Karnick and Henry Jenkins. New York: Routledge, 1995. 123–46.

Kelly, Dorothy. *Telling Glances: Voyeurism in the French Novel.* New Brunswick: Rutgers UP, 1992.

Kendall, Elizabeth. *The Runaway Bride: Hollywood Romantic Comedy of the 1930s.* New York: Alfred A. Knopf, 1990.

Kierkegaard, Søren. *Either/Or I.* Trans. David F. Swenson and Lillian Marvin Swenson. Ed. Howard A. Johnson. Princeton: Princeton UP, 1971.

———. *Either/Or II.* Ed. and Trans. Howard V. Hong and Edna H. Hong. Princeton: Princeton UP, 1987.

———. *Stages on Life's Way.* Ed. and Trans. Howard V. Hong and Edna H. Hong. Princeton: Princeton UP, 1988.

Klinger, Barbara. *Melodrama and Meaning.* Bloomington: Indiana UP, 1994.

Knuth, Deborah J. "'There is so little real friendship in the world!': 'Distant Civility,'

Conversational 'Treats,' and Good Advice in *Persuasion*." *Persuasions: The Jane Austen Society of North America* 15 (1993): 148–56.

Kuntzel, Thierry. "The Film Work." *Enclitic* 2.1 (Spring 1973): 38–61.

———. "Le Travail du Film, 2." *Communications* 23 (1975): 136–89.

Lent, Tina Olsin. "Romantic Love and Friendship: The Redefinition of Gender Relations in Screwball Comedy." *Classical Hollywood Comedy*. Ed. Kristine Brunovska Karnick and Henry Jenkins. New York: Routledge, 1995. 314–31.

Levin, Harry. *Playboys and Killjoys: An Essay on the Theory and Practice of Comedy*. New York: Oxford UP, 1987.

Lloyd, Rosemary. *Closer and Closer Apart: Jealousy in Literature*. Ithaca: Cornell UP, 1995.

Loraux, Nicole. *Tragic Ways of Killing a Woman*. Cambridge, Mass.: Harvard UP, 1987.

Maltin, Leonard. *Movie Comedy Teams*. New York: New American Library, 1970.

Mandelker, Amy. *Framing "Anna Karenina": Tolstoy, the Woman Question, and the Victorian Novel*. Columbus: Ohio State UP, 1993.

Marc, David. *Comic Visions: Television Comedy and American Culture*. Boston: Unwin Hyman, 1989.

Marková, Ivana, Carl Graumann, and Klaus Foppa, eds. *Mutualities in Dialogue*. Cambridge: Cambridge UP, 1995.

Marks, Peter. "The Brief, Brilliant Run of Nichols and May." *New York Times*, 19 May 1996, section B, 31–32.

Mast, Gerald. *The Comic Mind: Comedy and the Movies*. Chicago: Chicago UP, 1979.

McClary, Susan. *Feminine Endings: Music, Gender, and Sexuality*. Minnesota: U of Minnesota P, 1991.

Mellencamp, Patricia. *High Anxiety: Catastrophe, Scandal, Age, and Comedy*. Bloomington: Indiana UP, 1993.

———. "Situation Comedy, Feminism, and Freud: Discourses of Gracie and Lucy." *Studies in Entertainment*. Ed. Tania Modleski. Bloomington: Indiana UP, 1986. 80–95.

Meredith, George. "An Essay on Comedy." *Comedy*. Ed. Wylie Sypher. Baltimore: Johns Hopkins UP, 1986. 3–57.

Meyer, Priscilla. "*Anna Karenina*: Tolstoy's Polemic with *Madame Bovary*." *Russian Review* 54.2 (1995): 243–59.

Mill, John Stuart. "Utilitarianism." *Utilitarianism and Other Writings*. New York: Meridian, 1962. 251–322.

Miller, D. A. *Narrative and Its Discontents*. Princeton: Princeton UP, 1981.

Miller, Jerome A. *In the Throe of Wonder: Intimations of the Sacred in a Post-Modern World*. New York: SUNY P, 1992.

———. "Laughter and the Absurd Economy of Celebration." *Cross Currents* 45.2 (1995): 217–33.

Modleski, Tania. *Loving with a Vengeance: Mass-Produced Fantasies for Women*. New York: Routledge, 1986.

———. "The Terror of Pleasure: The Contemporary Horror Film and Postmodern Culture." *Studies in Entertainment*. Ed. Tania Modleski. Bloomington: Indiana UP, 1986. 155–66.

Morris, Linda A., ed. *American Women Humorists*. New York: Garland, 1994.

Mortimer, Armine Kotin. *La clôture narrative*. Paris: José Corti, 1985.

Musser, Charles. "Divorce, DeMille and the Comedy of Remarriage." *Classical Hollywood*

Comedy. Ed. Kristine Brunovska Karnick and Henry Jenkins. New York: Routledge, 1995. 282–313.

Naremore, James. *Acting in the Cinema.* Berkeley: U of California P, 1988.

Neale, Steve, and Frank Krutnik. *Popular Film and Television Comedy.* London: Routledge, 1990.

Neibaur, James L. *Movie Comedians: The Complete Guide.* Jefferson, N.C.: McFarland, 1987.

Nelson, T. G. A. *Comedy: An Introduction to Comedy in Literature, Drama, and Cinema.* Oxford: Oxford UP, 1990.

Neupert, Richard. *The End: Narration and Closure in Cinema.* Detroit: Wayne State UP, 1995.

Nozick, Robert. *The Examined Life: Philosophical Meditations.* New York: Simon and Schuster, 1989.

Nussbaum, Martha C. *The Fragility of Goodness: Luck and Ethics in Greek Tragedy and Philosophy.* Cambridge: Cambridge UP, 1989.

Oppenheimer, Jess, with Gregg Oppenheimer. *Laughs, Luck . . . and Lucy: How I Came to Create the Most Popular Sitcom of All Time.* Syracuse: Syracuse UP, 1996.

The Palm Beach Story. Dir. Preston Sturges. With Claudette Colbert, Joel McCrea, Mary Astor, Rudy Vallee. Screenplay Preston Sturges. Paramount, 1942.

Panofsky, Erwin. "Style and Medium in the Motion Pictures." *Film Theory and Criticism.* Ed. Gerald Mast and Stanley Cohen. 3rd ed. New York: Oxford UP, 1985. 215–33.

Park, Clara Claiborne. "No Time for Comedy." *Comedy: Meaning and Form.* Ed. Robert Corrigan. New York: Harper and Row, 1981. 58–64.

Phelan, James. *Narrative as Rhetoric: Technique, Audiences, Ethics, Ideology.* Columbus: Ohio State UP, 1996.

Phillips, Adam. *On Flirtation: Psychoanalytic Essays on the Uncommitted Life.* Cambridge, Mass.: Harvard UP, 1994.

———. *On Kissing, Tickling, and Being Bored: Psychoanalytic Essays on the Unexamined Life.* Cambridge, Mass.: Harvard UP, 1993.

Plato. *Symposium.* Trans. Walter Hamilton. Ed. Betty Radice. Harmondsworth, England: Penguin, 1978.

Peckham, Morse. *Man's Rage for Chaos: Biology, Behavior, and the Arts.* New York: Schocken, 1967.

Poague, Leland A. *The Cinema of Frank Capra: An Approach to Film Comedy.* New York: A. S. Barnes, 1975.

Prince, Gerald. *Dictionary of Narratology.* Lincoln: U of Nebraska P, 1987.

Purdie, Susan. *Comedy: The Mastery of Discourse.* Toronto: Toronto UP, 1993.

Rabinowitz, Peter. *Before Reading: Narrative Conventions and the Politics of Interpretation.* Ithaca: Cornell UP, 1987.

———. "Truth in Fiction: A Reexamination of Audiences." *Critical Inquiry* 4.1 (1977): 121–41.

Reardon, B. P., ed. *Collected Ancient Greek Novels.* Berkeley: U California P, 1989.

Richter, David. *Fable's End: Completeness and Closure in Rhetorical Fiction.* Chicago: U Chicago P, 1974.

Rimmon-Kenan, Shlomith. *Narrative Fiction: Contemporary Poetics.* London: Methuen P, 1983.

Robards, Brooks. *Situation Comedy and the Structure of Television: A Structural Analysis.* Ann Arbor: University Microfilms International, 1982.

Robinson, Fred Miller. *Comic Moments.* Athens: U of Georgia P, 1992.

Roth, Marty. "Slap-Happiness: The Erotic Contract of 'His Girl Friday.'" *Screen* 30.1–2 (1989): 160–75.

Rouner, Leroy S., ed. *In Pursuit of Happiness.* Boston University Studies in Philosophy and Religion 16. Notre Dame: Notre Dame UP, 1995.

Rowe, Kathleen. "Comedy, Melodrama and Gender: Theorizing the Genres of Laughter." *Classical Hollywood Comedy.* Ed. Kristine Brunovska Karnick and Henry Jenkins. New York: Routledge, 1995. 39–62.

———. *The Unruly Woman.* Austin: U of Texas P, 1995.

Rubenstein, E. "The End of Screwball Comedy: *The Lady Eve* and *The Palm Beach Story.*" *Post-Script* 1–2 (1981–82): 33–47.

Russell, Bertrand. *The Conquest of Happiness.* New York: The Book League of America, 1930.

Sacks, Harvey. *Structures of Social Action: Studies in Conversation Analysis.* Ed. J. Maxwell Atkinson and John Heritage. Cambridge: Cambridge UP, 1992.

Scarry, Elaine. *The Body in Pain.* New York: Oxford UP, 1987.

Schaar, John H. ". . . And the Pursuit of Happiness." *Legitimacy in the Modern State.* New Brunswick, N.J.: Transaction, 1989. 231–49.

Schultze, Sydney. *The Structure of "Anna Karenina".* Ann Arbor: Ardis, 1982.

Scodari, Christine. "Possession, Attraction, and the Thrill of the Chase: Gendered Myth-Making in Film and Television Comedy of the Sexes." *Critical Studies in Mass Communication* 12.1 (1995): 23–39.

Seldes, Gilbert. *The Movies Come from America.* New York: Scribners, 1937.

Shakespeare, William. *Antony and Cleopatra. Shakespeare: The Complete Works.* Ed. G. B. Harrison. New York: Harcourt, Brace and World, 1968.

———. *Much Ado about Nothing.* London: Penguin, 1968.

Shields, Carol. *The Stone Diaries.* New York: Penguin, 1993.

Sikov, Ed. *Laughing Hysterically: American Screen Comedy of the 1950s.* New York: Columbia UP, 1994.

———. *Screwball: Hollywood's Madcap Romantic Comedies.* New York: Crown, 1989.

Smith, Barbara Hernstein. *Poetic Closure: A Study of How Poems End.* Chicago: U of Chicago P, 1978.

Sochen, June, ed. *Women's Comic Visions.* Detroit: Wayne State UP, 1991.

Spoto, Donald. *Madcap: The Life of Preston Sturges.* Boston: Little, Brown, 1990.

Stam, Robert. *Subversive Pleasures: Bakhtin, Cultural Criticism and Film.* Baltimore: Johns Hopkins UP, 1989.

Staples, Shirley. *Male-Female Comedy Teams in American Vaudeville, 1865–1932.* Ann Arbor: UMI Research, 1984.

Stenbock-Fermor, Elisabeth. *The Architecture of "Anna Karenina": A History of Its Writing, Structure, and Message.* Lisse, The Netherlands: Peter de Ridder, 1975.

Stewart, Garrett. *Dear Reader: Conscripted Audience in Nineteenth-Century British Fiction.* Baltimore: Johns Hopkins UP, 1996.

———. *Reading Voices: Literature and the Phonotext.* Berkeley: U of California P, 1990.

Stone, Lawrence. *The Family, Sex and Marriage in England, 1500–1800.* Harmondsworth, England: Penguin, 1979.

Storey, Robert. "Comedy, Its Theorists, and the Evolutionary Perspective." *Criticism: A Quarterly for Literature and the Arts* 38.2 (1996): 407–41.

Sumner, L. W. *Welfare, Happiness, and Ethics.* Oxford: Clarendon, 1996.

Tannen, Deborah. *That's Not What I Meant!* New York: Ballantine, 1986.

———. *You Just Don't Understand.* New York: William Morrow, 1990.

Tanner, Tony. *Adultery in the Novel: Contract and Transgression.* Baltimore: Johns Hopkins UP, 1981.

Tave, Stuart. *Lovers, Clowns, and Fairies.* Chicago: U of Chicago P, 1993.

———. *Some Words of Jane Austen.* Chicago: U of Chicago P, 1973.

The Thin Man. Dir. Woody Van Dyke. With Myrna Loy, William Powell, Maureen O'Sullivan, Asta. Screenplay Albert Hackett and Frances Goodrich. Based on the novel by Dashiell Hammett. MGM, 1934.

Thorlby, Anthony. *Leo Tolstoy, "Anna Karenina".* Landmarks of World Literature. Cambridge: Cambridge UP, 1987.

Timmerman, John H. "Umberto Eco and Aristotle: A Dialogue on the Lost Treatise: Comedy." *Christian Scholar's Review* 17.1 (1987): 9–24.

Tolstoy, Leo. *Anna Karenina.* Trans. Louise and Aylmer Maude. Oxford: Oxford UP, 1990.

———. *Family Happiness. Great Short Works of Leo Tolstoy.* Trans. Louis and Aylmer Maude. New York: Harper and Row, 1967. 1–82.

Top Hat. Dir. Mark Sandrich. With Fred Astaire, Ginger Rogers, Edward Everett Horton, Helen Broderick. Screenplay Dwight Taylor and Allan Scott. Choreography Hermes Pan. Music and Lyrics Irving Berlin. RKO, 1935.

Torgovnick, Marianna. *Closure in the Novel.* Princeton: Princeton UP, 1981.

Turner, C. J. G. *A Karenina Companion.* Waterloo, Ontario: Wilfrid Laurier UP, 1993.

———. "Psychology, Rhetoric and Morality in *Anna Karenina*: At the Bottom of Whose Heart?" *Slavic and East European Journal* 39.2 (1995): 261–68.

Vatz, Richard E. "The Myth of the Rhetorical Situation." *Philosophy and Rhetoric* 6.3 (1973): 154–61.

Vernet, Marc. *Figures de l'absence.* Paris: Cahiers du Cinéma, 1988.

Wadia, Pheroze. "Philosophy as Literature: The Case of Hume's Dialogues." *Compendious Conversations: The Method of Dialogue in the Early Enlightenment.* Ed. Kevin L. Cope. Frankfurt: Peter Lang, 1992. 34–53.

Walker, Nancy A. *A Very Serious Thing: Women's Humor and American Culture.* Minneapolis: U of Minnesota P, 1988.

Warhol, Robyn R. "Guilty Cravings: What Feminist Narratology Can Do for Cultural Studies." *Narratologies: New Perspectives on Narrative Analysis.* Ed. David Herman. Columbus: Ohio State UP, 1999. 340–55.

Watt, Ian. *The Rise of the Novel.* Berkeley: U California P, 1957.

Weinsheimer, Joel. "Afterword: The Primacy of Dialogue." *Compendious Conversations: The Method of Dialogue in the Early Enlightenment.* Ed. Kevin L. Cope. Frankfurt: Peter Lang, 1992. 401–6.

Wexman, Virginia Wright. *Creating the Couple: Love, Marriage, and Hollywood Performance.* Princeton: Princeton UP, 1993.

Whitcomb, Curt. "Treacherous 'Charm' in *Anna Karenina*." *Slavic and East European Journal* 39.2 (1995): 214–26.

White, Eric Charles. *Kaironomia: On the Will to Invent.* Ithaca: Cornell UP, 1987.

White, Stephen. *Sovereign Virtue: Aristotle on the Relation between Happiness and Prosperity.* Stanford: Stanford UP, 1992.

Wike, Victoria S. *Kant on Happiness and Ethics.* Albany: SUNY P, 1994.

Williams, Raymond. *Television: Technology and Cultural Form.* New York: Schocken, 1975.

Wilson, Emma. *Sexuality and the Reading Experience.* Oxford: Clarendon, 1996.

Winnicott, D. W. *Playing and Reality.* London: Tavistock/Routledge, 1991.

Winokur, Mark. *American Laughter: Immigrants, Ethnicity, and the 1930s Hollywood Film Comedy.* New York: St. Martin's, 1996.

Wittgenstein, Ludwig. *Philosophical Investigations.* Trans. G. E. M. Anscombe. 3rd ed. New York: Macmillan, 1958.

Woolf, Virginia. *To the Lighthouse.* New York: Harcourt Brace Jovanovich, 1981.

Young, Kay. "Hollywood, 1934: 'Inventing' Romantic Comedy." *Look Who's Laughing: Gender and Comedy.* Ed. Gail Finney. Studies in Humor and Gender, vol. 1. Amsterdam: Gordon and Breach, 1994. 257–74.

———. "The Male-Female Comedy Team." *Performing Gender and Comedy: Theories, Texts and Contexts.* Ed. Shannon Hengen. Studies in Humor and Gender, vol. 4. Amsterdam: Gordon and Breach, 1998. 3–20.

Zimmerman, Gisela. "The Civil Servant as Educator: *Effi Briest* and *Anna Karenina.*" *Modern Language Review* 90.4 (1995): 817–29.

Index

The Theory and Interpretation of Narrative Series

JAMES PHELAN AND PETER J. RABINOWITZ, EDITORS

Because the series editors believe that the most significant work in narrative studies today contributes both to our knowledge of specific narratives and to our understanding of narrative in general, studies in the series typically offer interpretations of individual narratives and address significant theoretical issues underlying those interpretations. The series does not privilege any one critical perspective but is open to work from any strong theoretical position.

9206